·

TIME FOR HOPE

TIME
FOR
HOPE

PRACTICES
FOR LIVING IN
TODAY'S WORLD

Flora A. Keshgegian

continuum
NEW YORK • LONDON
www.continuumbooks.com

The Continuum International Publishing Group, 80 Maiden Lane, New York, NY 10038

The Continuum International Publishing Group Ltd, The Tower Building, 11 York Road, London SE1 7NX

Unless otherwise indicated, biblical quotations are from the New Revised Standard Version Bible, copyright 1989, Division of Christian Education of the National Council of the Churches of Christ in the United States of America. Used by permission. All rights reserved.

Cover design: Brenda Klinger

Library of Congress Cataloging-in-Publication Data

Keshgegian, Flora A., 1950–
    Time for hope : practices for living in today's world / Flora A. Keshgegian.
        p. cm.
    Includes bibliographical references and index.
    ISBN-13: 978-0-8264-1915-6 (hardcover)
    ISBN-10: 0-8264-1915-1
    1. Hope—Religious aspects—Christianity. 2. Time—Religious aspects—Christianity.
    3. Storytelling—Criticism, interpretation, etc. 4. Christian life. I. Title.
    BV4638.K47 2006
    234'.25—dc22
                            2006019628

Printed in the United States of America

06 07 08 09 10 11   10 9 8 7 6 5 4 3 2 1

In memory of Marlene
(who told me not to postpone joy),
Carol and Dick,
friends lost to cancer

And for all my friends
who nurture hope in life,
ongoing and abundant

CONTENTS

ACKNOWLEDGMENTS

Even though writing a book is often a solitary pursuit, it requires a whole network of institutional and personal support. I am grateful to Brown University and especially the Pembroke Center for Teaching and Research on Women, where I was a Visiting Scholar for much of the time I was writing this book, for providing an institutional home and enduring colleagues. Serendipitously, the theme of the 2004–2005 Pembroke Seminar, convened by Rey Chow, was "Orders of Time." That weekly, interdisciplinary gathering afforded a valuable setting in which to further explore, sharpen, and reinforce some of the perspectives of this book. Grants from the Conant Fund of the Episcopal Church provided needed support for research and writing. A grant from the Wabash Center for Teaching and Learning in Theology and Religion helped me initially to focus my topic and move toward a coherent proposal.

I am also grateful for all the people who accompanied me in the process of writing this book, especially Kay Johnson and Robin Rose for their devoted reading of the manuscript and their valuable feedback and spirit-lifting enthusiasm, and Susan A. Harvey and Tuck Shattuck for their care in reading and constancy in support. Patrick Henry provided acute editing suggestions on key chapters. Catherine Keller offered her insightful theological feedback and professional support. Heather Parr contributed research assistance and helpful suggestions in the early stages of this project. Paul Barton, Jane Elliott,

E. Angela Emerson, Cynthia Kittredge, and Janice Okoomian offered feedback and encouragement. Gail Tetreault and Kathleen Pappas made available concrete assistance when I needed it and made me feel welcome. During a crucial transition while I was in the midst of writing this book, many friends tended my spirit and sustained me.

I was elated and deeply moved by the awarding of the Trinity Prize for this manuscript. I thank the selection committee for that endorsement and affirmation of my work. Henry Carrigan, coordinator of the prize and my editor, deserves further mention for his gentle and caring guidance, especially for shepherding the manuscript through publication, and for sharing his knowledge and insight.

Stories of my family, especially from my childhood, are woven throughout this text. I trust I gave due honor to their memories, especially those of my grandmother and parents. The imaginative play my brother and I engaged in as children brought me joy then and lay seeds for the ideas in this book. I thank my brother, Albert Keshgegian, for allowing me to incorporate the fruits of his imagination. I am grateful for his presence and that of his family in my life, even more now that he and I have become the "older generation" in the ever-turning circle of time and life.

INTRODUCTION

We live in a world of change. Sometimes change is for the good. Everyday we are presented with new technologies and medical advances in an increasingly shrinking globe. At the same time, disaster and danger seem to haunt our every turn. We can no longer count on such essentials of life as air and water to be safe and freely available. Whether we fear terrorist attacks from foreign soil or our neighbors next door, we do not live as comfortably in the world as we once did. We are suspicious of what our elected leaders claim to be true and wonder whom in the world we can trust. Those of us who dreamed of a better life for our children now wonder whether they will be able to live as well as we have, or our parents did. Despite claims of progress, life is not necessarily getting better. For many, it is a struggle for survival.

How are we to sustain hope in this world that seems to offer little promise of a better future? Life seems less hopeful, the future less bright. Yet we long to find our way to a more hopeful life. We continue to read the signs of the time and look for indicators of hope. We yearn to make the most of the time of our lives. A desire for fullness of life seems to be "hard wired" into human beings. From a religious point of view, such desire comes from God, who created us and endowed us with mind and spirit, capable of imagination and endless creativity. We were made for hope.

This book explores the character of such hope in the context of today's world. It begins with the premise that to be human means to

1

live in time, to be time-bound creatures. Our lives are chronicled by their days and their years. Collectively, we live by the rhythms of decades and centuries. We inhabit time and it inhabits us.

The habitation of time is what is meant by history. We tell time, not only by clocks and watches, but also by the stories we tell about our lives. These stories shape our views about the world; they constitute our history. We live in these stories and the stories live in us.

We do not all tell the same story. We do not all live by the same narrative. To be sure, there are common elements—such as birth, death, work, family—but what these mean and how they are lived and experienced vary. These differences produce multiple stories. Tribes and nations develop group narratives, grand stories, that have the status of myth. When we live inside a myth, we forget that it is a story, simply one way to talk about life. We believe it describes and proscribes the way things really are and are meant to be. Among these myths are religious worldviews, which tell us about who God is in time and about God's relationship to our time. These narratives about God shape the meaning and nature of our lives. They tell the tale of hope: hope for history and for life.

This book will explore ways in which our telling of time affects our understanding of hope. It will examine how our narratives shape our lives. Along the way, I will consider such questions as: What happens when the stories no longer ring true, when changing circumstances make them hollow? What happens when we seem to misread the signs of the time? What do we do when our sense of hope feels threatened? I address these questions not for all times and places, but for right now and here, America in the period called postmodern. My exploration will pay particular attention to Jewish and Christian narratives that have so permeated and shaped the cultures of the West.

Judaism and Christianity have consistently maintained that God is in charge of history and that God's purposes are being enacted in and through history; in other words, what happens in history matters because it is God's work. Despite Christianity's emphasis on salvation of the soul and eternal life after death, despite even occasional attempts by Christian groups to deny the value of historical experience, the importance of history as an arena of God's presence and activity remains a central Christian affirmation.

For Jews and Christians, history has purpose and direction, an ending, a *telos*, which is both fulfillment and consummation. Jews wait for the Messiah; they anticipate the fullness of God's *shalom* (peace and harmony) as reflective of God's intentions. Christians say the kingdom of God is manifest in history, and/or they imagine an ultimate cosmic battle in which God will be victorious. They look forward to an ending in which God will set all things right. Jewish and Christian understandings of hope have been so molded by the conviction that time and history have a linear trajectory that other perspectives have scarcely gained a hearing. In the modern era, the grand or meta-narrative of the modern West appropriated and adapted this narrative to view time not only as linear but also progressive.

This grand narrative of the western view of history and hope no longer works. It does not feed our hope. Nor does it ring true to our experience. What if we paid attention to different narratives of time? What other ways of imagining time and history would emerge? Might these better account for the challenges and contradictions confronting us today? The goal of this book is to tell time differently, to offer a narrative better able to nurture hope today.

The questions I pose are real ones for me. This book grew out of my struggles with hope in this time. What I offer here is an extended meditation, a guided exploration of this particular terrain of time and history, which opens up to greater vistas, even imagining God's own. I begin with my own experiences, my own story, in which I trust readers will find resonances with their own. Setting out from those experiences, my exploration and meditation will be in conversation with the Christian tradition, and its Jewish roots, as well as with dimensions and contours of the current cultural and political landscape. In my exploration, I come upon hitherto neglected or overlooked perspectives that enrich the available resources. My desire is not to find simple answers, but ones complex enough to satisfy the contradictions and mysteries that attend life in this world.

How I Learned to Tell Time

I grew up and entered adulthood in the 1950s, 60s, and early 70s. I lived in two worlds: an "old world," located primarily in the Armenian American subculture of my family and community, and a "new world" of American public education and popular culture. In my late teen and early adult years, I identified with political movements that protested injustice, advocated change, and dreamed of a radically renewed society. My college years, textured by the civil rights movement and anti-Vietnam war movement, contained intense highs and lows: spontaneous joy the day Lyndon Johnson announced he would not run again for president and deep sadness when Martin Luther King Jr. and Robert Kennedy were assassinated within months of each other.

My generation combined its serious and intent political engagement with a wonderful sense of play and happiness in communal gatherings and festival occasions. At the end of the 1960s, I helped form an organization on my college campus called RALPH (Radical Action for Love, Peace, and Happiness) to foster community and authentic, as well as playful, encounters. We were going to change the world and have fun doing so.

In those years, I learned about power and social analysis, to look at the world as systems of power that had a life of their own, apart from individual behavior. Oppression in the form of "isms"—racism, sexism, militarism—would be remedied by programs of liberation. The world was riddled with problems, but my generation could solve them.

Naively, but earnestly, I brought these commitments and all that I was learning to Christianity, in hopes that it would "join the struggle." For me, the message of Christianity was about changing the world. The church was to be engaged fully in the world, for the sake of justice. I understood this to be the heart of the Christian Gospel. It is what drew me into ministry and the study of theology. In the writings of theologians such as Rosemary Ruether and Mary Daly, Gustavo Gutierrez and Rubem Alves, I discovered theology as a potentially life-giving discipline. With them, I adopted as a type of slogan Marx's dictum that the purpose of philosophy (read *theology*) is not to understand the world, but to change it.

One day many years ago, a seminary classmate and I were having a passionate argument about the nature of salvation. He quoted John 3:16—"For God so loved the world that God sent God's only son in order that the world might be saved through him"—as evidence that a personal relationship with Jesus is necessary in order to be saved. I pointed to the same verse to argue that God's saving work is for and of the world—"God so loved the *world*"—and that salvation is not an individual affair, but is all about saving, *changing*, the world.

With the somewhat overbearing but forgivable arrogance that accompanies youth, I, and others in my generation, intended to set the world aright, to make it better. Our grand dreams about what we were going to accomplish were fed by protests and sit-ins and the victories we dared to claim. The songs we sang, such as Bob Dylan's "Blowing in the Wind" and Pete Seeger's "If I Had a Hammer," gave voice to our vision and stirred us to commitment.

As we moved further into adulthood, victories began to seem less clear, accomplishments compromised. Returning Vietnam veterans were not the enemies we had portrayed, but men and women deeply injured by the traumas of war. The solidarity of movements for justice and change splintered into competition for resources. We were drawn into struggles over dueling oppressions. Was race more important than class? Was gender oppression more fundamental than race or vice versa? We hoarded power and privilege. The women's movement, critically important to my own journey, grew out of these other struggles, by claiming the specificity of its own oppression. As women felt the discrimination practiced against them within the civil rights and peace movements, they began to apply the analyses they had learned to their own situation and to organize on their own. But then the women's movement itself fragmented: straight and lesbian, white women and women of color, so-called radical and not so radical. Other movements splintered as well.

My commitment to changing the world and my faith in that possibility faltered yet remained central. It might be that we needed to learn more about the workings of power and become more practiced at solidarity, but our mission was still clear. Even that clarity, however, clouded as economic, social, and political events, many on a global scale, seemed to take on a life of their own.

In the last thirty years, this world has witnessed more radical change than my generation had expected: the collapse of the Berlin wall, the fall of the Soviet Union, and the end of state-sponsored apartheid in South Africa. In the wake of such revolutions, however, we learned that change—even desired changed—often does not produce what we had dreamed. South Africa struggles in fits and starts toward justice, even as its people are being ravaged by AIDS. The independent states of the former Soviet Union gasp for survival and jockey for position amid much internal chaos and contestation. The hegemony of global capitalism casts a menacing shadow over prospects for worldwide justice and makes inequity a rapidly moving, but ever growing, target.

I feel sobered about the possibilities for enduring justice and peace. I experience a certain measure of disappointment, if not regret, that my generation somehow failed to do what we set out to do. While we continue to practice our commitments to making a better world, I find myself confused at times about what that means and how to accomplish it.

Seeds of cynicism and even despair are sprouting within me as well. Recent events—the growing lack of faith in the truthfulness of our elected leaders, the callous manipulation of political processes to achieve partisan ends, the string of corporate failures due to executive misconduct, the shattering of America's sense of innocence with the terrorist attacks on the World Trade Center—have shaken our sense of trust in fundamental institutions and dimensions of our society.

These events eat away at the vision of a society that is just and fair, in which people act responsibly in freedom. They challenge our dreams of a world in which no one need be in want, in which plentiful resources are shared rather than hoarded, in which peace and harmony govern relationships between persons and nations. Instead we inhabit a world in which the gap between rich and poor grows more visible each day; in which war and terrorism, rather than mediation and cooperation, are preferred courses of action; and in which so many die daily from hunger and AIDS. Meanwhile our leaders offer little but self-serving sound bites.

This book is driven by a desire to relearn the contours of hope in this world that seems so far from what we envisioned. I do not want to turn away from history in disappointment, nor to abandon faith in history and focus solely on the self in a search for personal fulfillment. Rather I want to think differently about history and to keep hope alive, to quote Jesse Jackson.

What Else I Learned about Telling Time

The "old world" in which I grew up taught me different things about life in the world. My immigrant family and the Armenian American subculture in which we lived feared assimilation. Being Armenian meant not being American. But being Armenian was a fraught existence. By the time my family members immigrated to this country, they had already survived the Turkish genocidal campaign and its aftermath, including life as refugees. They carried in their bodies and spirits the legacy of threatened existence and identity. The prospect of assimilation only added another dimension to such dangers.

Armenians, as do many ethnic groups, divide the world into "us and them." When I was growing up, everyone who was not Armenian was an *odar*, which means foreigner or other. Our Armenian values and lifestyle were not just different, they were superior. Our distinctiveness was to be maintained through language, religion, social customs, and circles of affiliation and association. My family belonged to the Armenian Church, which was not only the religious but also the social center of our lives. I attended Armenian language school there, as well as Sunday school. We were often at church for festivals and banquets and performances. Outside of church our social life consisted of families who visited us and with whom we visited—usually relatives and always Armenian. During the summer, when we went to the New Jersey shore, we stayed at an Armenian-owned inn and planted our blanket on the Armenian section of the beach.

Armenian was the language of our home. I learned English first when I began kindergarten. Languages define worlds, and so my worlds were twin, Armenian and English. In Armenian, I inhabited a space that was of the old world; in English, I was American, an inhabitant of the new world.

Since I grew up before the days of home schooling and of ethnic day schools, public school introduced a whole new and competing world into my life. I experienced a clashing of cultures that I felt acutely, that impacted my sense of identity and identity formation, and that left me swinging between worlds. In school, I learned to value freedom and autonomy. I was taught to think critically, to analyze and to subject knowledge to rational arguments and tests. The education offered to me in modern day America carried a promise of redemption, a way to a new and different life. My teachers encouraged me to achieve and to make choices, free choices, about my future. They showed me that knowledge opens doors, and ignorance is to be spurned.

The education I received reflected the values of the Enlightenment: reason and freedom and individuality. So much of the Armenian "old world" practiced different values. I came to view that heritage as backward and "unenlightened." My grandmother's folk piety seemed like superstition. I was embarrassed by her warding off evil spirits with garlic and making a sign of the cross every time we drove by a church. I thought it odd that each Saturday at sundown she lit incense and carried it throughout our house to fill it with the smoke of blessing and to welcome the Sabbath. Yet decades later, on the day she died, when I was separated from family by hundreds of miles, I did not know what to do but light incense and carry it through my house. This gesture seemed a proper way to honor and remember her. In my youth, though, I wanted out of this "old world."

Other values my family embraced also seemed at odds with those I was soaking in at school. In the Armenian ethos, family and community overshadowed and took precedence over individuality. Religion and politics and ethnicity were one, so Armenians simply asserted that to be Armenian was to be Christian, specifically "in the Armenian Church." All Armenians were connected, though internal divisions and even animosities within the Armenian community meant that unity was not often practiced. Despite these tensions, a fierce sense of solidarity rooted in identity was in the air I breathed as a child. The fierceness was fed by our genocidal history, framing our identity as victims and survivors. We had to stick together. We had to maintain our distinctive identity, in order to survive. Our history seemed frozen in that event of genocide, long before my birth, that changed the Armenian people forever.

My father used to say to my brother, my only sibling, and me: "There is no mine or yours in this house." These words, often meant to end a quarrel or a competition over something we both wanted, reflected a set of values about individuality, privacy, and ownership different from the American norm. In our family, separateness and separation were not valued, not seen as good.

My father's declaration reflected his role as patriarch as well. His words were as much a statement about his power and its concomitant authority as about anything else. Even as a child, I knew enough to realize my father was telling me that everything in the house was really his after all.

I was also well aware that my family privileged my brother's achievements and aspirations over mine. The primary institutions of the Armenian world, family and church, offered proscribed options, especially for females. My future was to be a wife and mother. Having a career was not one of the given options—especially one as a priest and theologian. I rebelled against such restraints and felt I had to choose between the worlds in which I grew up. I opted out of the Armenian world.

I left it, but it never left me. It taught me about being part of a people, not as a voluntary association, but as blood ties that flow among all, blurring separations and knitting connections. Relation was valued over autonomy. Identity was marked not by individuation but by mutual participation. Time did not just flow forward. The webs of connection in time were multiple.

That "old" world also taught me alternatives to rationality as the way to knowledge and a good life. The Armenian church liturgy is an ancient rite, chanted in the haunting melodies of minor keys. Still now, after so many years, when I hear those chants, I cannot help but sing along. Those melodies live in me; they move me toward a mystery that is simultaneously approached and eluded by them. The Armenian liturgy is a tightly scripted and enacted ritual with clearly delineated roles for all in attendance. It is fully participatory (though such participation has fallen out of use as more and more of the congregational parts have been taken over by the choir). The liturgy engages the senses and the body. The scent of incense hangs in the air; the tinkling of bells accompanies the chant. Candles sparkle; the smell of wax lingers. Worshippers are bid to attend, not only by listening, but by standing and sitting and kneeling, as well as crossing themselves and bowing and dipping. The robustness of this liturgy stands boldly next to the pale and word-centered rites of the Protestant West. Western liturgies, especially their Protestant versions, are all about hearing and understanding. The power of the Armenian liturgy comes through the body and the senses and the emotions, as well as the intellect.

In fact, few understand the words of the liturgy. Still chanted in fifth-century classical Armenian, only the clergy have knowledge of the liturgical language and its meaning. As a child and young adult, I railed against this exclusiveness. I wanted to understand the words. I resented needing to follow along in translation. Doing so distanced me from the liturgy. I remember countless discussions at youth events, when we went round and round in circles of argument about the language of the liturgy. One time, a priest responded to our arguments for English language liturgies by declaring, "You don't need to understand what is being said; it is a mystery." My modern Enlightenment self was horrified at this dismissal of reason and its value. The intransigence of the Armenian church hierarchy to changes in the language of the liturgy is one reason I left that church.

Today I still would argue for English liturgies, but I am grateful for what I imbibed about mystery, ritual, and beauty by my regular presence at the Armenian liturgy. It nurtured in me ritual sensibilities that I continue to practice. I know that truth and knowledge are not only rational and intellectual. In fact, the mind sees only partially and dimly; it does not apprehend mystery as well as do the body and the senses, more receptive to that which is irreducible and even contradictory.

The Armenian liturgy communicates its truth as much through its aesthetics as through its words. Its rituals form participants and attune them to mystery that can be appreciated more than comprehended. The yearning toward is as valuable as the knowing. Indeed, there is no distinction in the end between the process and the goal. They are one.

The less formal and more "folk" rituals practiced by Armenians such as my grandmother also point to a different type of knowledge and way of being in the world. What I once deemed superstition, I now see as pointers in the webs of connection that bind all that is created. Science today touts the medicinal values of garlic. Scented candles and incense are everywhere. Prayer releases energy. Even seemingly barbaric practices such as animal sacrifice can be evidence of the honoring of ecological and economic balances. Such rituals recognize human dependency on other parts of the created order.

It is difficult for the western mind, trained in abstracted intellectualism and a narrowly rational morality, to grasp the more aesthetic and seemingly amoral values and practices of the "old world" cultures among us. These approaches clash, as loud, clanging symbols, producing a dissonant noise. Such clashing has reverberated within me for years. I ran to the "enlightened" side and stood with its judges, casting condescending looks toward the backward and inferior people, who at best were deemed superstitious or exotic.

Now I am looking for relation and balance amid the voices that clamor within me. I am finding that the most profound truths came to me early in my life. One day, when I was perhaps six or seven and at the church with my family for a social event, my brother and I sneaked into the sanctuary. The liturgy had ended hours earlier and no one else was there. The smell of candle wax greeted us when we opened the doors. The empty church seemed full of presence. In that moment, in that place, I sensed God in the silent stillness. I told my brother that we must be quiet because "God is here." The stillness resounded with a mystery that commanded our silence, our reception, our wonder. To disturb it would be to dishonor God.

That was many, many years ago, but part of me has been yearning ever since for such a sense of stillness and wonder. I have been searching for that moment when ordinary time seemed to stop and the universe felt present, intensely, fully, and forever present, in a way that takes our breath away—and makes us feel so very alive.

Expanding the Known World

I am not alone in finding value and meaning in my ethnic heritage and its religious and cultural particularities. In the last several decades, a number of previously silenced and submerged voices have been calling attention to long-neglected resources for thinking about history and time. These are challenging notions of linear, progressive time. Among them are the voices of the injured of history who bear the signs of trauma and those of the marginalized and the colonized whose overlooked histories and cultures offer different ways of being in the world. Also joining the chorus are advocates for the earth, which is increasingly threatened by our wanton abuse of natural resources.

First Nation peoples, for example, tell a very different story from what we read in textbooks about America and its commitment to freedom, human rights, and citizenship for all. America has not been the land of opportunity and freedom for all. In fact, American history is a story of conquest: those deemed to be in the way of the taking of this "promised land" were to be moved or eliminated. First Nations peoples are also reminding us of the ways in which the actions of the colonizers have scarred the people and the land. These voices challenge the dominant American tale of time and history as progress and achievement.

They are not alone. Ecologists and anti-nuclear peace activists are suggesting that there will be no future, no ongoing history, if we destroy the earth. Survivors of genocidal activity around the world are demanding recognition and challenging notions of historical justice. What some claim as progress, others experience as injury and loss. In our increasingly multicultural society, we are hearing more and more from those who do not think about time and history in the same way. The dominant western paradigms may be the loudest, but not the sole voice in a varied chorus.

The voices in this chorus are calling for a rethinking of the way in which we understand human existence and the contours of time. They are making us pay more attention to the viewpoint and content of the stories we tell about history and hope. I seek to be attentive to such voices and what they have to teach us about time and how we understand redemption in history. They are revealing the presence of God in perhaps unexpected and unanticipated ways.

As I write this book, I am also aware of the shifting of generations. The babies of my "baby boomer" generation are now adults and parents—and even grandparents—themselves. Those born in the last couple of decades are experiencing time and history quite differently than my generation did. The world these younger generations know and experience was barely imagined when I was growing up with the black and white television, and without PCs and cell phones. How are they to think about their lives and the future? What is the nature of their hope?

For many years, as a university chaplain, I mentored these succeeding generations. At Brown University, we, faculty and staff, understood our role as providing the environment, resources, and guidance for students to pursue their potential. We knew we were helping to prepare a future generation of leaders who were going to change the world. Our job was to guide them along the way.

As I listened to students talk about their lives and their futures and tell of their struggles and uncertainties, I came to understand how we live by "scripts," as one popular psychology named those stories that shape our lives. The students were all dealing with expectations, some laid on them by others, some their own, about who they were supposed to be. Often their struggles grew out of contradictions between the narratives they had grown up with and all that they were learning and experiencing in college, which challenged the old scripts or even revealed them as based on lies. Many students wrestled with ideas about success and what it meant to be successful. Some had to deal with clashes between their parents' desires for their futures and their own passions: whether to be a doctor or engineer as their parents wanted or become a dancer or an activist. Others found themselves remembering past experiences long buried, of abuse and violence, which required re-writing the family stories and even their own.

These students had to deal with larger narratives, too—the social and cultural scripts they had learned growing up: what it meant to be American or Asian American or Korean or gay or middle class; what success looked like; and what career and lifestyle choices were held in high regard. They were working through their values and who they wanted to be in the world. I was so often moved by students' earnest desires to be good and to do good. They could not, however, always clearly discern the path from desire to actualization. What was the good? And how might it be accomplished? These students felt pressure to be successful. But what were the measures of success? They wanted to change the world. But what should such change look like? Was innovation always desirable? How were these students to evaluate their choices and to move into the future with a confidence and hope that was authentic and responsible?

We all live within narratives. However we understand the process of formation and change, we know we are our memories and our stories. The same is true for society. There are stories we tell about what America is and how it should be and act. There are also stories we tell about who God is and how God acts and who we are in relation to God. We understand these narratives to be true and even *the* truth. We do not recognize them as fictional accounts, but as stating the way things are, as reflecting the nature of reality. The same is sometimes true for our personal narratives. Until they are challenged by some other story, some other voice, usually coming from outside our known world, we think they are reality, the only reality.

The narratives—personal, societal, or religious—are true in a couple of ways. These stories do reflect how we understand ourselves and our places in the world. They convey what we believe about ourselves, our histories, our lives, and the meaning of our existence. They are also true in the sense that they are not pure fiction. There is a relationship between what we think about God, for example, and what God is in Godself. There is also a relationship between what we say about society and the way societies function. But, in no case is the relationship a direct correlation. What we say about God is more ascriptive than descriptive. The same is true for what we say about society.

And these stories, including our theologies and social narratives, can be restrictive, even harmful, just as our personal ones sometimes are. One of the questions being asked by those who are marginalized and whose stake is not in the *status quo* is whether the social and religious narratives include their perspectives, their experiences. Women have wondered why God is nearly always imaged and named as male. Those who suffered in the Holocaust and other genocides have asked what it means to call God good and powerful if God would allow such atrocities. Many of the marginalized and victimized have noticed that all the benefits claimed for "progress" do little to help them. Others have been offering alternative stories that are significantly different from the ones that are most often told.

Attending to these questions and challenges, I want to learn to tell time differently so that we might be able to claim hope anew. Our dominant narrative of time has shaped our understanding of hope in ways that are not life enhancing. Maybe these ways were effective before, but they are no longer. It is time to look at the stories we have been telling and rethink these narratives, including the grand stories about the nature of history and time, God and hope. If God is a God of life, then only that which is able to promote life and well-being is of God. What are these narratives and truths?

In this book, I purpose to outline a theology of hope that is life giving and so appropriate and adequate for the historical, social, and theological challenges of life in America today. My work is meant as a contribution to cultural criticism and cultural construction. Theology is a cultural task. It is not about abstract and eternal truths, but about the modes and norms of living in specific social contexts, with a certain set of commitments, practices, and values. Hope is in history, yielding an open and creative, though limited, future. It is always contextualized.

In this exploration of time and hope, my primary conversation partner is Christianity, particularly the way in which the Christian story has been intertwined with the history of the West. So, another conversation partner is western thought and society, especially in its modern and postmodern manifestations. Other voices in this conversation include psychological theory, especially trauma theory, and social theory, as well as quantum physics and various alternative spiritualities and movements for change. Each of these enrich the conversation with the particularity of their perspective, which offer both criticism and creative alternatives to the more dominant modes of thinking and acting. Actually, my method is not one conversation with multiple partners, but multiple conversations happening at the same time. The "eavesdropping" that happens in such a process allows for different types of connections and creative insights.

The book unfolds in this way:

- Chapter one outlines, in broad strokes, the dominant Christian view of time, history, and hope, as linear and teleological (from *telos*, Greek for goal); examines its narrative form as comedy; and surveys the ways in which it has been so influential in the West.
- Chapter two reviews six contemporary challengers that are calling that dominant view to account and/or revealing its harmful and problematic consequences.
- Chapter three focuses on attempts to rethink linearity and to question the focus on comedic resolution, but still maintain historical movement as the arena of God's meaningful saving actions.
- Chapter four examines more tragic views of history and those that understand time as interrupted and unredeemed. These perspectives are particularly attuned to losses in history and a past that remains unresolved.
- Chapter five surveys an array of movements and perspectives that are broadening our thinking about history and time by offering more cyclical and present focused approaches. These approaches tend to intensify the value of time and to give more attention to place.
- Chapters six brings together the different threads of the book and discusses what it might mean to tell time differently.
- Chapter seven outlines practices and habits to help us live into a different narrative of time, history, and hope. Together these practices and habits form a vision of redemption as life, ever renewing, ever ongoing.

- The epilogue revisits the practice of telling time and offers narrative elements for improvisation and hope.

This book is meant to offer life-giving hope. Its intent is to keep such hope alive. I yearn for a quality of life that is fully engaged with the world. I still want to know, as I believed when I was younger, that what I do makes a difference and may even change the world; but I also seek to honor the complexities and limitations of historical action. My stake, my interest, here is in finding nourishment for life and in offering that nourishment to others who are also searching for oases in the desert of these days. I invite readers into this terrain of questions and exploration. This is not a journey to a final destination where all will be revealed. Rather it is an attempt to map a territory, so that we all may better find our way.

1

DIVINE COMEDY

Christian Narratives of History and Hope

A few times in my life, I have experienced a loss or some other troubling event as deeply shattering, in a way that affected and changed my life on many levels. I would not have chosen these moments. In fact, they seemed like assaults on my life. Whether it was the death of my father when I was still quite young or institutional changes that resulted in the loss of a job, I felt shaken in fundamental ways. Inevitably, in those instances, people told me that a greater good would come as a result and that I should have faith in such an outcome. Because God was in charge and God was good, all would be well. In the Christian narrative, resurrection follows crucifixion, as day follows night. All that happens does so for a reason. Faith in God means that all works ultimately to the good.

I never found comfort in such advice, nor felt such perspectives to be meaningful in times of grief. In fact, they felt like a dismissal of the pain that clung to me. I imagine parents who have just lost a child may have similar feelings when someone piously tells them that the death was God's will, that their child was now with God and so was in a better place. Such remarks offer little consolation. And yet, I also know there are people who absolutely believe that everything that happens is under God's control and that God has an ultimate, and good, purpose for even the most horrific of events. These believers can easily find warrant for their views in the history of Christian thought.

In much of traditional Christian thinking about time and history and redemption, God is the one who is in charge, despite any other appearances or evidence to the contrary. God is in control and God makes the rules. These rules do not necessarily follow the logic of our human thinking or our expectations about reality. In other words, what God is doing in history and in our lives may not always make sense or seem clear. However, the outcome is assured and it is good. From God's perspective and that of the redeemed, history has a happy ending. God is not only the author of time, creation, and history and the one in charge of all that occurs in the universe, but God is also good and loving. God may be unknowable and even untamable, but God's goodness is given. God will work things out in the end. "All's well that ends well," the title of one of Shakespeare's comedies, could well be the slogan for Christian faith in God's action in history.

This chapter will outline, in general terms, these Christian views of time and history, hope and redemption. Theologians, in trying to develop a comprehensive and coherent account of God and God's activities, employ a narrative framework, even though they may not be doing so intentionally. They tell a story, though it may not "read" like a story, about who God is, who we human beings are, and how God and we are in relation. Included in the narrative is an account of the way in which the world is related to God.

All stories employ a narrative structure. They use a specific form of emplotment, tell stories in a particular way. My argument in this chapter is that theologians have most often told the story of Christianity as a comedy, a divine comedy. To view the story of Christianity as a comedy does not mean it makes us laugh or that it is funny, but that everything is resolved in the end. There is a happy ending.

In a divine comedy, God is the one who will effect the resolution. God will bring everything to a happy conclusion, at least for those who are included in God's plan of salvation. The poet Dante vividly portrayed this journey of redemption in his *Divine Comedy* with its three levels of hell, purgatory, and paradise. The comedic ending is reserved for those who find themselves in paradise with God. Those who end up in hell or purgatory deserve to be there. In the next chapter, I will show the limits of a comedic plot line, especially for those who are attentive to the tragedies of history and to often overlooked perspectives. In this chapter, I will explore the dynamics of divine comedy.

The Christian narrative is rooted in the story of Judaism, as contained in the Hebrew Scripture. The books of what Christians often refer to as the Old Testament describe a God who is in charge of time, creation, and history. What happens in history is interpreted as God's actions. God is the one who chooses Abraham and Sarah to leave their homeland and become the forebears of a people. God is the one who calls Moses to lead the people of Israel and orchestrates their liberation from Egypt. The same God is the one who punishes Israel when it goes astray. God's punishment is enacted through historical events such as exile from Jerusalem. This God also redeems Israel and makes possible the return from exile.

Thus Jews seek God in history. History is the arena of God's activity. Not only are the events of history meaningful because they reflect God's will, but they are also purposeful for the future. God's action in history is directed toward the future and the coming of the Messiah. God is working out God's purposes in history, and that history will have an end, a *telos*, that is not only a culmination, but also a consummation. In other words, time and history will not only conclude but also will be realized in the way that God intends them to be. To have faith in God is to believe these things. Such faith is what enables God's chosen people, the people of Israel, to do as God asks. Abraham and Sarah have faith in God's promises, as do Moses and the prophets who communicate God's intents to the people. Such faith persists even when it seems directly challenged. Abraham is often portrayed as the supreme biblical example of such faith. He, along with Sarah, was promised an heir by God and waited a long, long time for such an heir to be born. Still he is willing to follow God's command to sacrifice his son Isaac, the one designated to inherit God's promise. The outcome of that seemingly gruesome and tragic story is also comedic. God spares Isaac and Abraham's lineage is assured.

Many of the writings of the Hebrew Scripture can be read as attempts to address, in one way or another, the vicissitudes of history faced by the people of Israel as well as the challenges found in living. There is no one answer. The different written traditions that were brought together into one Scripture often contain diverse perspectives. What is known as the Deuteronomist tradition most often interprets history as a drama of judgment and redemption. God has called Israel into a particular type of relationship, into a covenant that is dependent on Israel's faithfulness. Again and again, however, Israel is not faithful: the people construct an idol of a golden calf, which they worship rather than Yahweh; Israel chooses to have a monarchy despite Yahweh's warnings of the dangers of such a structure; and the Jewish belief in God's promise of a center in Jerusalem is so taken for granted that the Jewish people do not heed the prophetic warnings of how their actions will result in exile from Jerusalem. According to the Deuteronomist tradition, Israel's actions result in judgment that is manifest in history. So the Israelites have to wander in the desert for many years before coming into the promised land; the monarchy is beset by jealousies and competition and violence that produce destruction again and again; and Jerusalem falls to the Babylonians, and the Israelites are sent into exile for generations. After judgment and punishment come deliverance and restoration. Israel is redeemed; the covenant is renewed. Israel comes into the promised land; it returns from exile; and it is restored to Jerusalem.

This story of judgment and deliverance—or catastrophe and redemption—is told again and again in the Hebrew Scripture. While the scriptural narrative addresses what happens to the people on the corporate and historical scale, psalms of lament and comfort, confession and redemption may be read as the playing out of dynamics of catastrophe, judgment, and deliverance in a more personal mode. Even in the most accusatory of laments, in which the petitioner rails against God for all that has befallen her/him, there is a moment when s/he utters the "yet" that marks faith in the Holy One. And yet, the petitioner avers, I know that Yahweh is good and faithful and true. Hope is expressed through faith that God will respond.

This pattern is perhaps most dramatically and intriguingly played out in the book of Job. One could well argue that Job is the most well known of the Hebrew Scripture because it addresses the question of undeserved suffering that so often plagues the human condition. Job is a righteous man who, the text tells the reader, is being "tested" by God. God takes away everyone that Job loves and everything that he has. Job is left alone, seemingly without hope. The end of the story remains ambiguous. It does, however, contain Job's affirmation of "yet." "Yet I know my redeemer lives," says Job. Meanwhile, God's response to Job's challenges, in one of the most beautiful poems of Hebrew Scripture, affirms the power of God over all of creation. "Where were you?" God questions again and again. Where were you when I, the Lord of heaven and earth, created all that is and gave life to all?

Despite the many commentaries and interpretations of these words, their intent is not obvious. They could be read as upholding God's power as absolute, or as pointing to the mysteries of the universe, or as describing God's relationship of care for all that is. Job's seeming acquiescence is ambiguous as well. The reader does not know what kind of relationship characterizes their exchange. Job's final words in the story have been translated, from the Hebrew, most often as something like: "I despise myself and repent in dust and ashes." Those same words have also been translated: "I despise and repent of dust and ashes." These two translations have very different meanings. The ambiguity resides in the text, so it is difficult to know what the intent of the author(s) was. What the reader does know, however, is that this most tragic of stories ends as a comedy. All of Job's family, possessions, and wealth are restored to him. In that way, he is vindicated, and so is God.

From Hebrew Scripture, Christianity draws the basic elements of its view of history and of God's action in history: that God is the one who creates all that we know, including time, nature, and history. God is outside those things but directing them. That work of direction is referred to as God's providence. God provides all that is needed in creation and continues to take care of what God has created. Because things do not go as God intends, God's work also includes redemption, a restoration of creation, and a bringing back into faithful covenant all who have gone astray. Faith and hope are directed toward this God of promise and fulfillment.

Christianity also derives from Hebrew Scripture a view of history as having a *telos*, an end. As noted above, this end is both culmination and consummation as intended and effected by God. Time does not just stop, but is brought to completion. That completion is a realization of God's intended purposes. It is fulfillment, the outcome of hope. In the later books of Hebrew Scripture, when, because of the experiences and circumstances of the Hebrew people, it became more and more difficult to interpret history as the arena of God's purposes, different perspectives, such as apocalyptic thought, emerged. Apocalyptic suggests that God's presence is not to be found in the ordinary processes of history but in dramatic actions of God's breaking in to history. These actions affirm, by their very drama, the power of God in history. In apocalyptic thought, the *telos* is not so much a fulfillment or culmination, as a type of insertion or interruption. God will realize God's purposes despite the presence of historical obstacles. For Christians, the reality of Jesus as the Christ, the Messiah, is an apocalyptic realization, a new revelation of God's presence, changing and reforming history forever.

Types of Biblical Time

Before I elaborate on the Christian narrative and the ways in which it uses and adapts Hebrew thought, it is important to discuss the nature of time and what the understanding of time is in the biblical witness. It is commonplace to suggest that the biblical view of time is linear. Past, present, and future follow upon one another in succession. In the beginning, God created the heavens and the earth, and then on the next day, and the next day, and so on. The linearity is directional. Time is moving not only toward the future, but also that future arises from and is shaped by the past. Thus time has an end goal toward which it is directed. The outcome is contained in God's original intentions in creation. Even if such original intentions are seriously compromised, as the Christian narrative of the fall suggests, God's work of redemption will undo the effects of the fall in order to realize God's purposes. Just as at the end of a Shakespearean comedy all is revealed and resolved, so will God resolve history and make real God's promises. In this intentional, linear view of time, what happens in creation and history is not random. God, who is directing all to its intended, comedic end, is both powerful and good. Hope is given shape and character by this view of time as the working out of God's purposes. These purposes are messianic and redemptive. What God has created, God will fulfill; what is promised will be delivered; and what is lost will be redeemed.

Most often that linear view of time is compared and contrasted with a cyclical view of time. Again, it has been commonplace to suggest that Jewish and Christian views of time are linear in distinction to Greek and "pagan" views of time as cyclical. Cyclical time does not progress in a direction; it contains no "arrow" of time, but continues in an endless cycle of return. Time, in that sense, does not "go" anywhere, but constantly repeats. Modern perspectives on these two views added an evaluative element. Linear time came to be seen as better than cyclical time. Hope was manifest in linear time in a way that cyclical time, which keeps repeating endlessly and seems to go nowhere, does not allow. Later in this book, I will offer my own evaluations of such judgments and the interests they serve. What is important to note here is that biblical Judaism also reflected a cyclical view of time.

Biblical Jews were primarily an agrarian and ritual-bound people who paced their lives by the cycles of nature and the rituals that accompanied those cycles. Some of the rites practiced by ancient Jews marked historical events such as the Exodus; but others, especially the sacrificial system that was so central to Jewish life, focused as much on the rhythms and cycles of the seasons and of everyday life as on dramatic moments in history. Given the history of Judaism, including the destruction of the Temple, the dispersal of Jews from Jerusalem, and the shift away from temple sacrifice, these aspects of ancient Jewish life do not receive much attention. Because the biblical texts are read through modern views of time and history, these more nature-bound and ritual dimensions of biblical Judaism are often overlooked and neglected.

Wisdom literature offers yet another perspective on time. The biblical wisdom writings seem to turn away from historical events as the loci of faith and hope. The title of Elsa Tamez's book on Ecclesiastes, *When the Horizons Close*, captures well this sense that history holds little hope. For the author of Ecclesiastes, "there is nothing new under the sun" and all is "vanity." Change for the better does not seem possible; future time does not guarantee deliverance. Wisdom narrows focus and tries to find meaning in life itself: to "eat, drink, and be merry." It advocates affirming life by living it as well as one is able. Desire and faith are expressed through particular ways of living and the practice of certain attitudes and virtues, including faith in God as ultimately good and powerful.[1]

As noted above, the biblical witness also offers an apocalyptic view of time. One could argue that apocalyptic is not so much an alternative perspective on time as a way to think differently about linear time. Apocalyptic focuses on God's dramatic intervention from outside of what is known as historical time. Instead of linear time resolving itself successively or progressively, apocalyptic hope looks for an interruption that perhaps changes the direction of history or that ensures the realization of the original purposes.

In actuality, both linear and apocalyptic views of time contain the notion that when things do not go as they should, as they were intended to go, there is something wrong that must be corrected. The dynamics of judgment and restoration that play out again and again in the biblical narrative can be understood as such "course correction." Apocalyptic offers a more dramatic expression of that dynamic, a more radical course correction. One way to understand apocalyptic is an interventionist approach that seems to manifest when other avenues of hope appear to be unavailable.

Another way to think about apocalyptic is to see it as maintaining narrative tension. There is not necessarily much drama in a linear view of time that moves in a particular direction. We can consider this vectored time. What makes for drama and tension in that approach is resistance: that which does not allow the vector to move in its intended direction. Introducing an apocalyptic perspective allows one to account for the resistance and also to allow action that might change the direction of the original vector or allow it to break through the resistance. In other words, apocalyptic allows for dramatic change that cannot come from within the directional vector itself. Such possibilities also empower the seemingly powerless because they remind them of promised fulfillment and deliverance in times when such fulfillment seems elusive or impossible. They suggest that the future is open and that there is still the possibility of change in history, even dramatic change from "outside intervention."

The Christian Biblical Story

The biblical story suggests that Jesus was born in the "fullness of time." What does this phrase mean? It implies that there is a connection between Jesus and the realization of God's purposes in time. New Testament texts claim that Jesus is the Messiah, the one who will save the people and bring history to its fulfillment. This expectation is full of narrative tension. As we read in the Gospels, this savior appeared among a people long suffering under the yoke of imperial rule. For these people, historical hopes seemed fruitless. Jesus preached about the reign of God that is present and not yet. This preaching played upon themes of promise and fulfillment. In his parables, Jesus spoke of the kingdom of God as manifest in people's lives, often in ordinary ways, such as the rising of yeast bread or the growth of a mustard seed. In his warnings against those who were not fully faithful, he offered dramatic portrayals of God's wrath and final judgment. "Woe be to you," Jesus cried out. Meanwhile, Jesus paid special attention to those who had reason to doubt God's favor: the poor and the marginalized, sinners, and those in need of healing. He seemed to point to a different type of hope: one that offered life and a sense of God's imminent presence.

The degree of dramatic tension in the books of the New Testament varied. However, all of those accounts were trying, in one way or another, to tell a story about the difference that Jesus and his message made. In the Pauline letters, which have been so influential in Christian theology, that message was merged more and more into the person of Jesus and, more particularly, into Jesus' crucifixion and resurrection as being at the heart of what God was about in Jesus the Christ. In other words, what Jesus means, the difference Jesus makes, was contained in the cross and the resurrection. Jesus' preaching and life actions, his healings and teaching, played little part in Paul's telling of the story of redemption. New life, hope, and redemption were through the cross and resurrection. For Paul, the fruits of this new creation, the consequences of God's action, so to speak, were to be manifest in the Christian community, the body of Christ, and how its members lived their lives. Thus Paul's focus was not on history so much as community. New life in Christ was lived in and through Christ's body, the community of the faithful.

One place in which Paul did focus on history was in the opening chapters of Romans. His narrative intent in those chapters was to show that human beings had not been faithful to God, but had turned to sin. They had not lived the way God had intended them to live in creation. In Romans, Paul told the story of human faithlessness, which set the stage for the ultimate faithfulness of Jesus. God's good creation was harmed and deflected from its natural purposes by the unnatural and sinful behaviors of human beings acting against God, one another, and creation itself. The groundwork was laid to argue for the need for redemption and a savior. In those chapters in Romans, Paul affirmed God both as author of a good creation and as power in history. Paul also described human corruption and estrangement from God's original purposes. He pointed to a fundamental rift between God and creation that needed to be mended and transformed. Jesus Christ's actions were about setting right this relationship between God and humanity. Jesus Christ effected justification, which is the bringing back the estranged into right relation.

Paul is also the New Testament author who introduced a comparison between Adam, the first "man," and Jesus. Over the next couple of centuries, Christian theologians would develop that comparison more and more until the Genesis account of creation and the fall into sin became central to the Christian story of history and redemption. Even though the New Testament makes scant reference to the opening chapters of Genesis (and the Gospels make only one, and that in the context of a discussion about divorce), those chapters and interpretations of them became absolutely foundational to Christian theological thinking in succeeding centuries.

Also in those first centuries of Christianity, there occurred a shift in the way Christians approached time. The sense of narrative tension, of the imminent expectation of Christ's return, which so permeated the early books of the New Testament, decreased. As a result, the time of God's reign was stretched out more and more toward an unseen future. Rather than imagining the "kingdom of God" to be at hand, Christian theologians, increasingly influenced by Greek philosophical thought forms, found themselves imagining the fullness of God's presence as not here and not now. Hope for redemption came to be seen as a future promise, realized in a place called heaven; redemption was in an afterlife, rather than in this life.

As any sense of imminent expectation dissipated and the future moved more and more forward toward an unknown time of ending, human time and God's time, earth and heaven, split further apart. Eschatology came to be about God's time and about the end, the last things. In systematic theologies, it has characteristically been the last topic to be considered, listed at the end of the table of contents. Eternal life, the promise of life with God, came to be defined as timeless, rather than as the fulfillment of time. It would follow upon a last judgment, when all would appear before Christ and receive blessing or curse. Such shifts have held profound implications for Christian thinking about history and the presence of God's actions in and through history.

Augustine the Theologian

By the time Augustine of Hippo emerged on the theological scene, a few centuries later, these shifts and developments were well in place: especially ideas about original sin and Jesus Christ's work of redemption as a necessary remedy for original sin, and eternal life as discontinuous with earthly life. Augustine further developed, firmed up, and added nuance and systematic thought to a tradition that had already been taking shape. Because of his immense impact on western theological thought both in the past and still today, the influence of his theology cannot be underestimated. Augustine's theology of sin and redemption and his view of history, of God's time and our time, continue to dominate Christian thought on those topics.

In his magisterial tome *City of God*, Augustine outlined his theology of history and redemption. The "City of God" exists in contrast to the "City of Man," which is under the sway of sin. To understand the origin of sin, Augustine, along with many of the theologians who came before and after him, turned to the Genesis story. As Augustine told the story, God is the author of all that exists. God creates out of nothing, which is to say, that God is not part of creation, but is totally other. God's creation is good and it is ordered. God does not create evil.

It is, however, very apparent that evil, sin, and disorder abound. How did Augustine explain this? Included in God's good creation were the first man and the first woman, Adam and Eve. God created them also as good and ordered them to live in a particular relationship of obedience. Out of goodness, God gave these human beings freedom, but they abused their freedom. They disobeyed God by eating the fruit of the forbidden tree. By this "original sin" of disobedience and a misuse of freedom, the first humans presumed to make choices that were God's to make and theirs to follow and obey. Their behavior brought sin and disorder into God's good creation. What was done could not be undone. So, Augustine argued, the disobedience of Adam and Eve affects all of humanity. All human beings are born with original sin. Such sin so infects the human will that human beings, on their own, are not able to choose the good. Their free will is forever compromised. Without God's grace, they can only choose evil. Human beings are also responsible for introducing evil into the world by the misuse of their free will. God's gift of free will is a good thing, but human beings have used it for a bad end.

If the story ended here, it would be a tragedy. God's good purposes were brought to naught by human willfulness. God, however, originally authored a comedy and so did not leave humans in their predicament. God sent a savior, Jesus Christ, a sinless man whose offering and sacrifice of his life righted the wrongs that had been committed and made possible the healing of the wounded souls of human beings. In contrast to the sin of Adam and Eve, Jesus Christ embodied righteousness. His death and resurrection functioned to rebalance what was amiss in the universe.

Through grace, human beings are able to participate in Christ's saving actions. Such grace is a gift from God, given to those whom God chooses. Even though Christ's work of redemption is accomplished and, therefore, the outcome of history is assured, the drama continues in "human time." Only at the end of time, only when the "City of God" is made manifest, will the sorting and winnowing be complete. Thus, the assurance that God is bringing all to good purpose is ever yoked to the calling to account of the last judgment. Salvation in history remains a promise that, in the end, the redeemed will be delivered into eternity and God's embrace.

For Augustine and for much of Christian theology, the story of time, history, and redemption is of paradise given, paradise lost, and paradise restored. It is a narrative of Eden, fall, and redemption. There is a cyclical quality to this narrative in that restoration or redemption can be seen as a return to a state of original righteousness, but the story line moves primarily in a linear fashion. Eden is in the past, and fully realized redemption is in the future or beyond time. Even though redemption is a restoration, it is not a return. Rather redemption is realization of the promises that were present in original creation. Restoration enables those promises to be fulfilled.

Not only is redemption fulfillment of the original promises, but, as theologians have argued, Jesus Christ changes history decisively, which is to say that with Christ, time and history are forever different. The practice of designating calendar years as "Before Christ" and "After Christ," or *Anno Domini*, (B.C. and A.D.) is one familiar manifestation of that belief. Time is measured by the Christ event; the eras of history are defined by it.

Even though the event of Christ has already changed history, Christ's saving work is ongoing in the dynamic of crucifixion and resurrection. That dynamic is a primary way Christians understand what happens in history. Just as the Hebrews interpreted their history through the lens of catastrophe and redemption, Christians view historical events through that of crucifixion and resurrection. Jesus Christ died once and for all, but as long as human history contains the workings of sin and evil, God's presence will continue to be manifest as crucifixion and resurrection.

For Augustine, the "City of God" and the "City of Man" were parallel histories, existing alongside one another, until the end of human time. Only the inhabitants of the "City of God" would be saved, but as long as human beings were in time and history, those inhabitants were not known. The "City of God" was not to be identified with any earthly institution. Though the church was the place where God was most likely to be encountered, the church itself was not to be equated with the "City of God." Only at the end of time, only when God's reign was fully established, would the "City of Man" disappear and the "City of God" be established clearly and decisively. In the meantime, Christians were to live as if they were inhabitants of the "City of God," but in the knowledge that the "City of Man" was necessary for the conduct of human affairs. Both cities had ends and goods proper to them. In that sense, they were both necessary for their own specific purposes. Ultimately only the "City of God" was eternal, but because both cities had their proper ends and purposes and because history was not complete, there was a sense in which both existed in time. In that way, Augustine gave a value to history and time. What happened in history did matter, even if it did not ultimately affect redemption. Redemption history and human history were two distinct cities, but both were under God's providence.

These perspectives, firmly established in Augustine's thought, dominated Christian theology for centuries. God's history, salvation history, was not human history, even though human history had its own significance. Life on earth, whether individual or corporate, was always shaped by sin. Therefore, the drama of human existence was one of paradise lost. Hope lay in God's redemptive activity. God was bringing time and history to completion through the ongoing dynamic of crucifixion and resurrection.

There would be an end point that signaled both finality and consummation, accompanied by judgment and transformation. The great medieval cathedrals of Europe fixed the scene of the last judgment, with Jesus Christ enthroned in glory, over their portals. The message was abundantly clear. All who entered the heavenly realms did so through the gate of judgment, by way of Christ.

Moving into the Middle Ages and the Early Modern Era

Augustine's thought was so influential that, over the centuries, other theologians may have provided some different insights about these matters and so changed theological thought somewhat, but the overall schema that Augustine spelled out stayed in place. For example, Martin Luther developed a theology of two orders, divine and earthly, in a way that gave more value to human institutions such as marriage and the state. Human action in both orders could be expressive of God's intent. Yet the division between God's realm and the human realm remained intact. John Calvin also tried to infuse human work and life with divine virtues, to give them a value intended by God in creation. But, at the same time, he strengthened the absolute sovereignty of God and God's power as determinative. God was fully in charge and directing history toward God's purposes. Time and all of life were in God's hands. Humans, on their own, were only capable of sin, of the dissolution of time and history. Hope lay in God's grace and providence. History was a *divine* comedy.

Even though God's purposes were fulfilled only at the end of time, in classical Christian thought, future time was not privileged. The past, the value of tradition, held the premier place in theological thought, even in the Reformation era. Indeed, the Reformation can be read as a retrieval of tradition, a returning of the church to its pristine origins and a correction of the inevitable distortions that come with time. Time was not valued for what new things could happen in it. It was seen more as the environment for doing wrong and going astray. Better then to preserve the past against such threats in the present and the future and direct faith toward the new age to come, at the end of human history. Better to set one's sights on entry into God's eternity.

Before the modern era, more cyclical views of time also had value and held a place, especially in Christian liturgical and ritual practices.

Most Christians in the Middle Ages did not live their lives according to the arguments of theologians, but by the rhythms of the church and its cycles of time: daily, seasonal, and annual. While theologians wrote about time and history, redemption and eternity on a grand scale, the church developed ways to connect Christianity with people's everyday lives. In the agrarian societies of Europe, the *angelus* would ring out times for prayer each day. The cycles of feasting and fasting ordered the lives of most people. Time was marked by these events, which in turn were shaped by either the liturgical calendar or the agricultural one or more often, a combination of the two. Christian celebrations were held for fertile fields and for good harvests. Life was lived according to the rhythms of these cycles. Daily life was ordered by periodic reminders of eternity.

There were some variations on these themes, although not ones that necessarily moved to the center of Christian theological thought. In the Middle Ages, Joachim of Fiore took the idea of a linear view of history and introduced a progressive element. Joachim saw history in stages, corresponding to persons of the Trinity. The age of the Father paralleled that of the Old Testament; Jesus Christ inaugurated the age of the Son, which was to be followed by the age of the Spirit, which would witness the rise of new religious movements. At the end of the age of the Spirit, God's reign would be fully established on earth. In Joachim's imaginings, the ages were not only successive, but also progressive. They were generative, as was hope. Each era lasted for a designated period of time: forty-two generations, lasting thirty years each. By that calculation, the age of the Spirit was to be inaugurated in 1260 C.E. Joachim, whose dates are considered to be 1132–1202, was himself living in the last years of the age of the Son.

Joachim's ideas influenced millenarian and even revolutionary thinkers, those who liked to "count" and categorize God's time or who wanted to advocate for change in history. His views had an impact on Reformation figures such as Thomas Müntzer, leader of the peasant rebellion in Germany, and others associated with the Radical Reformation. Müntzer's call for changing the social order was opposed by Luther, who, siding with the princes, argued for maintaining the divinely established order of government.

Others turned to Joachim's ideas to try to imagine God's timing. Such millenarian thought is characterized by efforts to predict the course of history and to identify God's actions and purposes in history. Sometimes these millenarian predictions have had an apocalyptic tone. The end of history would involve a dramatic intervention by God. Other times they were more progressive in tone, as in Joachim's case. Depending on the perspective, adherents would look for different signs of the times. If they thought the end would be a dramatic intervention, they would look for indications that things were getting worse, that history was crying out for God's action. If they thought history was more progressive, then they would look for positive signs, instances of God's presence and action being manifest.

The more apocalyptic strain has persisted and received much attention, especially in what is referred to as dispensationalism. Dispensationalism reads the biblical witness as narrating successive "dispensations," distinct periods of salvation history, under the direction of God, culminating in the final dispensation, as recounted in the book of Revelation. This approach to time is embraced by segments of American society today, as evidenced by the popularity of the *Left Behind* book series, by Tim LaHaye and Jerry Jenkins, that focuses on the final rapture. Such dispensationalism is not only about predicting and describing the end; it is also about having a kind of control over it and over who will and will not be saved. This contemporary expression of dispensationalism is modern in its sensibilities, even though it represents itself as counter to modernity's thinking about history and time, redemption and hope. It is shaped in reaction to Enlightenment thinking.

Following the Enlightenment

Beginning in the seventeenth century, the Enlightenment represents a monumental turning point in the history of western thought and practice. For our purposes here, what is most important about Enlightenment thinking is that it shifted attention to human history, with the human person at its center. God was no longer the only author of time and history. Human persons were fully engaged as sole or co-creators. Life was not about taking one's place in the world but about making and shaping the world. History was not only linear but also progressive. As human persons made the world, they were changing it for the better. History was the story of freedom and development, ever growing toward completion. Human reason and intelligence were capable of great invention. They were the sources of true knowledge and the arbiters of value.

For the next several centuries, theologians, philosophers, and theorists proffered, elaborated, and debated these assertions. We today are heirs of these centuries. We live in post-Enlightenment time, the era of modernity, now declared past, but whose ghosts still haunt and inform the ways in which we view the world. Postmodernity is shaped by modernity. We continue to play out modernity's legacies in one way or another.

In the last several centuries, what human reason makes possible has been celebrated in previously unimaginable ways. Technological reason, the type of thought that figures out how to do things and whose value is measured by what it produces, took on its own unparalleled value. Invention and achievement became the measures of success. Other more contemplative and wisdom-seeking notions of reason, which had reigned supreme previously, lost status and were marginalized in both academic circles and society in general.

The scientific discoveries and technological advances of the last several centuries have been immense: from the telephone to the television, from the printing press to the computer, from the steam engine to the space shuttle, from the automatic pistol to the nuclear bomb, from the microscope to the MRI machine. Human invention propelled knowledge forward and continues to do so. Our science fiction writers imagine worlds of the future with even more sophisticated technology and capabilities. It seems there is no end to human knowledge and what human persons can discover, invent, and make.

Modernity changed the human relationship to time and the world. Technology and its inventions profoundly affected the character of human living. The hope contained in all these discoveries and creations was to make our lives easier, healthier, and better. In many ways, technology has done that. Modern medicine is able to treat diseases long deemed mysterious. The daily chores of life do not consume so much of our energies. Theoretically, we should have time for more devoted leisure and other pursuits. Airplanes and computers make the spaces between people in different parts of the globe smaller and more easily traversable. We can travel around the world in a day, communicate across continents in an instant.

Television allows us to see immediately what is happening thousands of miles away.

Not only is the world smaller, but we view it as ours in a way that is different from the past. Because we not only take our place in the world but also make the world, we human beings think of the world as the raw material of our invention. We are free to use and manipulate its resources in the name of discovery and progress. No longer is God the author of history: we are. Our actions, whether they produce technological development or revolutionary change, alter the course of world.

We human beings see ourselves as being at the center of this world. Everything is about us and revolves around us, not God. We are the final arbiters. The Christ of the last judgment has been dethroned and replaced by progress. The measure of success and even of salvation has become such progress. Achievement is the ultimate value.

As a result of all these changes, the relationship between salvation history and world history seemed to shift. Theologians labeled this change "secularization." The sacred had given way to the secular. The workings of the world and of human existence were no longer the mysterious province of God. They were accessible through human knowledge. Theologians responded to these shifts in a variety of ways. Some denounced secularization and called for unswerving allegiance to the sacred. Others embraced it and tried to rethink traditional Christian categories in light of it. More recently, the distinction itself, between sacred and secular, has been questioned and criticized for setting up a false, problematic, and unhelpful dichotomy.

Whatever the attitude toward secularization, there is little doubt that modern thought influenced and impacted Christian understandings of time and history. Many theologians no longer view salvation history and world history as two separate and totally distinct processes. They are not two "cities." Rather there is one history. Nor is judgment reserved for God, to be revealed at the end of time. History contains its own judgments and its own dynamism for good or ill. For the historical optimists, the forward march of time is a story of progress.

In the nineteenth and early twentieth centuries, what has been called Liberal Christianity understood Christianity to be about establishing God's reign on earth. Christians were to be engaged in action for social justice and charity that would make more real the ethics of

God's reign and that would establish justice, peace, and harmony. Progress was not only technological; it was also human and ethical. Paradise could be approximated on earth.

Though the schema of Christian history as paradise given/paradise lost/paradise regained continued to dominate Christian theological thought, there emerged a different view about where and when paradise would be regained. It was no longer only what would be bestowed on the chosen ones in eternity; now, it was a possibility on earth, in and through human action. The divine comedy had become a human comedy.

Such thinking extended beyond Christian theological thought itself. Indeed, it permeated American ideologies of manifest destiny and America as the promised land, if not paradise itself. From its origins, those who landed on American shores were in search of a new and better life. America offered, if not heavenly salvation, a promised land, a place of deliverance. These attitudes continue to play themselves out in the way America conducts itself in the world and in its social policies at home.

Yet, just as the Israelites' move into Canaan was at the expense of the Canaanites, so was American manifest destiny, whether in the northern or southern hemispheres, at the expense of those already inhabiting the land. And just as the biblical witness is written from the point of view of the Israelites and so silences, and is even critical of, the Canaanites, American history has tended to be written only from the perspective of the colonizers. Those whose lands were taken, whose lives were lost, are only now beginning to have their story told and their claims recognized. As we will see in the next chapter, these emerging voices are challenging the dominant American narrative. They are suggesting that it is a story of imperialism masking itself as a redemption narrative.

Theological Developments in the Last Century

Challenges to optimism about approximating God's reign on earth arose almost immediately. Events in history, especially World War I, made claims to human progress in goodness seem naïve, at best, and even ludicrous. Theologians such as Karl Barth denounced the proponents of human progress and declared the absolute sovereignty and judgment of God over all human inventions and institutions. God was still in charge of history. But for the grace of God, humans lived only in sin. Other theologians, such as Reinhold Niebuhr, affirmed the necessity of human power and action, while maintaining the inevitability of sin. All human action was under judgment, but action for the good was possible through grace. Even then it was never without sinful motivations and consequences. Niebuhr updated Augustine's view of two cities by declaring that both goodness and evil were growing in the world. What seemed like progress was always accompanied by a potential for more evil. Only at the end, in God's time, would evil be eliminated.

Still others, while forgoing optimism about the possibility of eliminating evil completely, looked for different ways to understand the relationship of human history and God's history. They continued to read divine and human history as one. The German theologian Dietrich Bonhoeffer, writing during World War II, spoke of human persons "coming of age in the world." For so long, Bonhoeffer argued, we human beings had relied on God to explain and make sense of the world, but now, given advances in knowledge, we had ways to account for much of what had once been seen as God's province or God's doing. God needed a new job description, so to speak, and we human beings needed a different kind of relationship with God. For Bonhoeffer, God was not to be found at the edges of our knowledge or in the "gaps" between what we knew and did not know. This God of the gaps, whose primary job had been to explain and give reasons for what lay beyond our understanding, played less and less of a role in the post-Enlightenment world of discovery and scientific explanation. God was to be found in our midst, and especially in the reality of human historical existence, characterized by suffering. Bonhoeffer offered no easy optimism about human history. He lived, after all, in Nazi Germany. But he did not turn away from history either. God was to be found in the world, in and through human history.

Bonhoeffer communicated these ideas in letters he wrote from prison, where he was being held because of his participation in a plot to assassinate Hitler. Tragically, Bonhoeffer was executed just before the prison was liberated by the Allies, and his theological career was cut short. The intriguing thoughts Bonhoeffer offered in those last letters, however, continue to capture the imagination of many theologians, who, in turn, attempt to rethink these questions of God's relationship with the world and with human persons.

In the last several decades, liberal, political, and liberation theologians have been at the forefront of such attempts. They persist in seeing God's history and human history as ultimately one. Therefore, God's action for redemption is historical. What happens in history not only matters, but history is the arena of God's saving work. Redemption is not simply about consummation in eternity, defined as beyond time or timeless. Redemption has to be in and through history. Otherwise, human life and indeed creation do not really count in God's saving drama. They are devalued.

Such assertions naturally lead to the question of how are we to know what is and what is not God's action. Most liberal and political theologians have been reluctant to point to any specific historical movements as of God. They affirm that history is the arena of God's saving work, but do not identify or equate God's action with any particular historical manifestation. They are more confident about pointing to what is not of God, than what is of God. Since these theologians occupy positions of relative privilege and cultural, social, and political dominance, this holding back makes sense and can be indicative of an admirable humility. Given that America and the European nations are complicit in so much of what ails the world today, the practice of a critical stance toward modern western society seems appropriate and fitting. Thus Roman Catholic theologian Johann Baptist Metz could insist on the importance of hope in history and yet be critical of any specific naming of that hope. Likewise, Protestant theologian Paul Tillich wrote of an "eschatological proviso," which suggested that any historical actions or accomplishments fall short of God's redemptive purposes. For Tillich, all historical judgments are provisional, pending final judgment at the end of time. Alongside such reservations, these theologians have still embraced and pointed to general trends or movements in history, such as the growth of freedom or justice or humanization, as signs of God's presence and activity. In other words, God is working in history in particular directions, toward more freedom and justice, toward making human life more human. As long as God is active, history is a comedy, divine and human.

Liberation theologians, who identify with and write from the perspective of those who have suffered grievously in and from history, have sought more concrete evidence of God's actions in history. Motivated by the desire to change the conditions of oppression in specific political contexts, these theologians have found it important and even necessary to support particular historical strategies and movements. They have pointed to the rising up of subordinated peoples as an expression of God's intent and action. Commitment to the growth of freedom ought not simply gesture toward a general movement in history, but it needs to actively support and be in solidarity with specific actions and campaigns. Concern for justice has to translate into concrete social programs. Humanization must be identifiable in a people's sense of themselves as agents in history. So Latin American liberation theologians have written of the "power of the poor in history"; Black theologians supported and embraced Black power; and feminist theologians, inspired by the women's movement, claimed women's self-transformation to be revelatory of God.

What is common to all these theologies, whatever their approach to concrete events and dynamics of history, is a view of time and history as linear and moving toward a *telos*. Even if theologians are critical of historical progress and wary of naming historical accomplishments as evidence of divine action, time is still viewed as directed toward a culmination. Even if they advocate the need for revolution in history, the movement of revolution is toward a particular, future end, often imagined in utopian terms. Salvation history and world history are directed toward an end that will be realized. Redemption is defined by that end, that eschatological conclusion. Thus, theologians speak of eschatological promises being fulfilled or of realized eschatology. As feminist theologian Mary Daly has done, they may write of the Second Coming of women. Or as liberation theologian Gustavo Gutierrez has, they may point to the poor as the locus of God's ongoing revelation. There is no doubt that sin and evil continue to be obstacles and problems in history, expressed in systems of oppression as well as in human behavior, but paradise is being regained by actions for transformation and liberation. God or the divine is clearly on the side of such movements for transformation and liberation. What makes for liberation is of God; what does not is against the divine intent.

These liberal, political, and liberation views of history and salvation history further refine and define modern perspectives on time.

They emphasize continuity in history. To say that history is linear and progressive is to imply that the present follows upon the past and the future follows upon the present in a way that is free of radical breaks or departures. To say that human history and salvation history are one is to view God's actions through the lens of linearity and continuity. Occasionally a theologian, such as Johann Baptist Metz, adopts the tones of apocalyptic to offer a counter-narrative to what he understands as the dominant ethos of complacent linearity. Although his definition of religion as "interruption" and his advocacy of imminent expectation seem to suggest that salvation will come from outside history, Metz's aim is not to leave history behind but to read better the signs of the times and to aid discernment.

In modernity, even ideas about revolutionary change are characterized by a certain linearity and teleological determinism, whether it be Hegel's rendering of history's progress as thesis, antithesis, and synthesis or Marx's views about the rise of the proletariat and the necessary march of history. The tensions and discontinuities of apocalyptic approaches have been "tamed," so to speak. Or they have been relegated to the marginalized religious expressions of millenarian sects and to the pages of science fiction. These tensions, however, may assert themselves occasionally and find expression in our anxieties about time and history.

There was evidence of such an "anxiety attack" as we approached the turn of the millennium at the end of 1999. In the months preceding the new year, the "hype" about the immensity of that change and about all the dangers of Y2K resulted in countless amounts of time, money, and energy spent to prepare for what turned out to be a rather smooth transition. The dire predictions did not come true. In the end, the new millennium came in with a whimper and not a bang. Despite our anxieties, linearity and continuity ruled the day.

Theologians, such as Paul Tillich, have attributed these experiences of anxiety to our human condition, caught between finitude and infinity. We can see the stars and try to reach them, but our reach exceeds our grasp time and again. What distinguishes us from other animals is not our limitations, but our awareness of them. To be created is to be limited. Finitude is intrinsic to our creaturely condition. But that we know our limitations and can imagine other possibilities produces a disease and anxiety in us. Paul Tillich and Reinhold Niebuhr, among other theologians, related that anxiety to our condition of sin, our inability to be content with what God has given us. So we disobey and seek for more than God has allotted us in our creation. We eat of the forbidden tree.

These theologians have further suggested that such anxiety, to a certain extent, drives history. It is a source of both creativity and destruction. Anxiety feeds into and reinforces our future orientation. What is yet to be—possibilities—seem always more attractive than what we have—actualities. More is always deemed better. There is then a connection between linear, progressive views of time and history and our seeming inability to find satisfaction, to know, have, and be enough. Thus we are left to flounder in our anxiety.

Another key aspect of linear and progressive views of history is thinking that what happens in history has to be meaningful. It needs to be accounted for. In the divine/human comedy, there is nothing that can be deemed fate or chance or in the realm of the inexplicable. Everything serves a purpose and, history being a comedy, ultimately a good purpose. A case in point is human suffering. We humans do not simply accept the conditions of suffering, but ask why and to what purpose. Theologians have spent immense amounts of time and energy trying to find meaning in suffering and to have it fit into a grand, purposive scheme. Most often, such explorations and justifications are under the umbrella of theodicy, which is about justifying God and preserving God's goodness and power. But they are also about the human search for meaning and for accounting for everything that happens in history so that history is not the realm of the arbitrary, the capricious, the inexplicable. Such a pursuit of explanation and meaning creates it own problems, however, especially when the immensity of evil and suffering, such as in the case of the Holocaust, defies any purpose the suffering might possibly serve. I will explore this challenge more in the next chapter. For now, it is important to note that there is a connection between this quest for meaning and justification and a view of history as linear and comedic.

Triumph of the Good

Thus far, I have been arguing that the Christian tradition produced a view of time and history, hope and redemption that is linear and teleological. Time and history are moving forward toward an end. That end is the realization of the promise of God's redemptive activity. We are assured a happy ending, even if the world is destroyed in the process and not everyone is saved. Even then the story remains a comedy, a divine comedy. Since the Enlightenment, that divine comedy has become more and more a human comedy as well. Not only should God's purposes be realized but so should human ones. We expect time and history to fulfill our desires and to have a happy ending.

Into this wedding of linear time and comedic narrative, I would introduce another factor: the question of what is deemed valuable. Platonic thought emphasized three categories of value: the good, the true, and the beautiful. All three were important and necessary. In modernity, I would suggest, we have witnessed the triumph of the good, and what I would consider its more base forms of the effective and the efficient, over the valuing of truth and beauty.

Classical Christian thought tended to privilege truth. The goal of theology was orthodoxy, correct and right thinking about God's revelation. Reason was in the service of explicating that revelation, received as truth. God's truth was ultimate and absolute. As such, truth was to be honored, preserved, and awarded central place in any considerations. The good and the beautiful were evaluated by their correspondence to revealed truth. So, for example, something was deemed beautiful because God had created it or because it reflected truth. Something was good because God had designated it as such. The theologian's job then was to seek truth, revealed through creation and in Scripture and tradition.

The Enlightenment challenged classical understandings of revelation and reason. Truth was not given; it was not revealed. Nor was reason subordinate to revelation. Rather revelation was subject to reason. So, for example, miracles were no longer accepted as true but were questioned according to the rules of nature. Only that which made sense and could be demonstrated was to be considered true. Reason was now used to criticize authority and to aid in discovery. Practical and technological reason joined hands with criticism. A concern with truth was replaced with a concern for morality. What was right became more a question of morality, of the good, rather than of the true.

This concern for the good developed in different directions. On the one hand, it was expressed in a growing interest in justice and the common good. The practice of goodness was to be manifest in history through work for just, free, and caring communities. God was the source of such goodness. God's love was to be experienced as care, as providence, and as redemption, the transformation of society. This commitment to goodness has perhaps reached fullest expression in liberation theologies in which truth is understood to be practical: what is of God is known by its effects. Truth is what we practice. God is present where justice and good works are manifest. Biblical passages cited to support this perspective include Micah 6:8: "What does the Lord require of you but to do justice, and to love kindness, and to walk humbly with your God?" Another oft cited passage is Matthew 25, in which Jesus suggests that whenever his followers have fed the hungry, provided drink for the thirsty, or visited those in prison, they have done those things for him. Jesus conveys a similar message—that actions for justice and transformation are manifesting God's work— when John the Baptist's followers question him as to whether he is the Messiah or if they should wait for another, and Jesus says, "Go and tell John what you have seen and heard: the blind receive their sight, the lame walk, the lepers are cleansed, the deaf hear, the dead are raised, the poor have good news brought to them" (Luke 7:22; also Matthew 11:4–5).

Christianity is thus as true as the goodness and justice it demonstrates. What is true is that which contributes to the good. It is effective in making a difference in people's lives. This equation of truth with morality has been said to transform—or reduce—theology into ethics. It reflects the shift from reason that is in the service of wisdom and contemplation to reason that is concerned with practical effects. This shift may highlight the importance and necessity of justice, but, as I will show in this book, it may also produce problematic consequences for the ways in which we view time and history.

For one thing, in the industrial West, the concern for practical effects has too often been translated into an emphasis on productiveness. Goodness is equated with productiveness. Combined with capitalist economics, such a perspective measures goodness, along with truth and beauty, by the bottom line. What is true and good and beautiful is assessed by its use value, effectiveness, and efficiency. If something is not useful, then it is not good or true or beautiful. There is a conflict inherent in these two approaches to the good as justice and as efficiency. Often what is most just is neither efficient nor even necessarily productive. Too much concern with efficiency tends to erode a commitment to goodness as justice. The implications of the conflict between efficiency and justice will be discussed further in the next chapter. The point I am making here is that whether in the form of morality or efficiency, goodness has become the primary category of assessing value in western societies.

The Promise of Comedy

In the Jewish and Christian narratives discussed in this chapter, there needs to be a happy ending. God and/or the good must win out. Otherwise, God is not God. Otherwise, redemption is in jeopardy and humans are left vulnerable to what has been called the "terror of history."

When we go to the movies, whether they be romantic comedies or thrillers, we can give ourselves over to and even enjoy the "comedy of errors" depicted or the tragedies that befall the lovers or the horrors that terrorize the actors, because we know all those "bad" things will be followed by a "Hollywood ending." Before we leave the theater, we expect a resolution: lovers will be united, heroes will prevail, and evil forces will be defeated or, at least, judged in a way that foreshadows their ultimate defeat by goodness. We have come to expect the happy ending. We have difficulty understanding or accepting any other plot lines.

The same is true in our thinking about God and history. We claim the assurance that God will act in a way that makes right out of wrong and resolves the tensions, terrors, and losses of history. With God in charge, the outcome will be good. As the mystic Julian of Norwich imagined it: "All will be well, all will be well, all manner of thing will be well." In this comedic approach to time and history, tragedy and evil do emerge as powerful challengers. Their ultimate defeat is guaranteed, however, either in history or in eternity. Such is God's promise. This God of goodness will prevail; the goal of redemption, whether it is understood as restoration, resolution, or realization, will be accomplished. In the next chapter, we will examine several contemporary challengers who are calling into question that guarantee and promise, as well as the assumed resolutions and restorations of the comedic redemption narrative.

For Further Reading

For survey treatments of biblical and religious ideas of time and history, readers might consult *Religion and Time*, edited by A. N. Balshev and J. N. Mohanty, in the series Studies in the History of Religions, edited by H. G. Kippenberg and E. T. Lawson (vol. LIV; Leiden: E. J. Brill, 1993) and C. T. McIntire, ed., *God, History and Historians: An Anthology of Modern Christian Views of History* (New York: Oxford University Press, 1977). Helpful discussions of time and contemporary culture might be found in Jeremy Rifkin, *Time Wars: The Primary Conflict in Human History* (New York: Touchstone, 1989); Richard K. Fenn, *Time Exposure: The Personal Experience of Time in Secular Societies* (Oxford: Oxford University Press, 2001); and Helga Nowotny, *Time: The Modern and Postmodern Experience* (trans. Neville Plaice; Cambridge, UK: Polity Press, 1994).

Christian theologians' reflections on time and history may be included in the categories of eschatology or salvation. Sometimes theologians develop a theology of history. Augustine's *City of God* is without doubt the most influential, if not the first fully formed theology of history. Many translations (from the Latin) and versions of that work are available. A more recent theological treatment is Langdon Gilkey's *Reaping the Whirlwind: A Christian Interpretation of History* (New York: Seabury Press, 1976). Gilkey's text provides a good introduction to a modern Protestant perspective on time and history from a Christian perspective. Readers might also consult Peter Hodgson's *God in History: Shapes of Freedom* (Nashville: Abingdon Press, 1989), which will be discussed further in chapter 3; the works of Jürgen Moltmann, especially *Theology of Hope, God in Creation*, and *The Coming of God in History*, all of which are translated by Margaret Kohl and published by Fortress Press; Reinhold Niebuhr, *Beyond Tragedy* (New York: Charles Scribner's Sons, 1937) and *Faith and History* (New York: Charles Scribner's Sons, 1949); and Rosemary Ruether, *The Radical Kingdom: The Western Experience of Messianic Hope* (New York: Harper & Row, 1970). Johann Baptist Metz in *Faith in History and Society* (trans. David Smith; New York: Seabury Press, 1980) and *Theology of the World* (trans. William Glen-Doepel; New York: Herder and Herder, 1969) offers an approach to political theology as a Roman Catholic theologian. Metz's ideas about apocalyptic will be discussed in chapter 4, but much of his work concerns the impact of modernity on attitudes toward time and history. See also Karl Rahner, "History of the World and Salvation-History" in *Theological Investigations* (vol. 5; trans. Karl H. Kruger; Baltimore: Helicon Press, 1966). In *Letters and Papers from Prison*, Dietrich Bonhoeffer also offers reflections on how modernity affects the ways in which we live in history and understand God. Multiple editions are available, including one edited by Eberhard Bethge and published by Macmillan.

More recently, South American and other liberation theologians have offered their own perspectives, from the viewpoint of the poor and powerless. Beginning with Gustavo Gutiérrez's groundbreaking book, *A Theology of Liberation: History, Politics and Salvation* (trans. Matthew J. O'Connell; New York: Orbis Books, 1988), which was first published in Spanish in 1971, theologians from around the globe have been developing culturally specific theological resources for thinking about time and history, hope and salvation from the perspective of the marginalized and oppressed. Gutiérrez has also developed his own ideas in numerous books, including *The Power of the Poor in History* (trans. Robert R. Barr; Maryknoll, NY: Orbis Books, 1983). For other South American perspectives, see Rubem Alvez, *A Theology of Human Hope* (New York: Corpus Books, 1969), as well as Elsa Tamez, *When the Horizons Close* (trans. Margaret Wilde; Maryknoll, NY: Orbis Books, 2000).

Michael Walzer's *Exodus and Revolution* (New York: Basic Books, 1985) offers an interesting perspective on Jewish views of history and revolutionary change, and their influence on western and Christian thought. For theoretical treatments of time and narrative, see Hayden White, *Metahistory* (Baltimore: Johns Hopkins University Press, 1973); Paul Ricoeur, *Time and Narrative* (vol. 3; trans. Kathleen Blamey and David Pellauer; Chicago: University of Chicago Press, 1988); Larry Bouchard, *Tragic Method and Tragic Theology* (University Park: Pennsylvania State University Press, 1989); and James Berger, *After the End: Representation of Post-Apocalypse* (Minneapolis: University of Minnesota Press, 1999).

Notes

1. See Elsa Tamez, *When the Horizons Close: Rereading Ecclesiastes* (trans. Margaret Wilde; Maryknoll, NY: Orbis Books, 2000), especially the introductory chapter.

2

OUTSIDE THE LINES

*Contemporary Threats
and Challenges*

If Christian and western perspectives on time and history are so relentlessly comedic, is there room in the narrative for voices that do not fit within that plot line? What happens when those voices try to edge themselves onstage? Or when someone begins to wonder whether the comedic narrative makes sense anymore? In the last several decades, more and more challengers have arisen to question and indict modern western views of history and its attendant beliefs, such as in progress or resolution. Some of these challengers also raise questions about the ways in which Christianity has defined the nature and purposes of God. How do we account for experiences and events that seem to contradict a view of God as powerful and good? What happens to our beliefs when other perspectives, long unknown or excluded, present themselves and demand recognition?

Such questions often arise when we experience a big change in our lives. Change affects us, and our place in the world, profoundly. Some changes can be accommodated within our existing ways of understanding the world and the divine, and some cannot. When changes do not fit in our worldviews, we experience dissonance. This process is similar to a phenomenon that is at work when we watch a movie or read a work of fiction. In those instances, we practice what is known as "the willing suspension of disbelief." We willingly accept things we know are not true or real, because we want to experience the fiction. So, for example, when we watch adventure movies, such as the Indiana

Jones series, and see Indiana Jones engage in all sorts of daredevil stunts, or when we see the character of "Neo" in *The Matrix* spin in the air, we shut off that part of the brain that says, "nobody can do that" or "that can't be done." We want to accept what we are seeing; we want to enjoy the fiction. Sometimes, however, because the movie is so badly done that it does not pull us into the fiction or because the moviemaker does not stay within the lines of what we can allow ourselves to accept, the part of us that says "this can't be" begins to assert itself, and we find ourselves no longer "willing to suspend disbelief."

The changes and events discussed in this chapter are ones that get in the way. We are not able to pretend them away or to dismiss them. We cannot make them fit into our inherited worldviews. Even if we wanted to ignore them, we cannot. We have to deal with them in some way.

Many of these changes also cause us to feel more vulnerable, to feel more acutely the fragility that seems to accompany human existence. We human beings have always felt life as contingent. People living centuries ago were subject to the kinds of elemental risks we still experience today: earthquakes and tornadoes, hurricanes and sweltering heat, disease and injury. At any moment, some disastrous act of nature could wipe out the crops that would feed them for the year, fire could destroy their dwellings, or infection might ravage a whole population with disease. In addition, people of previous centuries did not have the kinds of warnings we do today or an understanding of the conditions and causes of these threats. They did not have weather forecasters who would track and predict the course of hurricanes, nor did they know the connections between infection and disease. They did, however, experience their lives as vulnerable and fragile. They lived in and with that awareness.

They also lived more circumscribed lives. They did not dwell in a global community with all its complexities. Their horizons were more closed in. Nor did they have the capacity to inflict the kinds of harm on one another that advances in technology have made possible. In the Middle Ages, disease might spread through a village or perhaps a region. The plague, perhaps the worst disaster of that time, did affect many parts of Europe and killed a significant portion of the population of the continent. Today, however, a SARS outbreak in China is a threat to the whole world. The repeated label "weapons of mass destruction" carries power because of the "mass destruction" capability of such weapons. Hand to hand combat or even the use of cannons could not produce the kind of devastation caused by bombs, at least not as quickly nor as easily.

Our time is different from the past. We know more, and that knowledge increases our capabilities. We are able to imagine and do remarkable things: cure disease, fly across continents and oceans in a matter of hours, view the paintings in a museum, or listen to thousands of songs on a computer. We can also build bombs capable of destroying the earth. So our abilities do not necessarily make life better. Some of our accomplishments create their own problems and potential disasters. Viruses, whether human or computer, can travel around the globe at alarmingly fast rates. Industrialization continues to disturb the balance of the world's ecosystems. If such effects are left unchecked, the earth will become ultimately unfit for human habitation.

Such differences give our time in history a particular character and texture. They pose certain challenges and threats not only to those of us living in the world today, but also to the way we inhabit the earth and live in time. They call us to rethink the stories we tell about our lives. As I have argued in the previous chapter, the dominant narrative in the Jewish and Christian West has read time and history as linear and moving toward a future end. That end is also a resolution. The outcome is already given as promise even though it may not yet be realized. Modernity has added to that view of time a fixation on progress. The movement forward is progressive. I have hinted that such a view is no longer tenable or even faithful. In this chapter, I will outline and describe dimensions of life today that raise questions about such linear and progressive views of time and history. I will explore the landscape of this particular time and place in history and the ways in which the contours of that landscape are calling for new understandings of time and history and, therefore, changed narratives.

A simple and straightforward way to state what feels different today is that we are becoming more aware of the tragic and even ironic, rather than the comedic, dimensions of life. But that is too simple a view. We might also suggest that we are more aware of our responsibilities in history and, as a result, are trying to think about what it would mean to live more faithfully in history and on this earth. To be sure, not all the challenges we encounter today are threats. They are not all bad news But they are challenges. And as a traditional hymn suggests, new occasions teach new duties. This chapter is about examining the occasions.

There are six occasions or dimensions of life today that are affecting our thinking about time and history: (1) the emerging voices of oppressed and marginalized groups and their insistent "intrusion" into conversations about history and theology; (2) awareness of the immensity of harm in history that human beings perpetrate against each another; (3) the growing realization that we may be destroying the planet and ourselves in the process; (4) the seeming triumph of global capitalism and the pervasive ideologies that accompany it; (5) postmodern thinking that seems to challenge so many of our basic assumptions; and (6) the recognition of pluralism that asks us to reconsider how we relate to one another. I will briefly consider each of these and how it contributes to changing perspectives.

"Whose" History?

At the center of the Enlightenment project was a call to freedom. Whether we focus on Enlightenment thinkers who challenged traditional forms of authority and claimed autonomy of thought, or turn to the age of revolution and the revolutionaries' cries for liberty and justice, or take note of the Hegelian view of history as a movement toward freedom, the modern era extols individual and historical freedom. Again and again, the modern West has made liberty a value and freedom a goal in ways that were different from other times, locations, and cultures. Such freedom, if it was to be real, needed to be accompanied by justice and equality, by certain rights.

Americans point to the Declaration of Independence as our founding document of freedom. The Declaration of Independence states: "We hold these truths to be self-evident, that all men are created equal, that they are endowed by their Creator with certain unalienable Rights, that among these are Life, Liberty and the pursuit of Happiness." The Declaration of Independence was written to claim the colonies' freedom and to provide justification for the war of independence from British rule. It argued for the right to the pursuit of life, free from outside restraint. Though a historical document, it continues to inspire American ideals. Orators and politicians, freedom fighters and justice seekers quote it and refer to it again and again. The Declaration of Independence is viewed as formative of the American character and purpose, as the defining document of what America is meant to be and what Americans value.

Yet we now know that the declaration of freedom contained in the document was not for "all." The authors of the Declaration of Independence, all white, propertied males, were referring only to themselves. "Life, liberty, and the pursuit of happiness" was intended for them and them alone. Embedded in the Declaration's call to freedom and equality was the exclusion of women, non-whites, and the poor, those who did not own property.

In the last centuries and decades, these excluded groups have increasingly insisted on their own right to freedom, as well as to equality and justice. They have raised their voices and made their presence and desires known, not only in America but throughout the world. Colonized and subjected peoples, those who have been marginalized and oppressed, have come forth to claim power and freedom.

Around the globe, revolutionary activity increased. The twentieth century witnessed movement after movement to "throw off the yoke" of imperial and oppressive rule—from India to the Congo, from Poland to Haiti. The colonized fought for self-rule. The oppressed struggled to be included fully in political processes. They, too, wanted to participate in governance and to have a say in the decisions that affected them. A new term was coined—*subalterns*—to refer to those who had been excluded from political processes and had not been recognized as historical subjects and actors. Subalterns, hidden and overlooked in the politics of the world to which they were the most vulnerable, were under the radar screen, so to speak, of historical action. These groups were silenced and excluded from prevailing discourses. They had no voice in the halls of power.

In their quests for freedom and power, these peoples and groups came to a growing awareness of the silence that surrounded them. They realized that the dominant historical narratives did not contain their experience or speak of their lives. These narratives told the story from the point of view of the privileged and those who had been in power. They reflected the dominants' interests and biases. Even though partial and biased, the dominants claimed these narratives to be universal, speaking for all.

The Declaration of Independence is a case in point. As I have indicated, its promise of freedom and equality was limited and partial. The God-given rights it declared were not meant for everyone. Such partiality was not accidental. Women, African Americans, and the poor were excluded intentionally. The document served the interests of a few, those already with some measure of power. This would not be so problematic in and of itself, if the bias and partiality were admitted. But they were not. The history of America has been and continues to be told as if the Declaration of Independence, as written, included everyone. Every time the story is told in that way, it perpetuates the exclusion and silencing of those who do not have full freedom, equality, and access in our society.

What is true of the Declaration of Independence is also true of so many of the narratives—both historical and theological—that shape our identities and our lives. In school, I learned that Columbus "discovered" America. I was also taught that Indians were savage peoples who had to be contained "for their own good" or that they were simple and innocent people who welcomed the new settlers and were easily convinced to give over their lands. Today the story of the "first Thanksgiving" is still often recounted as that of friendly Indians who helped out the Pilgrims who then responded in gratitude. Telling the story in that way implies that the Indians were content to have these settlers take over their lands. These narratives, as I was taught them, present the point of view of those in power. The stories work to their advantage.

Again, this would not be such a problem if we recognized these narratives as biased. All narratives are told from a particular point of view. Problems arise when one perspective asserts itself as the sole truth or when the narratives are used by the powerful to justify the abuse of power, such as when one country invades another and calls it an act of liberation.

As the excluded and marginalized add their views, these dominant narratives change to become more inclusive of different perspectives on history. Borrowing philosopher Michel Foucault's term, the "insurrection of subjugated knowledges" alters the stories we tell. For example, when the native peoples of the western hemisphere speak of the arrival of Columbus and European settlers, they do not talk about discovery and freedom, but of invasion and conquest. For African

Americans the journey to America was not to freedom, as it was claimed to be for so many who came to America's shores, but to slavery and the loss of freedom.

Because the "grand narrative" of America's past has so often been told as a tale of deliverance and redemption, of arrival in the promised land, these emerging voices, in effect, ask us to think about redemption differently. From their perspective, this grand narrative is not a story of redemption, but its opposite. In that grand narrative they are damned, demonized, and brutalized. They are robbed of and displaced from their lands, denied their freedom, labeled as primitive and savage, and forced into giving up cultural and religious practices—all in the name of civilization and salvation.

The redeeming story, for the perspective of these displaced and brutalized peoples, would necessarily be different. For example, Steven Charleston, a member of the Choctow Nation and an Episcopal bishop, notes that when Native Americans read the story of Israel's exodus, deliverance, and entry into the promised land, they identify not with the Israelites, but with the Canaanites whose land the Israelites invaded and took over. The Jewish Old Testament, suggests Charleston, does not, therefore, function as "good news" for Native Americans. Native Americans have their own traditional stories about the land and the past that can function as "testament" for them. Their "saving story" includes their own histories, traditions, and experiences.[1]

As Charleston makes clear, not only the American grand narrative but also the Christian one has been told from the perspective of the dominants and so has excluded other voices. As it stands, the Christian story cannot be a redeeming story for all. Each silenced and excluded group needs to tell the story of redemption from its own perspective in order to make the Christian narrative a saving story for them. For example, feminist theologians have been arguing for several decades now that the story of redemption, as traditionally told by Christianity, not only excludes women but also often demonizes them. They point out that in much of Christian theology, all women are viewed as descendents of Eve, the original evil woman who is responsible for sin being in the world. This narrative, predicated on women's sin and subsequent taint, makes women's redemption secondary and derivative. The history of Christian thought has played out that founding myth again and again by viewing women as evil or, if not evil, lesser than or other than the male norm. A vivid example of such thinking is evident in the argument that women cannot be priests or ministers because they are not able to image Christ and/or because the God-given order does not allow them to have authority, especially over men. One of the projects of feminist theology has been to demonstrate again and again the bias in such theological perspectives. And beyond bias, feminist theologians point to the harm done to women by these views that have allowed and fostered an atmosphere in which domestic and sexual violence can be hidden and even justified.[2]

Not only are women viewed as evil or lesser, but women's own experience and understanding are also not included in the formative stories of religious traditions. Women are silenced and/or rendered invisible. Feminist biblical scholar and theologian Elisabeth Schüssler Fiorenza, in *In Memory of Her*, revisits early Christian history to demonstrate the exclusion of women in the narratives, even though women were fully active in the communities.[3] Throughout Christian history, this pattern of women's presence—rendered silent and invisible—is played out again and again. Occasionally women move toward the center of the picture, especially in periods of change and transition when institutional arrangements might be more in flux, only to be marginalized again by institutional practices and theological teachings.[4]

For their part, feminist historians have challenged the "grand narratives" that so many students of history take for granted, including the notion that things are moving toward greater freedom and rights. For example, Joan Kelly-Gadol questioned the traditional views of progress by asking whether the Renaissance was such for women. She argued that legally and socially women were often better off in the Middle Ages than in the early modern period.[5] Kelly-Gadol and other feminist historians are not only raising questions about the historical narrative but also are attempting to change it to reflect more fully and accurately the story of women's lives. After all, women were not granted suffrage in the United States until the twentieth century, decades after white men without property and African-American males were given the vote.

There are many more instances of these dynamics of historical erasure and silencing and of theological exclusion and demonization. Colonized peoples around the globe are beginning to uncover and reclaim their own pasts that were either wiped out or driven underground by colonizers. In the process, they are challenging the ways in which Christianity defined their identities and served the interests of those colonizers. Ethnic minority groups are rediscovering their own traditions and histories, including submerged religious traditions. All these groups of people—the poor, the colonized, people of color, and women—continue to struggle for inclusion and for a historical narrative that tells their story and speaks to their experience. In their struggles, they are raising loud voices of protest and critique, change and creation. They are making clear that the story most often told is not their story. It not only overlooks them but also often harms them. For them, it is not a comedy.

Violence, Violence Everywhere

Many of the marginalized and silenced peoples discussed in the previous section are not the victims of innocent exclusion or even a simple narrowness of perspective. Most often they are the objects of violence and hatred, persecution and abuse at the hands of others. Violence takes many forms: along with physical violence, we human beings harm one another emotionally, socially, economically, and politically. All these forms of violence seem rampant in our world. They operate on all levels, from the interpersonal to the global. A husband who dominates and mistreats his wife by controlling all the family finances so that she has no access to household monies is not unrelated to wealthier nations manipulating and controlling world economic markets in ways that keep other nations dependent and poor. Violence is everywhere.

The twentieth century has been labeled the bloodiest in history. It has also been called the century of genocides, beginning with the genocide against Armenians early in the century to the Holocaust in the middle and ending with ethnic warfare and cleansing in such places as Rwanda and Bosnia. The term *genocide* was coined by Raphael Lemkin in the 1940s in order to identify the form of violence that is intended to wipe out a people. The term *ethnic cleansing* was introduced in the 1990s to describe the movement to eliminate a particular population within a state or region. Debates continue as to what constitutes genocide and what the differences are between genocide and mass persecution and ethnic cleansing. However, what remains indisputable is that persecution and the killing of masses of people keep happening again and again, all over the globe.

It does not seem as if such violence will end any time soon. One could argue that mass violence has always been present in the world. Did not ancient peoples enslave the vanquished, rape the women of the conquered, and engage in wholesale murder? Were not civilizations wiped out? Was not the witch craze in the late Middle Ages and early modern period a genocide against women? Did not the European colonizers push native peoples out or subject them to violence—physical, social, political, cultural, and economic? Is this kind of violence not just part of life on earth that will always be with us?

While the answer to these questions is "yes," there is more to be said about differences between the past and the world today. In modernity, technology has made it possible to kill massive numbers of people at once and to do so more efficiently. The gas chambers of Auschwitz are testimony to that. The bombing of Hiroshima is but a foreshadowing of the worldwide destruction nuclear weapons make possible. Such weapons give us the power to destroy all the peoples of the earth and to make the earth uninhabitable for humans.

Another way in which our age is different is that our narratives of progress led us to believe that we could end such violence. Wars were fought (and are still being fought) "to end all wars" or "to make the world safe for democracy." Little attention has been or is given to the ways in which violence breeds violence, whether on the mass or interpersonal level.

The unrelenting prevalence of massive violence and the potential for nuclear devastation, along with growing awareness of the forms of interpersonal violence that assault people on a daily basis, leave us questioning the goodness of life and of God. Attending to violence directs us to the question of theodicy: how can a good and powerful God allow the death of thousands and millions of human beings or the loss of a child's innocence by sexual molestation? The theodicy question is speculative. It tries to imagine God's motivations and actions and to make sense of the senseless. Its intent is to justify or explain God's behavior. As more and more theologians have been suggesting, traditional approaches to theodicy do not respond to the immensity of horror contained in the violence around us.

Ongoing violence reveals the brokenness and woundedness of the world. The ruptures caused by violence are so deep that they cannot be easily folded into explanatory models. They remain as open wounds. There is no closure, but only cries for remembrance and a sense of loss and eternal mourning for those who live with the trauma caused by violence. The field of trauma studies has emerged to address the dynamics and conditions of victimization, as well as to offer ways to deal with and treat traumatic wounding. Those who study trauma do not so much explain violence and its aftermath, but suggest ways to respond that honor the rupture and the extensiveness of harm. They seek ways to attend to the wounds and promote recovery.

As I have already hinted and will explicate further in chapter four, the narratives of God's care and of redemption no longer seem to fit or work so easily, especially in situations of violence. The promise of redemption often remains elusive and faint for the survivors of violence. The sense of history as a progression, moving in a set direction, also does not work. Nor are the schema of catastrophe/restoration or crucifixion/resurrection, as they have functioned, adequate for attending sufficiently to depths of violence and trauma. They move too quickly to resolution and do not give the immensity of harm its due. Trauma interrupts all the ways in which we try to order our lives. It defies order and resolution. Life today is rife with such disorder, bred by violence and the legacies of trauma.

The Fragility of Earth

We human beings are not only violent toward one another, but our harmful behavior is directed toward the earth as well. Yet another challenge facing us today is the condition of the earth, threatened by human misuse and abuse. The ecology movement is pointing out how our practices and attitudes are destroying the earth and its atmosphere and endangering life on our planet. It is asking us to respond by changing the ways we live and by reexamining our thinking about time, history, and redemption. The destruction of the earth is by nature slow and gradual. It is not instantaneous and dramatic as the harm wrought by nuclear bombs. Yet the danger is real and present nonetheless and will result in a similar end: making the planet uninhabitable for most life forms.

This danger has many dimensions: Carbon-based emissions are resulting in the slow destruction of the ozone layer. The felling of the rain forests effects atmospheric changes. Imminent overpopulation threatens the world's resources and produces fears of scarcity and its attendant violence. The ways in which we practice agriculture and mining deplete the earth's resources and pay no attention to their restoration or to the dynamics of the ecosystems in which we exist. The waste we produce and the ways in which we dispose of waste, either industrial or household, are causing pollution. The air we breathe and the water we drink, both absolutely necessary for all life forms, are less safe because of pollution. Species are disappearing daily. Forms of vegetation struggle for life. Global warming is affecting the ecological balance. Slowly, we are making the earth uninhabitable.

These changes are subtle and almost imperceptible, especially for those who live with abundance. Such people have the option to shield themselves from or compensate for the effects of our abuse. If the days are getting warmer, they can live in air conditioning. If their drinking water is less safe, they can buy bottled water. They know there will be plenty of food available in the supermarkets, more variety than they can sample. In fact, there seems to be even more to choose from as "seasonal" products are now available year round. The poor, however, and those not in the industrialized West, those already vulnerable, are rendered more so. They are subject to drought and starvation and to the effects of wanton misuse of the earth.

Theologians and ethicists who are trying to respond to the ecological crises have drawn attention to the ways in which the Christian narrative has shaped and contributed to the abuse of the earth. The creation story in Genesis, even though it declares creation to be of God's making and good and necessary, has been read to imply a hierarchical order with human beings at the top. In Christian theology, God's giving of "dominion over the fish of the sea and over the birds of the air and over every living thing that moves upon the earth" to human beings has most often been interpreted to mean that human beings are in charge and that all other creatures are subject to them. Human beings are also the beneficiaries of the abundance of creation. The created order exists for human use, so that Adam and Eve might be fed and enjoy companionship and beauty.

In the modern era, processes of industrialization drew upon and extended the idea that human beings are meant to dominate the created order. In agricultural societies, human beings tend to live with a more humble attitude toward nature. They are aware of their dependency on the earth, its resources and its forces. Industrialization, however, separates humans from nature. Its rhythms no longer order human life. For example, the production of electricity and the light bulb meant that workers could be productive around the clock, day and night.

Industrialists think that we can manufacture anything we need. Manufactured goods originate in human ingenuity. The earth offers only raw materials. Industrialists who exploit the earth's resources have been able to use the biblical creation story to justify their practices, albeit by interpreting that story to fit their agenda.

Such a distortion of the biblical narrative would not have been so easy to accomplish had not the Christian tradition privileged time and history over space and nature. The narrative of redemption has been primarily about history and time, not nature or the earth. To be fair, Hebrew Scripture described catastrophe and restoration in ways that affected the natural order as well as history. The faithlessness of Israel caused disharmony not just among the people but in creation. God's redeeming actions then restored right relationship to the created order, too. Some of the New Testament writers, notably Paul, also pointed to the ways in which sin disrupted creation. Redemption was a new creation. However, what happened in and to the earth has not been understood to be of ultimate significance. In the end, creation would pass away; it was not necessary to redemption. The ideas of heaven and eternity took redemption out of this world. Redemption was to be in another place and time. What was of ultimate value was not of this earth or earthly time. Human persons were but strangers passing through this life, in but not of the world.

Christian thinking about redemption also focused on the infinite and on immortality. The finite is tainted by sin and will pass away. Even though such ideas reflect more the influence of Greek philosophical thought than the biblical narratives, they became embedded in Christian theological thinking and have been very influential. As a result, the biblical narrative was read through Greek philosophical lenses and notions of the soul and eternity. Dualistic thinking about body/nature and soul/spirit was incorporated into Christian thought. The body/nature side of the dualism was devalued, as was all that was associated with it, such as the female, more "primitive" peoples and the created order. Redemption implied a transformation or a leaving behind of the bodily and the natural.

All these ways of thinking have contributed to the ecological crisis we now face. I am not suggesting that they caused that crisis or that Christianity is to blame for it. But Christianity has been complicit and has offered few resources in its dominant traditions for thinking differently. Only recently, as theologians and ethicists have tried to respond to the ecological crises we face, has the tradition been mined for other perspectives and narratives. Even then, some of those looking for alternatives, such as ecological feminists, have found richer resources in other traditions, including those of native peoples.

Whatever their differences, all those concerned with the fate of the earth are trying to warn us that time is running out and that the future of the earth is at stake. If we do not find new ways to inhabit this earth, if we do not begin to think and act differently, then history, time, and life on this earth will end. And its demise will be by our own hands.

The Triumph of Capitalism

The modern era is also characterized by the marriage of capitalism, accompanied by industrialization, with technology and instrumental reason. This marriage is so successful that we cannot imagine life any other way. The ideologies and worldviews of this marriage so pervade the ways in which we think and operate in the West that most of us are not aware of the partiality these perspectives reflect. In the last decades, with the dissolution of the Soviet Union and the disintegration of other Communist countries, capitalism has claimed a moral as well as an economic triumph. It has presented itself, with little opposition, as the hope for the future, an infinite future of growth. With no alternative lifestyle choices, this merger of capitalist economics and technology with social ideologies of progress and growth is able to claim universality.

Indeed, capitalist ideology has become like the air we breathe. We are so immersed in it, we do not see or notice it. It pervades our language and our ways of thinking. We use the terminology of capitalism and of the marketplace to describe all dimensions of our lives: terms such as "bottom line" and "pay off" and "market value" and "growth potential" and "supply and demand" are in everyday usage. Any of us might say, on any given day: "The 'bottom line' is I just don't have the energy to exercise (or prepare a healthy dinner or clean my house) at the end of the day." "But," a friend might reply, "the pay off would be worth it."

We live by the quantitative and the quantifiable. Our lives are defined more and more by what we own and how much we possess. Success is measured by the size of salaries and by the number of possessions. If we live in a big house and drive an expensive car, we deem ourselves successful. Value is determined by usefulness and productivity. What is of little use or unproductive in our world is considered to be of little value, including the elderly and those who are ill. Efficiency is a key indicator of value as well. What is good is what is efficient. Efficiency in turn is measured by productivity. We extol the value of multitasking as a way to get more things done, which is to say, to be more productive.

In this late capitalist world, everything has become a commodity to be bought and sold. The field of medicine, for example, is no longer defined as being about service or healing or human well-being; it is an industry. The product of this industry is health care, which has itself become a commodity. More and more, decisions in medicine are made by the operating principles and values of the marketplace. Those seeking medical attention are consumers. Hospitals operate by the bottom line. Managers determine the kind of care someone will receive. There is no question that these values guide for-profit hospitals, but they drive the workings of nonprofit hospitals as well.

Education, too, has become a commodity. Students are consumers. Education is a product that students pay for; school systems are run like businesses. The goals are efficiency and quantifiable results. School systems and accrediting agencies stress student assessment. Standardized tests are used to evaluate a school's success. Students' test scores are the measure of their education. Learning outcomes need be set and measured in order to determine an education's worth.

At many American colleges and universities, students now "shop around" for courses during the first one or two weeks of each semester. Students visit a variety of courses in this "shopping period" before deciding which ones they will take for that semester. Faculty members may compete for students by pitching their courses so they will appeal to these consumers.

I imagine the reader might now be asking: what is wrong with students shopping for courses or for schools and hospitals to be concerned with efficiency and productivity? In order to consider that question, we need to examine what is excluded when education and health care become commodities and consumer products. When the bottom line and measurable productivity become the sole means of evaluation, then relationships and community, love and beauty, mystery and even the moral tend to get short shrift. Without attention to and the practice of relationships and community, love and beauty, mystery and ethics, we are diminished. Capitalism, technology, and instrumental reason are reductive ideologies. They reduce human beings to objects and consumers. They impact the quality of the life we inhabit.

For example, shopping around for courses does not seem, at first sight, to be a bad practice. It maximizes students' ability to choose and encourages them to "sample" a wider variety of subjects than they might otherwise. It also may result in professors thinking more about their teaching and the appeal of their courses. But the practice of course shopping also breeds individualism and puts so much emphasis on personal choice that it devalues other dimensions of the educational experience. Students make decisions rather exclusively on the basis of what works for them and what they personally will get out of individual courses. They do not reflect on what they might offer to the courses or to the communal nature of education. Their commitment is to themselves and not to their classmates or to the educational process. Faculty members who might be trying to build a sense of community and mutual responsibility in the classroom are thwarted and at best delayed by not even knowing who is in their classes, often until the third week of a semester. Given these dynamics, education becomes something students receive and consume, rather than an experience in which they are full participants and actors.

The liberal arts are themselves at risk in such an atmosphere because they are viewed as having no market value and, therefore, being of no use. Since instrumental reason only considers what is useful and productive, it does not offer a way to value things such as wisdom or beauty, other than as consumer products. Those who argue for the value of a liberal arts education often have to do so in the terms that the culture will hear. For example, they point out that students will learn critical thinking, which is a useful skill in a variety of businesses and professions. In other words, the advocates are pointing out that a liberal arts education is marketable; it can have market value.

Such thinking may accommodate to the dominant culture, but it distorts the nature of education and other affected dimensions of our lives, such as medicine. Education and medicine are not simply industries, businesses, and products. Teaching and health care are services and person-centered arts. When their results are measured only in quantifiable terms or when their practice is so regulated that practitioners cannot make judgments about how much time and attention are necessary, case by case, then it is difficult to main a service, person-centered orientation.

Rather than becoming more human or having our humanity deepened and enhanced, the cultural dominance of capitalism is diminishing our humanity. Capitalism produces reductive ideologies that ultimately define human beings as products and outcomes. Such ideologies set limits on our imaginations and our abilities. We end up living less full lives with reduced connection to others and to sources of mystery and meaning.

In this world of late capitalism, religion itself has become a commodity. Religion is something we consume. We assess our participation in religious practices and communities by how satisfied we are. Combined with the individualism of capitalist ideology, we are becoming more and more self-centered and narcissistic. Our culture breeds narcissism with personal satisfaction as its chief value. Satisfaction, in turn, is measured by production and consumption. If we personally are not "getting anything out of" our religious practices, we look elsewhere.

Ironically, focusing on personal satisfaction and the dimensions of our life as commodities actually threatens our existence rather than enhancing our lives. We often pay so little attention to that which takes us out of ourselves and allows us to experience ourselves as part of a whole, that we end up isolated and numbed to the fullness of life.

The capitalist drive also distorts our understanding of time and history. The future is always beckoning to us with the potential for more production and consumption. As a result, we pay little attention to the present and none to the past, except as it offers opportunities for the marketing and consumption of nostalgia.

Again this is ironic. Current movements of nostalgia lead to a proliferation of industries of memory. The antique business is one example of a desire to purchase the past. In literature, the memoir, which is about retrieving and making sense of the past, has become a popular genre. Both the purchasing of antiques and the reading of memoirs can be seen as expressing a desire for nostalgic return. Yet these are also evidence of the triumph of capitalism and instrumentality and reductive ideologies. If we have to buy the past, then we are not so much historical and social agents as consumers.

Consumption breeds consumption that in turn feeds the capitalist machine and keeps it going. It becomes very difficult to have a sense of anything being enough or to feel real satisfaction. The system requires that there always be more unmet desires for consumption to fill. Because nothing is deemed of value in and of itself, including life, there is really no way to experience satisfaction. Only the elusive promise of better things to come and the relentless drive of technological progress persist without end. We seek to be redeemed through possessing and consuming.

Capitalism is wedded with technology and technological progress. Technological discovery and innovation both helped make capitalism work and keep it going. Machines of mass production moved industry out of shops and into factories. Ongoing technological advances allow for more and better mass production. At the same time, they keep the consuming desires alive. The latest and best version of a product render the model we purchased last year obsolete or no longer desirable. There is now a version that can do more and do it faster. Products are not built to last, but to offer short-term satisfaction that will feed the desire to find even more satisfaction in the next product feature to be introduced. In these ways, technology serves the consuming drive of capitalist ideologies.

These ideologies are problematic for all the ways in which they shape us and potentially distort our lives, but even more insidious is their pervasiveness. Given that these ideologies have invaded all dimensions of our life and are like the air we breathe and with no viable economic alternatives to capitalism on the world stage, it is difficult to recognize, let alone challenge, their power and ubiquity. The world has become one big marketplace.

The triumph of capitalism does not present itself so much as a challenge to the linear and progressive view of time and history as it displays the logic of such thinking. The threat contained in capitalism and consumerism is not to the comedic narrative, but to the character of human life. Left unchecked consumerism may consume us all.

The Postmodern Situation

Thus far I have been discussing modernity and the social conditions of late western capitalism. Culturally, however, the West has actually been moving into what has been labeled the "postmodern era." Postmodernism emerged out of the seeming collapse of modernity and the dissolution of its projected historical goals. For our purposes here, there are several dimensions of what Jean-François Lyotard named the "postmodern condition" to consider.

In postmodern thinking, the idea that something is a universal or that it is given "by nature" is regarded with suspicion. Claims to fundamental and foundational ordering principles are challenged. Postmodernism was first recognized as a movement in architecture in which traditional forms of order and design were fractured. The categories of outside and inside were no longer recognizable: staircases might be on the outside of a building; gardens inside. For example, Opryland, a "hotel" and "conference center" near Nashville, Tennessee, contains a total landscape under its roof, consisting of gardens, a "river," and trees. Its design includes "neighborhoods" and "commercial districts." A guest's hotel window looks "outside" onto vegetation, which is actually inside, under the roof. Perceptions of reality—of in and out—are thus challenged, as is any notion of "nature" being natural. What one sees along the walkways and outside one's balcony in Opryland is "manufactured nature."

Postmodernism raises questions about what is "nature" or "natural." It also challenges notions of representation and of images corresponding to reality. For example, the artist Magritte paints a picture of what you and I would recognize as a pipe and then writes on the same painting in French: "this is not a pipe." He forces the observer to question the relationship of object and painting and naming. The observer is left to wonder whether objects have any reality, substance, or representational value that is given.

Postmodernism also raises questions about human agency and the autonomous human subject as the director of historical action. In other words, it challenges the notion of a centered human subject who is an independent agent and source of action. In the form of deconstructionist theory, postmodern thinking radically adopts and adapts the legacies of Nietzsche, Freud, and Marx, who viewed human behavior as grounded in forces and drives that were in some sense directing that behavior. Correspondingly, the idea of God, the divine, as being in charge of history is severely criticized and becomes almost incomprehensible in a postmodern framework.

Indeed, in postmodernism, no *one* is in charge. What happens in history and in our lives is the product of forces and dynamisms that are not being directed by an agent of any kind. History is characterized by contingency and chance and fragmentation. Power and truth, according to the French philosopher Michel Foucault, are produced in systems by interactions of forces that form into regimes of control and regulation. These then are externalized and normalized and designated as givens that may even be characterized as eternal or inherent. Such "knowledge," however, is itself the product of power.

There are no transcendent realities in this view and no master narratives other than those produced by regimes of power. In a way, any master narrative is the perspective of the "winners" in history or of the regulatory mechanism. Such narratives are ideologies of control and regulation. For Foucault, such master narratives include our understandings of sexuality, crime, mental health, and other social institutions. In other words, the ways we think about and practice sexuality or define sexuality are products of the workings of power. The same would be true of other dimensions of social life.

Postmodernism and deconstruction clearly pose great challenges to theological claims and to notions of truth as representing or reflecting reality. Those seeking to do theology with an appreciation for postmodernity have had to find different ways to understand truth and make truth claims. A number of these theologians have been turning toward a view of theology as a practical discourse. The truth of theological claims no longer is measured by correspondence to received revelation or to given, foundational norms, but by what those claims make possible or occlude. In other words, the "truth" of a theological claim is tested by what it "produces."

Such an approach holds implications for how we think about redemption. Redemption itself becomes a practical claim, to be assessed by what it makes possible. There is then no master narrative of redemption, but only rhetorical strategies that may or may not function as redemptive in particular contexts.

In postmodernist thinking, time is not ordered in a progressive, linear, and teleological way. Rather thinking about time tends toward a type of timelessness. According to deconstruction, time itself is an ideological construct, as is history. History is always the story of the present, projected into the past. Thus deconstruction can state that, in actuality, there is no time and no history. In a way, postmodern time collapses on itself or becomes an ever-changing dynamism.

Contemporary science, especially physics, has been developing similar perspectives on time. Ever since Einstein proposed his theory of relativity, we have known time to be relative and not fixed. Past and present change depending on the speed of motion. The determination of something as past or as present or as future is a function of one's perspective and position that are ever changing.

These mind-bending ideas are also time-bending. They challenge so many of the ways we think and view the world. They disturb our sense of order, as set by the clock and the calendar. That sense of order is characterized by fixity and progression and purpose. Living in a universe governed by randomness undermines the security that order provides. We feel disturbed and unsettled. This dimension of the postmodern condition also suggests that everything is provisional. There is no permanency. Nothing is given or set forever. Living with fluidity and ambiguity and a sense of contingency characterizes postmodernity.

Some responses to the postmodern situation attempt to reassert fixity and order. They resist going where postmodernism seems to be taking us. Other responses see opportunities within a postmodern framework for re-imagining life and our place in the universe. Whatever the response, however, we are all having to deal with a world that is changing rapidly and in ways that require re-imagining things that many of us took for granted, such as trees and gardens and rivers being outdoors.

Pluralism without Oneness

The American motto *E Pluribus Unum* ("Out of Many One") does not adequately describe American society and actually never has. America has never been "one" or "unified." It has always been plural, although not recognized as so. In recent years, as silenced and marginalized groups have asserted themselves and challenged the dominant discourses and as the ideology of master narratives has been revealed, we in America have come to some recognition of the range of religious, ethnic, sexual, and other identities present in American society. Many of us are defining ourselves more by those identities, at the same time that we are paying more attention to the multiplicity around us. In a seemingly contradictory way, those identities are both overvalued and relativized.

When I was growing up in the 1950s, an image that was often used to describe American society was that of a "melting pot." In the melting pot, the different ethnic and racial groups were joined together, to be mixed and blended into Americans. In the outpouring from the pot, the different groups would be indistinguishable. Out of many would come one.

In the 1980s, the rainbow emerged as an alternative image. Mel King, in Boston, and Jesse Jackson, nationally, founded the Rainbow Coalition as a political movement with a goal of inclusiveness. Since then the rainbow flag has become a symbol for gays and lesbians. In the rainbow, the colors are and remain distinct. They are present, side by side. The rainbow is made up of all the colors. Unity is determined by inclusion, not by blending.

The rainbow also represents the challenge of our society: how do we include everyone, with distinctions and differences intact? How do we honor those differences, but not make them so determinative and even divisive that they cannot be held together in some way?

A key factor in dealing with such questions is the nature and status of identity. The old image of the melting pot was based on the belief that as different immigrant and ethnic groups became part of American society, they would eventually forego their ethnic differences in order to become part of the "pot" of America society. There is no doubt that such processes were at work. The arguments I had with my parents in our immigrant household were often in some way about my desire to blend and fit in with American culture and their desire to maintain our distinctiveness. Those debates were quite illustrative of classic clashes between the first and second generations of immigrants. As I grew older, however, rather than discarding my ethnic identity in the interests of blending, I have come to regard it as more central to my sense of self. In this country, we went from being Americans, to being hyphenated Americans, to dropping the hyphens. I consider myself an Armenian American, but in everyday conversation, if I am asked to identify myself among Americans, I say simply that I am Armenian.

In so doing, I am not different from many others in this country who claim a distinctive ethnic, racial, or religious identity. The importance of identity is affecting our society on so many levels. Businesses market to identity groups. They ask what will sell to Hispanics or to Christians. Politicians worry about the ethnic vote and the opinion of ethnic constituencies. They wonder how the Vietnamese community will react to proposed legislation.

Not only are identities more important, but difference-based identities are proliferating. In addition to the standard categories of difference—race, ethnicity, religion, gender, and sexual preference—more and more claims are being made for other differences. For example, some argue that being hearing impaired or deaf is not only a difference but an identity. They claim there is a distinctive deaf culture, with its own language (sign) and other cultural markers.

Another example of proliferating identities emerged from the presidential election of 2004. What began as a convenient and easy way to display the way states voted—as red (Republican) and blue (Democratic)—became markers of identity. Given the way these terms came to be used, residing in either a red or blue state revealed much more about the people of that state than how the majority of voters cast their ballots. The color of the state became an indication of values, behaviors, and culture. The country was turned into a pattern of red and blue.

If identities are proliferating and all are claiming that their identities are distinctive, we might anticipate two contrasting social outcomes. On the one hand, we might see more recognition of diversity and a valuing of pluralism. Pluralism means that differences are taken seriously and honored. It seeks unity not through the blending together of differences so they are no longer distinguishable—the melting pot—but the juxtaposition of differences so they are connected, but remain intact—the rainbow. The unity of the whole—and the wonder and beauty of it—are in and through the differences. Unity is not uniformity. There is no need for one outcome or one look or one agenda for everyone. In a genuinely pluralistic society, the emphasis shifts from the one to the many.

On the other hand, when so much emphasis is put on the distinctiveness and importance of identities, those identities tend to become too fixed and determinative. And many more differences may claim to be identities, each with distinctive and different cultures. Such a proliferation of identities leads to questions about what constitutes an identity and what is meant by culture. It may also result in conflicts among identities and so-called "culture wars." The culture of blue states is pitted against that of red states. Those who extol rap music claim it as a cultural icon, whereas others abhor it as a debasement of culture. These dynamics get so heated and the category of culture so broad that it may lose its usefulness as a descriptor.

When identity becomes fixed and determinative, then it becomes more difficult to question it. Those who do so tend to be accused of prejudice and bias. In intellectual circles, debates abound about the status and nature of identity. For example, is sexual orientation by choice or by nature? Is sexual identity fixed, or is it, as Judith Butler argued, performance? In political circles, however, it is very difficult to raise such questions. In fact, many identity groups find themselves arguing for the givenness of their identities, often for political and strategic reasons. Gays and lesbians claim that sexual orientation is by nature, that they were "born that way," because that makes it easier for others to accept their difference. However, such a political move essentializes identity in a way that can carry dangerous implications. Identities do not only define us; they also can confine us. Often it is those at the margins—or the intersections—who reveal the limitations of rigid identity definitions: for example, transgendered persons, by their existence, call for an examination of the nature of gender; and multi-racial persons raise questions about the identifying character of race.

There is no doubt that the question of identity is a complex one that haunts our society in many ways. We struggle to recognize multiplicity, however that may be defined. Globalization has moved these tensions and debates onto the world scene. Is globalization a movement toward homogenization, that all may be one? Or does it hold the potential for living with multiplicity in new ways? Whatever the answers to those questions may be, just posing them represents a challenge that puts added strain on traditional modes of thinking about life in the world. If we embrace multiplicity, then we need to rework our understandings of what it means to be in relationship and what value we give to differences.

Remapping the Lines

In this chapter, I have outlined six dimensions of life today that, in different ways and in varying degrees, challenge or expose some of our traditional ideas and perspectives, especially about history as linear, teleological, and progressive. Not all of these dimensions pose the same challenge nor do they carry equal weight. There is tension and even contradiction within and among them. The triumph of capitalism both feeds into and contradicts the postmodern condition. The intrusion of previously silenced voices correlates with the multiplication of identity, but at the same time challenges some notions of identity. Together, these six dimensions constitute a patchwork of social conditions and dynamics.

No neat picture emerges. The lines are blurry in some places, crisscrossing in others. What is clear, however, is that these conditions and threats demand some response, or, at least, some rethinking of established patterns and modes of thought. We can no longer assume a straight and forward march into the future, especially if we think that future will be better than the past. Our hope can no longer follow the line forward to a greater glory. Nor can we assume that history, the story we tell about ourselves, is one. The presumption that any single worldview—whether it be Christian or not—can claim universality, that it can hold all truth, is revealed as a masking ideology. What then? The next chapters are by way of response. They are about telling time differently and seeking for alternatives for a renewed vision of hope.

For Further Reading

The themes I explore in this chapter are catalogued in many contemporary theological works. Part 2 of Peter Hodgson's *Winds of the Spirit: A Constructive Christian Theology* (Louisville: Westminster/John Knox Press, 1994) focuses on the emergence of postmodernity, of marginalized and oppressed voices, of ecological consciousness and of pluralism. Sallie McFague's works also treat a number of these themes, especially the ecological. Readers might consult her *The Body of God* (Minneapolis: Fortress Press, 1993) and *Life Abundant* (Minneapolis: Fortress Press, 2001). Three collections of essays that contain helpful articles are *Reconstructing Christian Theology*, edited by Rebecca S. Chopp and Mark Lewis Taylor (Minneapolis: Fortress Press, 1994); *Lift Every Voice: Constructing Christian Theologies from the Underside*, edited by Susan Brooks Thistlethwaite and Mary Potter Engel (rev. ed.; Maryknoll, NY: Orbis Books, 1998); and *A Dream Unfinished: Theological Reflections on America from the Margins*, edited by Eleazar S. Fernandez and Fernando F. Segovia (Maryknoll, NY: Orbis Books, 2001. Other relevant resources include Sharon Welch, *Communities of Resistance and Solidarity* (Maryknoll, NY: Orbis Books, 1985); Paul Lakeland, *Postmodernity* (Minneapolis: Fortress Press, 1997); and Flora A. Keshgegian, *Redeeming Memories* (Nashville: Abingdon Press, 2000).

The Holocaust, in particular, and ongoing violence and historical suffering, in general, including the dynamics of poverty, oppression, and marginalization, have exercised an enormous impact on many theologians of the twentieth and twenty-first centuries, including German political theologians, Jürgen Moltmann and Johann Baptist Metz. Along with their works already cited, see the collection of essays by them entitled, *Faith and the Future: Essays on Theology, Solidarity and Modernity* in the Concilium series (Maryknoll, NY: Orbis Books, 1995). See also the works of German political theologian, Dorothee Soelle, including *Suffering* (trans. Everett R. Kalin; Philadelphia: Fortress Press, 1975); *Theology for Skeptics: Reflections on God* (trans. Joyce L. Irwin; Minneapolis: Fortress Press, 1995); and *The Silent Cry: Mysticism and Resistance* (trans. Barbara and Martin Rumscheidt; Minneapolis: Fortress Press, 1995). For a recent collection of essays dealing with violence and hope, see *Surviving Terror: Hope and Justice in a World of Violence*, edited by Victoria Lee Erickson and Michelle Lim Jones (Grand Rapids: Brazos Press, 2002).

For accessible introductions to quantum physics and its cultural import, see Roger S. Jones, *Physics as Metaphor* (Minneapolis: University of Minneapolis Press, 1982) and Shimon Malin, *Nature Loves to Hide* (Oxford: Oxford University Press, 2001). Another helpful text is Julian B. Barbour, *The End of Time: The Next Revolution in Physics* (Oxford: Oxford University Press, 1993).

Notes

1. Steven Charleston, "The Old Testament of Native America," in *Lift Every Voice: Constructing Christian Theologies from the Underside*, edited by Susan Brooks Thistlethwaite and Mary Potter Engel, (rev. ed.; Maryknoll, NY: Orbis Books, 1998), 69–81.

2. See, for example, articles in Joanne Carlson Brown and Carole R. Bohn, eds., *Christianity, Patriarchy, and Abuse: A Feminist Critique* (New York: Pilgrim Press, 1989), and Carol J. Adams and Marie M. Fortune, eds., *Violence Against Women and Children* (New York: Continuum, 1995).

3. Elisabeth Schüssler Fiorenza, *In Memory of Her* (New York: Crossroad, 1983).

4. The articles in Rosemary Ruether and Eleanor McLaughlin, eds., *Women of Spirit: Female Leadership in the Jewish and Christian Traditions* (New York: Simon & Schuster, 1979) demonstrate such a pattern of women's leadership being marginalized or squelched again and again. When they had the opportunity, especially in periods of transition, women would assert themselves, and then with institutionalization and "normalization" they would be pushed aside or deemed outside of acceptable boundaries.

5. Joan Kelly-Gadol, "Did Women Have a Renaissance?" in *Women, History and Theory: The Essays of Joan Kelly* (Chicago: University of Chicago Press, 1984).

3

ARE WE THERE YET?

Rethinking the Journey

A number of years ago, two of my nephews were coming for a visit. I was to pick them up and drive them the few hundred miles to my house. When we were not yet out of their driveway, they piped up in unison: "Are we there yet?" This "joke" they had planned became the theme of our journey, as it has been for so many a ride with children. That day was one of the longer ones of my life. We arrived at my house exhausted: they worn out by impatience; I drained of patience.

My nephews could not appreciate the journey. They were only interested in the destination, the end. I had thought carefully about this trip and how to make it more enjoyable for them. There was a state park along the way, where I thought we could stop and the boys could run around and use up some energy. But my nephews opposed anything that would, in their minds, "prolong" the trip. The journey was to be endured as a means to an end. It had no value or purpose on its own.

Christianity has viewed the journey of history like my nephews viewed this trip. The journey is governed by its destination and end, the reign of God, return to paradise. So the abiding question in Christian views of history is: are we there yet? As we saw in chapter 1, Christian theology has offered a variety of responses to the where and the when of the reign of God, the promised consummation, paradise regained. Those different metaphors shape the way the end is imagined: as the fulfillment of God's intent in history or in an afterlife; as the establishment of something new or the reestablishment of what has been lost. However the process is imagined, whenever and wherever the journey is completed, it is understood as a divine comedy: we will arrive at the end, and there we will find God and it will be good.

In modern times, as Christian theologians have looked more and more to history to seek answers to the where and the when of God's presence and activity, the end has been defined in terms of justice, freedom, and peace, and the journey as progress toward these goods. God's intent, which is the goal of history, is for justice, freedom, and peace to be realized in history. I have argued that such views of history and salvation history have been severely challenged by historical events, especially the ways in which history itself is threatened by violence and by the voices of those who have not been in the "driver's seat." These voices are asking not only, "Are we there yet?" but also, "Where are we going and why?" What claims, if any, can be made for God being in charge of the journey of history and directing it toward consummation?

The next three chapters will pay attention to the journey itself. What happens to our views of time, history, and redemption if we attend to the voices and dynamics outlined in the previous chapter? In the next chapter, I will examine the impact of suffering and the tragic dimension of life: what might it mean to fashion our views of history in response to all the unresolved horrors of history, especially the claims of a traumatic past? In chapter five, I will focus on the importance of the daily, of being in the moment, of the rhythms and cycles of life that center us in the present and the everyday. In this chapter, I explore the lure of the future and the vision of a good society or a final consummation to which God beckons us.

To the extent that the future vision is understood as an end or the end, a given *telos*, it not only shapes but also devalues the journey. Not attending to and honoring the journey, in and of itself, gets in the way of working for justice in the world. It fosters "once-and-for-all" thinking. And it does not let the future be open and be, in that sense, future.

To honor the journey requires that we rethink linear views of time and history and question a focus on the end as destination and consummation. The dilemma is this: how do we hold onto a vision of life transformed, of the reign of God, but not a linear and progressive view of history? How do we keep working for God's justice, peace, and freedom without seeing those as goals to be accomplished? In the Christian tradition, answers to such questions tended to move the vision into a "where and when" separate from human history: at the end of time, in God's realm, but not possible on earth. The vision functioned in the here and now only as judgment and promise. It translated into an eschatological proviso: what was truly of God was the not yet, the not here. At its best it served as eschatological promise: God's ends were not to be measured in time and by history. Eschatological promises were more "real"' than what happened in history. Historical justice was not a bad thing to work toward, but it ought not be equated with God's work of redemption.

Liberation theologians, working from the perspective of the disenfranchised, the oppressed, and the marginalized, whose hunger and thirst for justice and care is a matter of life and death now, have challenged visions of peace and abundance that are only future and do not feed the souls and bodies of those whose needs are immediate. Such persons require visions to be actualized in concrete instances of justice and care: in food and safety, housing and health care, education, and dignified work. And they need to hear that God cares about their well-being here and now, not just in the future, in heaven.

The Bible, especially in the prophetic writings, contains promises of the hungry being fed, the imprisoned set free, the blind receiving sight, swords being beaten into plowshares, and lions lying down with lambs. God declares that all will be safe and not come to harm. The people will rejoice; they will dance and sing. Even the desert will bloom.

The Hebrew Scriptures speak of "God's shalom," which is more than peace and justice. It is the presence of harmony and an abundance of blessing. Paul, in the Christian Scripture, writes of "new creation" and "reconciliation" to describe the reality of redemption. We also hear of a "new heaven and a new earth." In the Gospels, we are offered images in Jesus' life of the dispossessed exercising power, of outcasts being included at table, of the ill and infirm being healed. All these images and stories represent the fruition of God's love and justice.

But when and where and how?

Once-and-for-All Thinking

This vision of God's shalom has become infected with once-and-for-all thinking. This infection privileges the destination over the journey and assumes that once we have reached a desired destination, residency is permanent. Is this infection inherent in the vision itself and the ways of thinking fostered by the vision, or is it from outside?

This question is especially difficult for contemporary Americans to answer, because the American dream—our vision of the good life—is so deeply etched in our consciousness that contrary evidence does not seem to erase it. That American dream is rooted, albeit with twisted roots, in Christian ideas about God's favor and God's promises. The American dream is this: that each generation is better off than the one before, that we are making progress economically, socially, and politically. But, as I have indicated, the evidence seems to indicate this is not true today. The middle class is disappearing. The American dream is fading into the shadows for the vast majority of people in America. Politics seems more fractious, indicating deep fissures in our social and political fabric.

My generation senses that it is not necessarily better off than its parents were, and our children face even more obstacles to a bright and secure future. But we continue to act as if life will get better, and we have few resources available for thinking otherwise. We think that once something is accomplished or established—whether it be legislation or economic growth—there will be no going back, no regression. When our imagined progress crumbles, when the houses we thought were built on rock wash away in the sand, we feel helpless. This linear, progressive view of history is one source of infection in our vision of God's shalom.

Another infectious agent is the conviction that God is in charge of history, and nothing can stop God's purposes. Eschatology points to the end time when God's reign will be realized, so everything in history is ultimately not important and need not be taken seriously. Christian triumphalism is the consequence of such eschatological thinking. Its most dramatic form, apocalyptic, abandons historical progress, but has God break into history in order to bring about God's intended end. This view does not keep faith in history as progressive, but it does maintain that the vision will be accomplished no matter what. God's outside intervention is what changes history. Promises of eternal life function to resolve the ambiguities of history.

Eschatological thinking has many progeny, including some that are more worldly. Manifest destiny is one: America, as the center of power, is simply fulfilling its role in history. Declarations of finality, such as claiming that a particular armed conflict is "the war to end all wars" or stating that passing legislation to insure or protect certain rights, such as voting rights, will take care of the problem forever, are also evidence of once-and-for-all triumphal thinking. More chilling instances are Hitler's declaration of the Final Solution or recent claims that we are at the end of history because world capitalism has triumphed.

Once-and-for-all thinking privileges the end over the means; it turns visions into utopias, transforms imagination into wish fulfillment and hope into the eternal embodiment of desire. It ends up devaluing history and time by suggesting that history is not ongoing and the processes of history do not continue to play themselves out.

Such thinking also masks the workings of power. Power is not a fixed entity, as Michel Foucault taught us, but a fluid form that moves throughout systems. If it is blocked in one direction—by legislation, for example—it will find other means of domination. If we are not alert to this dynamic of power, we are surprised by new manifestations of what we thought we took care of. When we think the arrow of history moves only in one direction, we are not prepared for assaults from the rear and the flanks.

Yet another source of infection is our discomfort with finitude. Since God and God's reign are defined as eternal, infinite, and complete, we adopt these characteristics as measures for our visions and hopes. We find it difficult to embrace or value our finitude and attribute it to sin and the fall. Finitude is to be escaped; it is not intrinsic to creation.

All of these infections draw strength from dualism's either/or categories: we are either finite or infinite; historical action is either good or sinful; we are on the side of God or of evil. Dualistic thinking turns differences into oppositions: good and evil, oppressor and oppressed, rich and poor, male and female, white and black. In order for dualism to work, these dimensions require fixed boundaries. Hints of ambiguity and indeterminacy undermine such definitions. Fluidity, porousness—the messiness of life in history—do not fit into the neat packages that once-and-for-all thinking and its corollary, dualism, demand. And those neat packages, in the name of hope, choke hope.

The narratives of once-and-for-all thinking and of evolutionary and progressive views of history are also unabashedly comedic. There will be a happy ending. The good will win. God will make sure of that. In the standard Christian story, God has already accomplished the end, the promised redemption, in the life, death, and resurrection of

Jesus Christ. The victory over evil has been won, so history is actually only a "mopping up action." This way of telling the story offers few resources for dealing with the messiness of history, including its tragedies and terrors. For those whose lives are full of struggle and suffering, such a victorious approach to history feels dismissive of their experiences.

Utopianism in whatever form—this worldly or otherworldly—implies that our historical actions do not ultimately count. Assuming that the end of the story is already known, or already accomplished, privileges the outcome in a way that devalues the journey. The question "Are we there yet?" suggests that "there" and "then" are all that matter, and the journey is something simply to be endured.

Alternative Approaches to a Redemptive Vision

How do we maintain a vision of love and justice, freedom and peace, without a prior assumption that the vision will necessarily be realized? How do we act for the good without guarantees of success or progress? What would be our view of history if we paid attention to the journey itself and not only its destination? Answers to these questions need to find different ways to think about time and history than those most often provided by the Christian tradition and its modern secular off-spring in theories of progress and historical finality.

Although many theologians have taken seriously the challenges to progressive and linear views of history and time, most of them continue to maintain that history has a goal or *telos* that determines its meaning and purpose. That *telos* is of God and so is good. It will be realized. History, therefore, remains vectored: pointed in a particular direction. Its end is also known. There may be deviations, detours, and roadblocks along the way, but the destination will be reached. God makes sure of that. The character and content of Christian hope is then shaped by such knowledge and faith in God's actions in and beyond history.

These theologians do not really change the conversation. They continue to discuss the relationship of world history and God's history as it has been posed since the Enlightenment. They may disagree about the ways in which God will resolve history and its ambiguities, but not whether. In that sense the outcome is given. The destination is still what guides the journey. The end overshadows and determines the process.

For other theologians, however, the questioning goes deeper. They are less quick to turn to God's power to resolve. All is not determined by the end. In examining the perspectives of theologians Rubem Alves, Peter Hodgson, Rosemary Ruether, and Sharon Welch, I am looking for resources to help with my questions: How do we maintain a vision of love and justice, freedom and peace, but find other ways of thinking about history and what happens or is possible in history? How do we practice hope when the outcome is not known? I choose these four theologians not only because they have contributed significantly to this conversation about hope and history, but also because they have been companions on my own theological journey.

Rubem Alves

When I first read Rubem Alves's book *Tomorrow's Child: Imagination, Creativity, and the Rebirth of Culture* over thirty years ago, I was drawn to his ideas and language in a way I have not often experienced. I felt a deep connection with his questions and his struggles about how to live faithfully in the world. Alves, a South American liberation theologian concerned about justice, social transformation, and hope, specifies that he wrote that book especially for North Americans. He argues that North American culture and its values are bankrupt and headed for collapse. Alves likens the culture of North America to the dinosaurs who, he suggests, became too large and absurd for their own systems. So, too, American culture is ultimately absurd and will become extinct. Alves sees American culture as governed by the law of entropy, moving toward disorder and disintegration. The desire for power and continued, unquestioned economic and political growth have created a system that devalues life. Instead of power serving life, life serves the thirst for power.

Alves employs not only social analysis but also psychoanalytic categories. Misuses of power result in repression that chokes life. Imagination and creativity are an antidote to such repression, opening up to possibility and a future not closed down by the logic of the system and the seeming fixity of reality. Hope is fostered by the practice of magic, by play and by utopian imagination that will transform everything for the good. These alternative practices also function as forms of resistance to the totality of the overpowering system and its logic.

In fact, Alves does not believe our actions can change the dominant system. And they do not need to. That system will fall into oblivion from its own contradictions and absurdity. The role for communities of faith, in the meantime, is to keep hope alive and to practice disciplines that will allow for a different future when the time comes.

In the meantime, Alves's suggestions seem to be more tragic in tone than comedic. To hope in the present is to live "as if" our dreams and visions are more real than the overriding givenness of the world we inhabit—which is to say, that to hope is to live in resistance and to be countercultural. It is to establish communities that maintain and practice a different vision and alternative values. These communities are committed to life itself, as an end in itself, and to creating culture, a counterculture. They are aware that success is not guaranteed and that immediate results are an illusion. They do not practice once-and-for-all thinking, but its opposite, a hope for the future they may never see.

The biblical narrative Alves references is not the Exodus and the coming into the promised land, but Israel's exile and captivity. Drawing upon Jeremiah, Alves gives advice to those who must live their lives in a "foreign" land, under the rule of a conqueror. Just as Jeremiah told the captives in exile to live their lives, to build houses and inhabit them, to plant crops and harvest them, so Alves advises his readers in North America to continue living with intent for the future, so as to guarantee that there will be a future even though its contours cannot be seen nor is its outcome assured. He describes this process as one of planting dates, a crop that takes many years to come to fruition, as opposed to pumpkins that grow immediately and produce quick results.

Alves offers a hope that is not guaranteed in this world but is not otherworldly either. His vision is not a divine comedy. Nor is it determined by its end, though there is direction and intentionality in imagining a different future. For Alves, God is present in the journey, even when the path takes us into exile and captivity. Life itself is journey and its own end. Life continuing life with imagination and play, embodied and able to dance, is participation in redemption. As he writes so eloquently:

The culture-creating act is no more than a sabbath: a resting place in an unending journey. It is an *aperitif* which always says there is still something to come. Have you ever tried to reach the horizon? Every horizon denies itself, for there is always a beyond. Life is never exhausted. There are new possibilities ahead, new occasions for joy, new pregnancies to be conceived.

So there is no end?

This really should not be the question. The question is whether a situation will ever exist in which a new beginning is impossible. And what I am saying is that, because of imagination, life can always begin again.[1]

For Alves, "Hope is hearing the melody of the future. Faith is to dance to it."[2] Hope and faith are found in and through community and creativity.

Alves's vision is defined by ethical commitments, but it is textured by aesthetic sensibilities and a valuing of beauty for its own sake. His description of what we need to be and do, beautiful and haunting in its poetic tones, remains temporary; the journey will be superceded. Ultimately, even without investment in a *telos*, Alves remains utopian in his imagination and his hope.

Peter Hodgson

In *God in History: Shapes of Freedom*, Protestant theologian Peter Hodgson struggles, as I do, with the liberal theological tradition that put so much faith in history and that correlated salvation with the outcomes of history. Hodgson's summation of his argument resounds with the themes we have been exploring: "The mythos of salvation history, with its logic of triumph, its linear teleology, and its suprahistorical eschatology must be allowed to die out in order to salvage its enduring conviction that God acts redemptively in history, a conviction from which might be fashioned a new theology of the history of freedom."[3] Steering a course through postmodern challenges and movements of empowerment and liberation, he is trying to find a way to "rethink the relationship of God and history."[4] Hodgson's proposal is that God is in history and history in God "in the myriad shapes of freedom."[5]

As a scholar of Hegel, Hodgson is permeated with the language of freedom and spirit, though Hodgson's desire for what he refers to as finite, fragile, fragmentary, but nonetheless real, "shapes of freedom" in history is more modest than Hegel's. For Hodgson, history is always characterized by ambiguity and partiality, yet there is a movement, a shaping, of history toward freedom that is indication of God's saving work. This process of "configuration" will always be met by "deconfiguration" in history, so the praxis of liberation remains fragile—being undone, even as it is being done. It is not once and for all.

Hodgson's honoring of the ambiguity and limitations of action in history leads him to rethink the nature of the Christian narrative. He incorporates a tragic sensibility into the divine comedy of Christianity, but history remains comedic, or what he refers to as tragicomic. If tragedy were to become the dominant narrative, then, Hodgson argues, hope and historical action would be rendered ineffective. Hodgson's struggle is to honor all that is suffered and so to recognize the tragic in history, yet, at the same time, not to give the tragic too much power.

Although human history is tragicomic, God's action is ultimately comedic. There is no final resolution toward the good in history, but God will bring all to the good beyond history. Hodgson concludes: "Whatever happens in the worldly history of freedom, whether it is itself a failure or a consummation or an ambiguous mixture, will be annulled and transfigured in the "eternal history" of freedom that is God."[6] Even though Hodgson seems intent on viewing God in history, ultimately God remains outside of history. The only way to maintain hope *for* history, Hodgson argues, is to have hope originate *beyond* history, in and from the divine.

This perspective shapes Hodgson's understanding of time. Time is not linear, but moves in a helical, spiral pattern: "a coiling through constantly changing planes." Therefore, the direction of time is not given or unambiguous. Though there is still a general directionality and divine intent of movement toward freedom, the path toward the future is neither straight nor straightforward. Nor is the future determined. Hodgson suggests an "open teleology." Because of finitude, history will have an end in the sense of "terminus." But whether human history will end as a "consummation" or a "failure" is unknown.[7] In the meantime, history is the dynamic realm of God, "shaping" and "luring" toward freedom and justice and wholeness. Since human freedom is real, God's actions cannot be determinative in history, but they do affect it.

Hodgson seems to teeter on the brink of giving himself over to the tides of time and history without the anchor of a given *telos*, but he holds himself and God back for the sake of freedom and of God as "the One who loves in freedom."[8] Ultimately, Hodgson leads us to a deeper appreciation of the process of history and helps us to act in it in a more "worldly" way, but there remains a goal at the end that is more real and more desirable than the journey. Freedom is the goal and not just the commitment human persons embrace.

Rosemary Ruether

In *Sexism and God-Talk*, feminist theologian Rosemary Ruether moves beyond the opposition of linear and cyclical ways of thinking about history to suggest a cyclical model of historical time within which there is direction and linearity. She sees this model as "based on conversion or *metanoia*":

> Conversion suggests that, while there is no one utopian state of humanity lying back in an original paradise of the "beginning," there are basic ingredients of a just and livable society. These ingredients have roots in nature and involve acceptance of finitude, human scale, and balanced relationships between persons and between human and non-human beings.[9]

In *To Change the World: Christology and Social Criticism*, Ruether defines social change "as conversion to the centre, rather than to a beginning or end-point in history."[10] The goal of salvation history is not a future end point or a return to an "original paradise," but an ongoing process of movement and return—conversion—to core values and principles that ground and direct our lives.

As warrant for this understanding of temporal existence, Ruether draws upon an ancient resource. The Jubilee tradition, referenced briefly in Hebrew Scripture (Leviticus 25:8–12), is based on the model of the Sabbath, which sets aside times for rest and restoration. The Jubilee tradition assumes that, just as individuals (every seventh day) and even the land (every seventh year) need rest and restoration, so do communities and societies (every fiftieth year, after a forty-nine year cycle of seven times seven). In that fiftieth year, the community is to stop and readjust itself. It is to practice restorative justice: debts are to be forgiven, lands returned to their original owners, slaves released from bondage, and other inequities corrected. Lands, animals, and people are to rest and restore themselves. Though there is little historical evidence of these Jubilee practices, in recent years, a number of Christian denominations have turned to the idea of a Jubilee to argue for debt forgiveness for many struggling nations, as well as to advocate for other programs of social restoration.

The Jubilee tradition incorporates a view of historical processes as cyclical but not as endless return. History is not just repeating itself. Changes and developments are happening all the time, but not always or necessarily in a desirable direction. At each Jubilee time, there may be new achievements as well as new problems. Ruether points out that while the Jubilee tradition recognizes the possibility of changes toward justice and harmony, it does not support once-and-for-all or utopian thinking. Because of human finitude as well as human inclinations to do other than the good, problems, abuses, and inequities will inevitably arise. So there will ever be the need to stop, survey, and restore.

For Ruether, the Jubilee tradition is based not on the idea of endless return but of endless correction. In recognition of human limitations and tendencies toward sin, it eschews any notion that change for the good is forever. Rather it ensures that there will be regular periods of evaluation and adjustment. The Jubilee tradition maintains hope not only in the possibilities of making life better in history, but also in the ability of human beings to correct what is wrong and to change again and again.

Ruether's approach does not assume a *telos*. There is no set direction in which history is moving. Nor is God's intent going to be manifest in another place and time beyond history. Rather than seeing God's work as the consummation of history, of bringing it to a particular end, Ruether sees God present in the commitments to life and to living rightly, enacted in history. For Hodgson, this is not enough. He criticizes Ruether for not wanting more for the future, for not positing a clear enough direction in which history is moving into the future, even if that direction is not given and remains open, as it is for Hodgson.[11]

Ruether's vision is of a sense of home and of return to home, of living in harmony and balance with creation and with the Holy. She names this harmony as the Shalom of God that is the "true connecting point of all our existences." "Redemptive hope is the constant quest for that Shalom of God which holds us all together, as the operative principle of our collective lives."[12]

Living the Shalom of God requires the practice of justice, freedom, and peace. Ruether's understanding of such practices is shaped by biblical and western traditions of thought. She does not universalize her particular configuration of them. Nor does she eternalize them. What is eternal is life, life seeking life. As long as there is life on the earth, there is hope. Redemption is in and through life sustaining life.

I wonder, though, if Ruether has replaced the end with the beginning: a sense of original wholeness and of home derived from a transcendent vision of the divine. In contrast to Hodgson, who seems to be lured by the future and its unfolding of freedom, Ruether seems to be lured by this sense of home. She has bluntly stated that there is no original paradise to which we are to return, yet her vision posits an embodied harmony that seems to be original and drives our vision of what ought to be. Though the imagery she uses is more of return to the center than to the past, this place to which we are to return is more desirable than the one we inhabit. There remains then, in her perspective, a possibility of ultimate harmony, a vision of our true home.

Sharon Welch

Feminist ethicist Sharon Welch's goals for history are more modest still. Of the theologians considered here, she is the one who claims the least for history and for what is possible in history. This does not mean she has abandoned history; indeed, she sees nothing beyond history. As a postmodern thinker, Welch has embraced finitude and instability and has let go of transcendence beyond history. Yet she is hopeful. Her hope remains in and for history, for life.

In *A Feminist Ethic of Risk*, Welch asks questions similar to mine: How are we to practice faith and hope when our historical projects do not materialize as we have imagined? How are we to maintain commitment to social and political justice when we do not see the goals of justice come to fruition? The specific case she examines is the American anti-nuclear peace movement, whose ranks are filled mainly with members of the middle class. The dynamic Welch is most interested in exploring is the lack of persistence by these middle class Americans, whose lives are ones of relative comfort.

She finds that dualistic and clear-cut categories of good and evil do not work, even though such thinking is often the fallback position in theological analysis. She sees such categories as the result, not the source of the problem. The problem itself is rooted in attitudes and practices that constitute an ethic of control. Such an ethic practices once-and-for-all thinking that does not see value in partial and/or temporary solutions. Rather, it seeks security and finality. An ethic of control turns to utopian thinking that eschews pluralism and the inevitable complexities and conflicts that come with pluralism. Beneath this ethic and its accompanying attitudes and practices is a fear of difference and of chaos.

An ethic of control also produces a "cultured despair," an inability to sustain hope. Welch argues that such despair and cynicism are supported by liberals' views of eschatology. As we have seen, Christian theology has been reluctant to identify any concrete historical action with the kingdom of God. This reluctance, often referred to as the eschatological reservation or proviso, recognizes the limitations and incompleteness of human historical action. Since we are finite and fallible, since we cannot see all the implications of our actions, we cannot assume that anything we do is "of God." Welch disagrees not so much with the recognition of the partiality of our accomplishments as with the reasoning behind that judgment: "It is a social imperative that this disparity between intent and consequence be acknowledged, yet it makes all the difference in the world if the source of such knowledge is a contrast between human power and absolute power or a positive recognition of the complex structure of the web of life."[13] The latter perspective is a positive "appreciation" of the limitations of human life; the former is negative and critical about the human condition. In other words, if we accept finitude and limitation as part of the human condition, then we will not see our destiny as somehow beyond them. We will recognize the life we have to be our home and not some way station on the journey to a final and better end, which by its nature ultimately negates this life. Partiality will be an inevitable dimension of our lives. All historical accomplishments will be limited and incomplete, but nonetheless valuable and necessary. As Welch argues: "The need for correctives and revision is not . . . a sign of the failure of action; it is a manifestation of the nature of human action."[14]

Welch sees a further problem in the way the theological tradition has defined power and rendered God's power as total and totally other than any other power. This produces what she calls "the erotics of domination," which is "the valorization of absolute power" and "the glorification of submission to the greatest power."[15] Even though the theological tradition maintains that only God's power is absolute, a notion of absolute power, especially as potentially good, can still foster a tendency to support dominating and coercive uses of power. An erotics of domination does not value finitude; it suppresses differences. In their place are to be found a desire for security and the search for absolute and final resolutions.

Welch draws on resources from African-American women's literature to offer an ethic of risk, solidarity, and difference and a theology of resistance and hope in which "finitude, interdependence, change, and particularity" are valued.[16] Life is best lived in awareness of the partiality of any of its manifestations. Nothing we do or accomplish is absolute or once and for all. Yet each particular, partial expression is valuable and important and necessary for life. The need to act in history will remain as an ongoing process; the risk that we ever take. There will never be an end to the problems that arise. Therefore, the practice of resistance and creativity will be ongoing as well.

For Welch, the "location" of hope in an ethic of solidarity is the "beloved community" that celebrates "limits, contingency, and ambiguity."[17] Alone, we are not able to do very much. Our ability to accomplish anything of sustaining value is dependent on our doing so in connection, not only in solidarity with other human beings, but with the world and creation that is the source of life. The ground of our acting is love and selves nurtured in and for love. Such love enables hope and joy.

Thus, our ability to act needs to be sustained in community with others, a community that embraces diversity and interdependence. The divine is engaged with and in community through creative power. For Welch, the divine is "the resilient, fragile, healing power of finitude."[18]

In *Sweet Dreams in America: Making Ethics and Spirituality Work*, Welch continues to develop her thinking about hope and the limitations inherent in processes of change and work for justice. If in *A Feminist Ethic of Risk* Welch was advocating a turn from control to risk, vulnerability, and resistance, in *Sweet Dreams in America* she discusses chaos and our inability to insure the uses of power. Moving further away from dualistic thinking about good and evil that can only render chaos as something to be overcome, Welch offers a definition of goodness, not as the opposite of evil, but as "an aesthetic of seeing and responding to conflict, chaos, and ambiguity."[19] Goodness and beauty are one: "The source of work for justice is beauty; being grateful for the gift of life, honoring it, celebrating it, playing our part in this chaotic, glorious adventure."[20]

Hope is about going on and living life with commitment and joy and respect. The practice of hope necessitates community and engagement with others, not only for companionship, but to keep us honest and accountable. Our companions need to be widely diverse, if we are to honor the differences among us and to learn more about ourselves.

Welch understands human action as fundamentally ambiguous. She eschews moral dualism and its promised final resolution. Indeed, it is precisely such dualism that Welch sees as problematic. "Evil" is produced along with good in the process of living and acting. We can rely on neither God nor ourselves to guarantee a utopian future. We are, however, called upon to do our best, along with others, to sustain life. Welch's vision might be viewed as dour, if she were not so grounded in joy—a joy in life itself as beautiful and celebratory.

Using jazz as her primary metaphor and resource for an alternative vision, Welch is able to enter into the joy of "virtuosity." In jazz, the music is created and exists in the moment. It is improvisational yet structured. Jazz musicians "play" off one another for the sake of pleasure and beauty and joy, for the love of the music itself. Jazz offers "a model of responsiveness without progress or repetition."[21] The music is constantly changing in the interplay between the individual and the group.

For Welch, justice is not a goal but a necessary ingredient of life. There is no ultimate end to be attained or delivered, only partial and fragile accomplishments. The source and goal of Welch's ethics is life. Instead of dreams of finality and consummation as motivators, she offers joy and gratitude in the wonder of life itself. Hope is found in sharing life and recognizing its gifts. In her more recent book *After Empire: The Art and Ethos of Enduring Peace,* Welch develops these ideas further into an "improvisational ethic" that practices an ironic spirituality able to appreciate beauty, honor suffering, and find joy in living.[22]

Keeping House

Rubem Alves, Peter Hodgson, Rosemary Ruether, and Sharon Welch are each attempting to think differently about our lives in time. None of them wants to privilege the end, the destiny, in a way that denies the journey. Nor do they want to engage in once-and-for-all thinking or to maintain a linear, evolutionary view of history. Yet they all have deep and abiding commitments to social change that they continue to act upon. In that sense they are also activists for justice and peace and freedom. Indeed, it is their desire for a more effective social analysis and action that propels their theological projects.

As we attend to their work, several changes in thinking about time and hope, history and justice begin to emerge. They shift attention away from the end to the process—unlike my nephews who were so fixated on the destination that they could not appreciate or enjoy the journey. The process is really all there is. Hope is in and through the process. Without a fixed *telos*, directing or propelling all, the action must become its own justification, even its own end.

For Alves and Hodgson, even though there is no clear *telos*, there remains in place a horizon of hope that guides the journey. In that sense, the metaphor of journey is still directional. It assumes a destination even if the destination cannot be fixed. Whether that journey is understood as a helical spiral (Hodgson) or a future horizon that draws us forward (Alves), it is moving in a particular direction.

The value of this metaphor of journey is its emphasis on the process and the importance of moving intentionally through time and space. It seems a fitting way in which to understand life and to give life and living value in and of themselves. Journeys are dynamic; there is constant movement and a sense of change as good and necessary. But the metaphor is limited because it is still so often shaped by its destination. Unless there is a direction in which we are going, we seem to be wandering aimlessly. Neither Alves nor Hodgson wants to fix that direction, but they do not let go of the need for it. Because chaos lurks in the shadows of the present, they turn toward the future for a horizon point to guide them.

Ruether and Welch do not focus on the future or the metaphor of journey, but on home or place, on maintaining a living environment. Ruether uses the image of home explicitly, Welch implicitly. Yet for both of them there is no once-and-for-all accomplishment of justice or peace or a livable environment. Nor is there a fixed point in the future that guides our movements. Rather than journeying to somewhere else, we need to embrace life and the universe as home. Acting for social change can be understood as a form of housekeeping.

This metaphor of housekeeping helps us imagine living in time differently. Housekeeping does not move us from one place to another. Rather it is about the quality and character of the life we live. The point of housekeeping is to clean up messes and set things aright in order that we might live well, in comfort and safety.

There is no such thing as cleaning house once and for all. Housekeeping is a constant and continual need and task. Dirt happens. Messiness, even a certain measure of chaos, is a by-product of living, not the result of evil or wrongdoing. Accepting the need for housekeeping as a given of life avoids dualism and the location of evil as outside ourselves.

The more fully we inhabit our homes, the more the need for housekeeping. There is no way to make a meal that is nourishing and enjoyable without needing to clean up counters and utensils, dishes and pans. The more people there are living in a house, the more mess there is likely to be. Yet a person living alone may feel less need to pick up after herself, because, after all, no one else will notice. However messy or neat we are, alone or together, none of us can avoid the build-up of dust and dirt. It simply happens, even if we, like Felix Unger in *The Odd Couple*, are obsessive about neatness and cleanliness. The laundry builds up; the kitchen sink fills up with dishes; dust descends on any available surface. If housekeeping is neglected for any length of time, it becomes a greater chore. The greater the delay, the more demanding the work of cleaning up will be. If the neglect is too great, a house may be beyond restoration, or it may require dramatic intervention, such as fumigation.

It is easy to apply this metaphor to our life together in the world. Implicit in social critiques of the lack of justice and freedom in the world is the sense that we have not kept house as we should have. We have denied comfort and safety and a decent standard of living to many of the world's people. The frictions among earth's inhabitants have caused massive harm to our communal life. Nor have we taken care of the planet and the created order as if we were responsible housekeepers.

We do not live on the earth and with one another as if we shared a home, as if we are a household. We act as if we live alone or are just passing through. Sallie McFague, in *The Body of God*, points out that we treat the earth as if we are living in a hotel and not in our home, that we are just sojourning and someone will clean up after us.

Housekeeping is not for the sake of the future or because of some goal toward which we are striving. Cleanliness is not an end. We keep house in order to maintain and enjoy our lives. The quality of our life here and now depends on how well we keep house.

Housekeeping is cyclical. There is no sense of progress *per se*. In fact, in ordinary housekeeping we simply return to where we began, but not in a pattern of endless return or a return to paradise. When we clean we get rid of dust and dirt, and we put things back in their places. And we do so knowing that as soon as we are done the need will begin to arise again. Dust will come in through the crevices; our shoes will track in dirt; laundry, mail, and trash will pile up; we will eat and more dishes will need washing. The only way to avoid these things is to stop living. So we clean house again and again and again.

Housekeeping is not only about maintaining our lives but about living them well. Our homes are not simply utilitarian spaces. However modest our resources may be, we decorate them. We put pictures on the wall and knickknacks on shelves. Since such things collect dust, something other than efficiency is guiding our decorating. We want to enjoy our homes and be comfortable living in them, so we pay attention to aesthetics and are intentional about the kind of life we want to live and foster. That is true not only for what we put in our spaces, but how we live in them, the habits and relationships we cultivate and nurture.

Our homes are living environments. Making a home and keeping house are about making life possible, good, and enjoyable. And they are about keeping life going. Babies and children need homes in which to grow and develop. The elderly need homes in which to feel connected and in which to die, a point made clear by the hospice movement.

If we continue to apply this metaphor, then history is our habitation, the earth is our home. We are not simply passing through. We are not just sojourners, stopping for awhile on a journey to somewhere else. We are inhabitants, long-term, lifetime inhabitants. And we need to take care of our home with that understanding in mind.

Justice and peace, freedom and beauty are no longer ends. They are the tasks of homemaking. We need to practice them if we are to live well. Making justice and peace are about maintaining a decent living environment for everyone on the earth. Restorative justice is about fixing what is wrong or broken. Freedom and beauty make life more livable. The end, if we can call it an end, is living itself. But living is a process. Life is its own justification. The measure of life is its going on and going well.

This metaphor is not without its problems. Two trends characteristic of our current society are particular danger areas. One is consumerism. Homemaking can become an end in itself, as it has in so many ways in this consumption-oriented society with its emphasis on "house beautiful." When homemaking becomes such an end, the intent of housekeeping is no longer about living, but about "showing off," what has been called "conspicuous consumption." Then we lose the ability to measure our living, to know what is sufficient. Consumerism breeds on itself. The more we buy, the more we want. Not only have we no sense of our true needs but even our desires become distorted. Accumulation becomes an end in itself: bigger houses with more possessions. The few live in incredible luxury while others go homeless. Keeping up these homes, keeping up appearances, consumes disproportionate resources. This type of housekeeping makes life more difficult for the majority of those living on this earth.

The other danger is privatization. Even though we do not intend it, focusing on home as a primary way to understand ourselves in the world can make us too preoccupied with ourselves and the quality of our own lives. Privatization goes hand in hand with consumption and the tendency to hoard; both privatization and consumption are fueled by the dynamics of capitalism. The more we have, the more our energy goes toward protecting our possessions. Not only do we live alone or in nuclear families, but we lock our doors, install alarms, and even withdraw into gated communities. We make our homes havens away from the world, rather than our way of living in the world. It becomes increasingly difficult to imagine living in connection with others.

In contrast, the slogan "it takes a village to raise a child" speaks to the need for community, the need not to carry the whole burden of living ourselves. Privatization opposes community and connection with others. It feeds a capitalist economy that requires that any and all resources be market products. In a privatized economy, we end up paying for things that in a community-focused environment would be part of communal living, such as people to watch our children, someone who will sit down and listen to us, or even someone to make our meals.

Obviously, housekeeping is a domestic metaphor and that, too, may be perceived as a limitation in a culture that tends to devalue the home and homemaking because they are associated more with women. However, domesticity is a strength and a value insofar as it honors life. Thus, this metaphor helps to raise questions about the spurious separations of public and private, domestic and civic spheres.

Housekeeping and homemaking are in the service of life and living. They are not ends in themselves. They are necessary tasks, to be accomplished again and again in order to make life happen and happen well.

Are we there yet? The answer is yes, because in every moment we are inhabitants of time, which is as it should be. There and then are not separate from here and now.

For Further Reading

The theological texts discussed in this chapter are the best place to begin for further reading: Rubem Alves, *Tomorrow's Child: Imagination, Creativity, and the Rebirth of Culture* (New York: Harper & Row, 1972); Peter Hodgson, *God in History: Shapes of Freedom* (Nashville: Abingdon Press, 1989); Rosemary Ruether, *Sexism and God-Talk: Toward a Feminist Theology* (Boston: Beacon Press, 1983) and *To Change the World: Christology and Social Criticism* (New York: Crossroad, 1981); and Sharon Welch, *A Feminist Ethic of Risk* (Minneapolis: Fortress Press, 1990), *Sweet Dreams in America* (New York: Routledge, 1999), and *After Empire: The Art and Ethos of Enduring Peace* (Minneapolis: Fortress Press, 2004). For Rosemary Ruether, see also *Gaia & God: An Ecofeminist Theology of Earth Healing* (San Francisco: HarperSanFrancisco, 1992) and "Eschatology and Feminism," in *Lift Every Voice: Constructing Christian Theologies from the Underside*, edited by Susan Brooks Thistlethwaite and Mary Potter Engel (rev. ed.; Maryknoll, NY: Orbis Books, 1998).

Sallie McFague's *The Body of God* and *Life Abundant*, listed in the previous chapter, introduce the metaphor of housekeeping. See also Paul Fiddes, *The Promised End: Eschatology in Theology and Literature* (Oxford: Blackwell Publishers, 2000) and Frank Kermode, *The Sense of an Ending: Studies in the Theory of Fiction* (new ed.; Oxford: Oxford University Press, 2000) for a discussion of the influence of Christian eschatological and teleological thought on western views of history and time.

Notes

1. Rubem Alves, *Tomorrow's Child: Imagination, Creativity, and the Rebirth of Culture* (New York: Harper & Row, 1972), 176–77.

2. Ibid., 195.

3. Peter Hodgson, *God in History: Shapes of Freedom* (Nashville: Abingdon Press, 1989), 50.

4. Ibid., 42.

5. Ibid., 44.

6. Ibid., 237.

7. Ibid., 243–44.

8. Ibid., 251.

9. Rosemary Ruether, *Sexism and God-Talk: Toward a Feminist Theology* (Boston: Beacon Press, 1983), 254.

10. Rosemary Ruether, *To Change the World: Christology and Social Criticism* (New York: Crossroad, 1981), 69.

11. Hodgson, *God in History*, 232–34.

12. Ruether, *To Change the World*, 69–70.

13. Sharon Welch, *A Feminist Ethic of Risk* (Minneapolis: Fortress Press, 1990), 108.

14. Ibid., 108–9.

15. Ibid., 117.

16. Ibid., 122.

17. Ibid., 158.

18. Ibid., 178.

19. Sharon Welch, *Sweet Dreams in America* (New York: Routledge, 1999), 50.

20. Ibid., 101.

21. Ibid., 16.

22. Sharon Welch, *After Empire: The Art and Ethos of Enduring Peace* (Minneapolis: Fortress Press, 2004).

4

BLACK HOLES AND
FRACTURED FAIRY TALES

Trauma and Tragedy in History

Before they settled in America, my parents and maternal grandmother were displaced persons. During World War I, the Turkish government carried out a genocidal campaign against its Armenian population that resulted in over a million deaths and made refugees out of the survivors. Forced from their homes and their native land, these refugees, my parents and grandmother among them, struggled in various locations to eke out a living and to make a life for themselves. My father's journey to America was the most direct, but even it took several years. He fled from Turkey into Russia and eventually made his way to Japan. There he was able to arrange passage to America. His older brother, who had immigrated to America years before, sponsored him and paid his way. I have known my father's story in broad outline but not in detail. He died when I was twenty years old, so our conversations ended long ago. Many years after his death, however, I came across a reference letter written for my father by a Red Cross worker in Vladivostok, Siberia. From it, I learned that my father had spent time in a refugee camp there. Dated April 28, 1919, the letter states: "Mr. Keshgagian [*sic*] escaped from the Turkish massacres in his own country, made his way across Russia to Vladivostok, and has been in our barracks for about seven months. Mr. Keshgagian [*sic*] expects to leave here is a few days for the United States. His conduct whilein [*sic*] the barracks leads us to believe he will make a desirable citizen."

My grandmother arrived in the United States a couple of decades later in 1940, and my mother followed several years later. After the genocide, they had returned to their hometown of Arapkir, Turkey, but the poverty there was unrelenting, and they moved on to Aleppo, Syria, and then to Beirut, Lebanon. My mother spent some of her years in Beirut, sleeping in what was essentially a hallway. Her journey to America, when she was finally able to acquire a visa and arrange for passage, was a circuitous one through several countries, including Egypt and the Sudan.

My family's experiences are not that different from the majority of immigrants who came to America not so much out of desire as need. The particular narratives of what drove people from their countries or forced them from their homelands may reflect a variety of reasons, but they convey a common motivation. There was little or no life for them in their home countries. Though their journeys to America were not necessarily direct or timely, pasts of persecution and deprivation and violence drove wave after wave of immigrants, including many of this country's founding fathers and mothers, toward America's shores. From the earliest Puritans who were looking for a place to live out their religious and social values, to the Irish escaping famine and persecution, to the more recent groups of immigrants from Southeast Asia and Eastern Europe who were fleeing from violence and war, America has represented a place of escape, refuge, and opportunity.

These immigrants may have been seeking a better life, but they were also bringing with them the burdens of the past. On these shores, they experienced more suffering. Each new group of immigrants encountered hardship and discrimination. For many, the welcome greeting offered by the Statue of Liberty was soon replaced with the humiliating ordeal that was Ellis Island. What often followed was brutal factory work, barely tolerable living conditions, the indecencies of not knowing how to negotiate a foreign culture, and exposure to discrimination and prejudice from the dominant culture.

Others, whose presence on America's shores was not the result of emigration, experienced even worse forms of persecution and deprivation and violence. Africans, brought to America against their wills, lived and toiled in slavery. After emancipation, African Americans were subject to continuing violence, poverty, and discrimination legislated by Jim Crow laws and embedded in racist attitudes and systems.

Mexican Americans and First Nations peoples had their lands taken from them. Many First Nations tribes were forcibly displaced to other areas of the country and/or put into reservations. The native peoples of Mexico were subjected to exploitation and discrimination by both Spain and America.

Given this history, traumatic suffering shadows much of the population of America. Indeed, we may be considered a nation of trauma survivors. If we allow for the effects of secondary trauma and hereditary trauma, such as the trauma experienced by witnesses and by succeeding generations, then there are few people in this country who do not carry a trauma history in some form. In this chapter, I will explore what difference this makes for how we might perceive not only time but also place—and for the stories we tell about ourselves.

In its public narratives, America is portrayed as a land of opportunity. It is the promised land, the place of deliverance. These narratives are fairy tales that end with "happily ever after." Their enforced comedic emplotment does not include either the circumstances that brought people to America nor what they experienced here, other than as plot devices to move toward a happy ending. All the "bad" is left behind or transcended in an ultimate good and happy resolution. Immigrants to America, whatever their motivating circumstances, have often adopted this narrative structure for their own stories. The accounts of their experiences may begin with tales of persecution, poverty, and even genocide, but they lead up to a comedic ending as these immigrants find work, start families, and establish lives in America. Their hope is directed toward their own survival and toward building a better life for their children and their children's children. The wonder is that so many of these immigrants were truly able to build relatively good lives for themselves and their families.

But the question remains: in the comedic narrative what happens to the unresolved, the horrific, the ongoing pain and struggle? In these immigrant accounts, such realities are often ignored, submerged, left behind, or recounted as a past that has been superceded by new and renewed lives. As a result, little attention is paid to the experience of traumatic suffering—other than as plot devices—in people's lives. The hurts of the past are denied in vain attempts to leave them behind. As long as the narrative structures used to tell the story of these suffering peoples do not name and give due place to their hurts and injuries, these parts of their lives remain unspoken. Happy endings are layered on top of trauma that lies hidden, unrecognized, and unprocessed. In order to begin to uncover the hidden suffering and to tell the stories differently, it is necessary to explore the world of trauma, including the ways in which trauma affects the experience of time. Those who study trauma are only beginning to understand the enduring effects of traumatic injury and the processes of coping and survival used by the victimized. The following section will offer an introduction to the dynamics most central to this consideration of time and hope.

Surviving Trauma

A *black hole* is a term in physics. It refers to a space in the universe that emits no light, from whose gravitational field nothing can escape, and in which time does not pass. It is also a metaphor or image that trauma survivors use to describe the chasm that separates their experience of trauma and "ordinary life." The trauma seems to exist in another space and time that is not continuous or even connected with the rest of a survivor's life in time.

Trauma is a complex, psychological phenomenon that describes the effects of injury, physical and psychic, on a person. It may be caused by war and torture, persecution and attack, physical and sexual abuse, and a host of other injuries. There is usually a physical threat or injury related to trauma, but it can also be caused by psychological and emotional assault. Traumatic injuries harm people's psyches and affect their sense of safety and orientation in the world. Trauma can shatter relationships of trust, not only with other persons but even with "reality." When people go to work, as they have done every workday for years, they do so in the trust that the buildings they enter will not collapse or someone will not shoot them as they stand in front of their classes. Then when buildings do collapse after being bombed or hit by airplanes or when students pull out guns and fire them, trust is deeply shaken, if not destroyed. When children go to bed at night in their homes, they expect to be able to sleep safely through the night. That expectation is shattered when parents enter their beds and sexually molest them. The injury is not only physical and sexual but psychic and spiritual. Trust and innocence are forever shattered.

This wounding of a sense of basic trust and safety goes deep. If the injuries are not attended to, if the trauma is hidden and not recognized, the wounds fester. Traumatic injury produces irreparable damage. Even if and when trauma is processed and worked through, scars remain as reminders of the injury. There is no healing that resolves the trauma completely. This dynamic applies to social groups as well as individual persons. Massive social traumas, such as genocide or the enslavement of one people by another or nuclear explosions, produce ruptures in history that cannot be erased or ever fully repaired. The impact of trauma is world shaking and world shattering. It is like Humpty Dumpty falling off the wall. No one can put all the pieces together again, at least not without visible signs of rupture.

As I have suggested, many of us live with traumatic pasts. For some of us the inheritance is fairly direct. My parents passed on to me feelings of dislocation and mistrust and anxiety. Their fears of the world, produced by their experiences as an occupied people, followed by genocidal persecution and years of displacement and poverty, pervaded the atmosphere in which I was raised. For others, the inheritance is less direct, but it still has an impact through attitudes and behaviors, as well as family and group narratives. The stories any person, family, or group tells about its past shape its way of being in the world, in the present. This is true for societies and nations as well.

If past trauma and injury are not recognized as such and if their ongoing impact is not accounted for, they will continue to produce harmful effects, generation after generation. America's inability to deal with its racial diversity or truly to own up to its past of slavery and cultural genocide is evidence of such dynamics. Often this inability is fueled by avoidance or unwillingness to let old narratives go. Sometimes it is a more active denial.

Denial is a key mechanism in dealing with trauma, used by victims, perpetrators, and even bystanders. Denial pretends trauma never happened. It keeps the effects of trauma hidden. Telling the story of our American past differently, as I have been doing in these pages, is a way of witnessing to trauma. It begins to break through mechanisms of denial and displacement. As a corporate narrative changes to include more recognition of the traumatic nature of past injury and the extent and depth of harm, those whose stories differ from the dominant one will emerge and add their voices. As these counter narratives are incorporated more and more, the corporate narrative will change even further. For example, the museum at Ellis Island now contains exhibits that make clear how difficult the immigrant experience was. They narrate the ordeals immigrants experienced on Ellis Island, at the same time that they tell of the desire for safety, freedom, and transformed lives that brought so many to America's shores.

To narrate the past as a mix of good and bad experiences helps to uncover trauma. But the dynamics of trauma often make it difficult to reach, name, and understand the trauma itself. One of those dynamics is that trauma does not seem to be experienced as it is happening. It is as if mental and other processing shut down during the assault or injury or whatever harmful thing is causing the trauma. Only later is the event taken in, "re-experienced" if you will. That subsequent experiencing is not the same, however. For one thing, it is already in another time.

Thus, the time of the original trauma remains separate, distinct, and unexperienced. To say that it is unexperienced, however, does not mean that it does not exist or assert itself. Trauma, in its time, tends to intrude and manifest in flashbacks and dreams/nightmares or in vague feelings of disease or depression. It may make itself present as an eruption or a transposition. When someone is in this trauma time, the traumatic past is present not only as memory but as event, as "reality." This does not so much mean that the past intrudes into the present as that the survivor is again in the past, but as another present, if you will.

Linear time language cannot adequately describe this phenomenon. It is as if the survivor is living in two times and even multiple places at once. Lawrence Langer, who has studied and analyzed the videotaped testimonies of survivors of the Holocaust, notes that while survivors are telling their stories, their affect and posture may change. In that instant, they are present in the events of their story and not simply reporting them. They are both in the present, in front of a video camera, and in the concentration camp or on the transport train. There is a simultaneity, a co-temporality, to this juxtaposition of experiences. It is as if the survivors are in two present times at once. The two events or experiences do not exist in linear succession, but occupy the same place and time.

When the trauma experience erupts or intrudes, physical and emotional responses are heightened. Neuro-psychologists are able to plot the difference in brain response and function. Body posture may change, as may voice and breath. In fact, trauma often manifests somatically. Cognitive awareness and naming often follow upon the physical sensations.

Therapists who treat trauma seek to help survivors deal with the "past/present" experience of trauma in the present and to enable them to connect trauma time with their life in the present. This is not an easy process. Connecting with trauma requires that survivors recognize and mourn the losses that accompany the traumatic wounds. But to mourn the losses suggests that the losses have been experienced. We can only mourn what we know has been harmed or is gone. The first step then is to experience what had not been experienced.

Even though I am presenting these dynamics as if they are sequential, they do not operate in linear time but in simultaneous times. The goal of connecting with the trauma is not then to integrate it into a cohesive, sequential narrative so much as to accept the non-sequential, simultaneous, separate experiences that are present and connected together. The more profound the injury, the more unexperienced the trauma, and the more separated off the experience of it, the more difficult it may be to make and sustain connections.

There are several dynamics that contribute to the difficulties. The nature of trauma—as being outside of linear time—is one. Because we are so schooled in linear narratives, it is as if we cannot help but see the world and experience it that way. If we are then trying to deal with something that is—but is not—"past," we may have no way to accommodate it in our "known world." More precisely, we may be able to construct a linear narrative that offers an account of the traumatic injury as event, but that is not the same as experiencing it. Experience involves our whole selves, including our feelings, not only our cognition or thought processing. For example, right after a rape, a survivor may be able to report to a police officer the event of her rape. She may be able to fix the time and place it happened, describe her assailant, and recount what happened to her. Such an account, however, is often separate from the experience of the trauma of the rape that a survivor may not access for months to come and only a bit at a time. Being able to construct such an account of the event and having it acknowledged may well help the survivor to access the experience itself, but the experience remains separate, in a different time.

Another difficulty in connecting with trauma is that survivors may resist facing the trauma. The reasons for such resistance are very complex, complex as trauma itself. In addition to issues related to different temporalities, there are a number of other dynamics to consider. One is that a survivor may feel a loyalty to the trauma itself, especially to others who may have suffered. Dealing with the trauma may be interpreted as a "leaving the trauma behind," and this may feel as if one is abandoning others. Soldiers and war refugees may be especially susceptible to this type of loyalty. "Survivor guilt" is another concept some use to describe the experience of survivors. I do not find this concept of guilt particularly illuminating. The phenomenon of trauma and surviving trauma are more complex than a concept of guilt can account for. Guilt connotes responsibility and even awareness that presupposes a different kind of agency and participation than is the case in trauma.

Part of the confusion and even resistance survivors experience stems, I think, from trying to understand and interpret traumatic events in ways that presuppose autonomous choice and agency. In the midst of trauma, however, people are faced with "choiceless choices," to use Lawrence Langer's term. They are forced to make choices, but have no control over the options available. They may have to act, but in ways that are contrary to their sense of self. A classic example is portrayed in *Sophie's Choice* by William Styron: a mother in a concentration camp is made to choose which of her children will live and which will die.

Another reason for the resistance trauma survivors feel toward dealing with trauma is the persistence of dissociation. Dissociation involves a separation or splitting of the self. Often victims of trauma dissociate during the event of trauma and even after it as a way to survive. They describe how they floated up to the ceiling or hid in a lamp during acts of sexual abuse or how they crouched in the corner while they were being tortured. These "selves" were separated from the experience of the trauma. Such dissociation may help to explain the ways in which the trauma is not experienced while it is happening. It also factors into the narratives of trauma and the connections between reporting and affect.

Dissociation is best understood as a continuum, with different "levels" of dissociative states. Survivors practice dissociation not only during the event of trauma but also afterwards as well. It may easily become a way of life for survivors that allows them to keep the "traumatized self" separate and hidden. Survivors may even develop dissociative identities or what have been called multiple personalities. In these cases, in order to deal with trauma, a survivor has to negotiate among all the parts of herself/himself, some of which may have to let go of their uniqueness for the sake of cooperation. These parts will resist any coming together.

Yet another factor that affects the processing of trauma is how much the trauma is hidden or denied, both internally by the survivor and publicly in society. One of the ongoing issues for survivors of trauma is the need to have their trauma acknowledged, even by themselves. The lack of public recognition or even public denial or refutation makes it all the more difficult for survivors to recognize and deal with their traumatic suffering. When there is public silence or denial, survivors are left feeling defective and alienated.

Veterans of the Vietnam War taught us this. Again and again, they confronted the public and the United States government with how they had been affected, not only by their experiences in the war but also by the lack of recognition when they returned home. Slowly, awareness of what that war did to its soldiers has been sifting into public consciousness and into veterans' programs.

The more public knowledge and support there is, the more possibility there is for dealing with trauma. That is why the stories we tell about our country's past and formation are so important. The narrative of immigration and of America's past with which I began this chapter is very different from the one I was taught in school. It allows people a framework for naming their experience as trauma.

There is then a vital relationship between a person's ability to recognize and face into a traumatic past and public recognition of the traumatic injury. If a person's trauma is overlooked or denied, there is much more of a tendency to split it off within oneself as well. This is what happens to many survivors of early childhood abuse whose families do not acknowledge the abuse and who, because of their young age and lack of knowledge of the world beyond their families, have no way of naming their traumatic injury as such. Therefore, in order to survive, they hide the trauma, so to speak, in an inaccessible part of themselves. Dealing with the trauma later on requires that they first come to recognize and accept the traumatic injury as part of their experience.

This mechanism operates with social groups as well, when their traumatic pasts are not acknowledged. Without such acknowledgment, it is difficult for them to have a context for dealing with the trauma. In the case of the Armenian genocide, the ongoing denial by the Turkish government that there ever was a genocide has complicated any efforts among Armenians to deal with the traumas of that past.

Strong feelings of fear characterize these mechanisms of resistance to trauma, as well as processes of dealing with trauma. It is terrifying to face the trauma at all, let alone acknowledge the existence of dissociated parts. It is frightening to assert one's experience in the face of non-support or denial. These fears are all real and powerful, but there is a more basic and primitive fear. It is the fear that is imaged as a black hole.

This image aptly describes a fundamental dilemma at the heart of trauma. Acknowledging and dealing with trauma, allowing the depth of traumatic injury to manifest itself, may feel as if one is falling into a black hole, experienced as that from which there is no escape. The black hole is utter darkness and hopelessness. It is ironic, if not cruel, that the only way to work through the losses associated with trauma seems to be to experience more loss and to risk losing self to hopelessness and oblivion. The black hole symbolizes this dilemma.

But there is more. Not dealing with the trauma also feels like being trapped in a black hole or teetering on its edge. Survivors may develop an avoidance of the trauma that is, in essence, an aversion to hopelessness. But that avoidance itself produces a kind of hopelessness, since survivors seem trapped in a dynamic of approach and avoidance.

Alongside these dynamics, the resilience of those who live with trauma is remarkable. Many, many trauma survivors develop lives that by most measures would be labeled full: they have successful careers, they enter into committed relationships and have children, they contribute to their communities and its institutions. On the surface and in everyday life, no one might ever know of their traumatic pasts. The resilience is evidence of the human capacity for life. Yet it can also be part of the dilemma survivors face.

Which life is real: the visible ordinary life or the hidden traumatized life? The resilience or the black hole? Are they both real? How are they related? I do not have simple or clear answers to these questions. Nor do others. The dynamics and effects of trauma, especially on a social scale, are only beginning to receive due recognition. We have much yet to learn and understand. Ongoing debates about the status of traumatic memories, the character and depth of traumatic injuries, and the nature of the victimization contribute to such understanding.

There are those, however, who are not interested in understanding, but in purposely challenging the existence and effects of trauma. For example, those who deny the existence of the Holocaust or argue that slaves on southern plantations lived decent lives are trying to "read" history in a way that denies victimization. These denials make it more difficult for those who live with traumatic legacies to overcome their resistance. Denial obscures the extent of the human capacity to do evil to others.

The forms of traumatic injury I have been considering are all historical. They consist of harm done by human beings to other human beings, whether it be the "personal" injury of childhood sexual abuse or the "social" injury of slavery or the "political" injury of genocide. To say that such traumatic injury is historical is not only to recognize the role of human agency, but also to suggest that the injury does not have to occur. It is not a necessary or given part of human existence, such as aging and death. We human beings all have to die. But we do not have to experience trauma in our lives. Trauma is not a given of human existence. Any death is a loss that calls for mourning. However, the losses generated by trauma are of a different order than the losses that are a necessary—and natural—part of finite human existence. As we learn more about trauma, we may become adept at perceiving such distinctions.

Traumatic injury is also historical in its effects. Although much more study needs to be given to the intergenerational and social transmission of trauma, it seems evident that trauma affects not only those directly injured, but also others, including family members and bystanders. After the attacks on the World Trade Center and the collapse of the towers, there was much talk of the secondary trauma experienced by those in the area, by family members of those who were injured and died, and even by people all across America. The attacks were also a triggering event for survivors of other traumas. The events of 9/11 evoked fears and traumatic symptoms.

The effects of trauma on family members can cross generations. Children of Holocaust survivors, among others, have studied the intergenerational dynamics of trauma, as it is passed on through families. Although our understanding of these dynamics is not fully developed, we do know that trauma leaves a wake. Its ripples are not confined to the persons directly injured. Indeed, the effects of trauma may fan out through a whole society or culture.

We also know that trauma time is discontinuous and non-linear. It makes present what has never been acknowledged or even experienced. It calls into question any simple sense of past or future or even present. When confronted with trauma, notions of continuity in history are revealed as faulty. Linear story lines cover over the ruptures and fissures that trauma leaves in its wake. Those story lines keep the trauma hidden.

Instead, the post-traumatic human condition needs to be acknowledged and described as fractured. The character of humanity is shaped by such fracture. We are not only limited creatures but also disjointed ones. Our history is not simply continuous; it contains discontinuity and non-linearity. There is a past that remains outstanding, in the sense that whatever happens in the present or future cannot undo or repair that past. It stands forever as judgment not only on notions of linear progress or even of sequential time, but also on our collective life story as a comedy. No happy ending can undo the suffering and losses caused by institutionalized social injustice and slavery, war and genocide. No redress, action for justice, or claim to a greater good is fully adequate to make right the injuries of the past.

So where does this exploration of trauma leave us in our consideration of traumatic suffering and narratives of time? As I have suggested, there is so much more to be learned about trauma in general and all its effects. Continued investigation is necessary in order to understand this complex phenomenon. Here, however, I would ask one basic question: do the ways in which we understand suffering and tell its story interfere with learning what we need to? In order to explore this question, I will examine ways in which theologians are attempting to acknowledge the impact of suffering and to fashion adequate responses.

Violence, Suffering, and Theology

Theologians have always addressed the question of suffering. Traditionally, responses were offered not from the perspective of those who suffered, but to affirm God as the one who is in charge of history and key to all that happens in people's lives. The goal was to reconcile the seeming contradictions between the harm people experienced and the nature and purposes of God. In the modern era, more attention has been paid to the experience of suffering. Such attention has, in turn, produced much discussion about the nature and causes of suffering and led to more nuanced perspectives on the relationship of violence and suffering.

Some Christian theologians approach the problem of suffering in history by paying attention to Christianity's complicity in perpetrating violence. Whether it be the role of Christian anti-Semitism in the Holocaust, or the participation of the church in empire building and colonization, or the church's ignoring and even condoning of sexual and domestic violence, including sexual abuse by its own clergy, feminist, political, and liberation theologians have been exploring the ways in which Christianity has allowed or supported violence.

Latin American liberation theology began as an effort to reform the church in Latin America, to have the church recognize its connections with governments and states that were oppressing the poor. Theologians called on the church to "convert" to the poor and enter into solidarity with them. Otherwise the church would continue to be in support of regimes of violence. If the church was going to be faithful to Jesus' teachings and resist institutional and state violence, then it needed to make God's "preferential option for the poor" central.

Feminist theologians have gone further: the problem is not simply the practices of the church but basic biblical and theological teachings. These theologians have repeatedly argued that violence against women and children, whether it be physical or sexual, is fueled by Christian thinking that supports hierarchies of control, domination, and ownership and that encourages women and children to be submissive and obedient to authority. Christian teachings about the character of sin, the power of God, the means of redemption, and the nature of gender and family relationships have provided ideological justification for those who inflict harm on women and children. These feminist theologians argue, therefore, that Christianity itself has to change if violence is to be curtailed.

Theologians are only beginning to take note of trauma and its effects in these discussions. My book *Redeeming Memories: A Theology of Healing and Transformation* is one such attempt. There are also works by pastoral theologians seeking to understand the religious dimension of treating trauma, such as *Trauma and Evil* by Jeffrey Means, or by feminist theologians attending to the abuse of women and other forms of violence, such as *Proverbs of Ashes* by Rita Nakashima Brock and Rebecca Parker.

Most theological reflection to date, however, has not been about trauma or violence *per se*, nor about the complicity of Christianity, but about the experience and meaning of suffering and/or the nature of evil. As discussed in the second chapter, one of the major theological challenges today is suffering in history, especially suffering that is caused by violence, carried out by human beings against other human beings. The suffering perpetrated by genocide or by the oppression of whole peoples or by the abuse of children is so horrific that it can be understood as world destroying for its victims, if not for all of us. Any suffering, but especially undeserved or what is often referred to as "innocent" suffering, raises fundamental questions about life, the meaning of human existence, and the divine.

The question most often asked about suffering itself is "why?" Why is there such suffering? Theological answers to the question of "why" attempt not only to find some explanation for the suffering but also to justify God in relation to it. If God is good and caring and is powerful and in charge, why is there so much suffering? Suffering also evokes questions about justice and right. If the suffering is undeserved, then where is the justice or how is justice to be obtained? These questions are not new. They have drawn the attention of theologians—and philosophers—for centuries. What seems different today is the sheer massiveness or horror of the suffering generated by genocide or by systematic abuse and torture that defies any attempts at explanation or justification. As I indicated above, our attention has also shifted more toward the victims and the imperatives their conditions pose. What happens to the question of "why" if we begin with the experience of the victimized?

Those who try to answer the question of "why" often look for meaning in suffering and a way to explain it. They are motivated by the need to put suffering and its causes in a moral framework in which there are clear distinctions between good and evil. The suffering is caused by evil, which is the opposite of good. But it is not enough to name what is evil. The source of the evil, and thus a place to lay blame, needs also to be identified. Who or what is to blame: is it God or humans or sin or some dualistic evil force ("the Devil made me do it")?

When good and evil are so split apart, however, "goodness" tends to eschew responsibility and claims innocence. Since God is good, God is innocent and not responsible. Thus, it is difficult to blame God. This innocent, good God is present to help those who suffer, but is not the cause of their unjust suffering. In the dominant strains of Christian theology, all humans are sinful and so, by definition, not innocent. They are, therefore, the ones blamed. Suffering is a result of sin and is, in that sense, deserved.

Theological approaches from the viewpoint of the victimized are quick to point out that such thinking is an example of blaming the victim. They argue that the victims are innocent and, therefore, not responsible for their suffering. If God and victims are innocent, then blame has to be directed toward either an outside evil force or the perpetrators alone or to society and social forces or some combination of those loci. Wherever the blame is cast, that force, person, or group is viewed as evil and even demonized. For example, the perpetrators of the 9/11 attacks were not only blamed for the suffering they caused by their actions, but they were demonized, as was the terrorist group with which they were affiliated, and as were, to some extent, all Arabs and Muslims. Meanwhile, the victims were viewed as innocent martyrs, as were the American nation and its centers of power.

There are many problems with such dualistic moral frameworks. Rigid categories of good and evil simply do not address the complex dynamics that attend the worst kinds of suffering. They may even interfere with the process of dealing with the suffering. To the extent that those who are victimized take on all the responsibility for their suffering, which is the logical conclusion of traditional notions of sin that hold human beings as fully culpable, then they have available to them scant resources for resistance and for navigating the terrain of victimization. But eschewing responsibility and claiming total innocence tend to undercut agency and so are also problematic.

Often the "why" question is motivated by the desire to preserve God's goodness and sovereignty and to maintain a comedic ending. God is working it out, as will be revealed in the end. If that is the case, then the suffering serves some purpose in God's grand scheme. Such a conclusion gives suffering a value it should not have.

In the end, asking the question of "why" is ultimately fruitless for the victimized because there is no satisfactory answer. Whatever explanations may be offered and however appropriate or illuminating they are, they still do not and cannot fully account for the harm done. Nor can such explanations undo the suffering.

They may even make things worse for the victimized. In many cases of violence, the victimized are also dealing with their own behaviors and what they did or did not do, felt or did not feel. Amid these complicated dynamics, clear-cut distinctions between good and evil are not necessarily helpful or fitting. Ambiguity and ambivalence almost always attend experiences of violence and the ways in which people are participants, either as victims or perpetrators or bystanders.

Tragedy and Theology

Theologians who are taking account of these complex dynamics and the inadequacies of moral dualism sometimes turn to tragedy to understand the experience of suffering and the anguish that attends it. From the perspective of tragedy, suffering is not necessarily the result of sin, and all suffering should not be reduced to sin. Though tragedy acknowledges the pervasiveness of evil, it seeks to move beyond moral dualism as a way to understand the relationship of good and evil. While not necessarily offering an explanation for the source of evil, tragedy recognizes its persistence and power. The category of the tragic thus allows room for the irreparable and irreducible dimensions of the violence in life.

At the end of a Shakespearean tragedy, there is more dissolution than resolution. Death abounds. Romeo and Juliet, the star-crossed lovers, both die because of a tragic mistake and the swirling forces of family feuding. Hamlet's death, as well as Othello's and Lear's, may be traced to personal flaws and blindness, but not to an evil nature. Not one of them "deserved" to die. That is the tragedy. The outcomes do not seem commensurate with the flaws or the mistakes. The plays may provide explanation enough for those outcomes and they offer closing comment, as a type of judgment or conclusion, but no explanation or comment can deflect the audience from the bodies, dead on the stage. There is no final resurrection—no adequate answer to the dilemmas posed. The implied moral judgments—that distrust and greed and jealousy and anger are destructive—do not satisfy either the questions or the longing that remain. In the end, observes Kathleen Sands, a feminist theologian who has written eloquently about the way in which the Christian theological tradition has ignored and evaded tragedy, tragedies "record the fundamental contradiction between reality and ideality: life is not as it should be; *we* are not as we should be."[1] These contradictions perdure.

A tragic sensibility would seem to offer an important corrective to the Christian comedic narrative, one that does not seek to resolve everything and bring it to a good and completed end. As we have seen, both Christianity and the modern spirit put too much stake in resolution and the triumph of the good in such a way that pain and suffering were always subsumed into the future and its final solution. Tragedy renders narratives of eschatological fulfillment suspect. It thus resists such closure.

Tragedy also honors the suffering. Suffering stands on its own as that which forever challenges narratives of historical progress. In tragedy, historical promises remain outstanding. Absence and loss are acknowledged. There is no predetermined resolution. Nor is continuity assumed or realized endings assured.

In these ways, tragedy points toward a different quality of time that interrogates the ubiquity and adequacy of linear and teleological notions. In the time of tragedy, what is considered in linear time as past and, therefore, over and done with, remains on stage, if you will. Just as in Greek tragedy, in which the chorus's role is to remember and remind, the recognition of tragedy serves as reminder. It demands of us ongoing remembrance. What tragedy bids us remember is neither past nor finished. It remains present before us, unaccounted for.

There are resonances between this time of tragedy and the time of trauma. The past is not simply past. It does not go away and will not go away. Kathleen Sands argues, "Tragedies are to history as trauma is to time. Traumas interrupt time. . . . In the same way, tragedies are not exactly part of history; they disrupt and defy the narration of time as meaning."[2] The difference between trauma and tragedy, for Sands, is found in tragedy's ability to narrate suffering and enact it ritually: "Tragedy, as an aesthetic form, consigns trauma to a ritual space where, rather than being silently reenacted, it is solemnly voiced and lamented."[3] This ritual narration may move trauma from the hidden spheres of silence. The repetition may spin slender threads of life-nourishing connection.

Tragedy is able to provide witnesses to trauma, but only if the witnesses do not impose their own narratives, if they do not read the story through their own interests. Because the Christian tradition has tended to put its own interests first, it has not been able to be a true witness for those whose suffering is the "stuff" of tragedy.

For Sands, Christianity's stake has been in a particular moral vision and defense of God: God is powerful and good. Evil is other than God and so not part of what God created. Even though evil is powerful in the world, it has no ultimate existence or power. In order for God to be good, evil has to be other than God.

Attending to tragedy moves us away from moral dualism into a world teeming with what Sands refers to as "elemental conflicts." This is the world we all inhabit in actuality. Our lives are textured and colored by competing goods and truths. We have to find our way amid ambiguity, multiplicity, and complexity. Conflicting demands and clashing loyalties are not problems and roadblocks to be overcome: they are the givens of life. Our duty to our country may pull us away from our duty to family. Our commitment to truth telling may cost us our livelihoods. We are forced to choose, again and again, among things that ought not to be set in competition, yet are. Other times, we cannot see our way for the complexities or the multiplicity. We think we are acting for the good only to find that our action has had harmful consequences we did not or could not foresee. We come to a fork in the road and have to choose a direction without knowing what will follow. And then there are times when we choose the evil or the wrong, not only out of malice, but because of ignorance or perversions that infect our souls and our societies.

There seems to be no getting away from tragedy. If we think we can banish it from our landscape or find smooth and straight pathways among the ambiguities and multiplicities and conflicts, we will discover ourselves lost in our own country, without the resources necessary to find our way through the brambles and rocky terrain. A tragic perspective gives us a way to read the landscape. It does not offer deliverance into a utopian promised land, but it does provide orientation and movement, a way to go on.

For theologian Wendy Farley, the author of *Tragic Vision and Divine Compassion: A Contemporary Theodicy*, tragedy helps us to recognize suffering and most especially, what she terms "radical suffering." Radical suffering is the species of suffering that dehumanizes and destroys a person. It leaves a person powerless and hopeless, "maimed beyond recovery."[4] Farley argues for incorporating a tragic vision into Christian approaches to suffering and evil in order to witness more adequately to the radical suffering that defies any justification. Such suffering ruptures the fabric of life and creation forever: "No explanation, no act of atonement, no consolation can heal the wound of radical evil. The goodness of creation is *essentially* violated."[5]

A tragic vision does more than offer a way to talk about the horror and distinctiveness of radical suffering, however. It also illuminates the human condition as characterized by finitude and freedom, each of which generates tensions and conflicts, possibilities and pleasures. Theologians, as we have seen, have long been concerned with the relationship of finitude and freedom. But most theologians have interpreted the ensuing conflicts to be the result of sin. For Farley, they are a dynamic of being human. They give our lives a tragic structure.

There is then no living without tragedy. The presence of God in the midst of tragic suffering does not take away the pain or erase the losses. God's presence is as compassion, which is, for Farley, "that power which survives to resist tragic suffering."[6] There is no final victory over evil, no end to tragic suffering. But there is resistance and persistence and resilience. Hope is in the going on and finding, in and through living, moments of joy and occasions of justice.

Thus, a tragic perspective offers us a way to account for the horrors of history by thinking differently about history. It expects less of history at the same time that it recognizes that there is no leaving history behind. There is no escaping our human condition—no rescue or deliverance into utopia. Tragedy accompanies our lives and our days.

In these ways, tragedy offers a way to understand and read trauma. Trauma, however, is not a condition or a sensibility or a viewpoint. It is an event; it is injury. To read trauma only through a tragic framework is, in a way, to give it more than its due. It may come dangerously close to making it a given part of life.

In both trauma time and the time of tragedy, hope may seem muted. From the perspective of those who look for the comedic ending, there may be few signs of hope. But for those whose bodies bear the trauma and whose eyes are fixed on the suffering, comedic hope is no hope at all. It feels more like a cruel joke: a further indication that there is perhaps little place for them in this world. Tragic hope, the hope of trauma, offers life to the living and the dead. Such life may be maimed, but it is not defeated. The past remains present, with its silent and unanswered cries.

Apocalyptic Versions

Apocalyptic thought offers yet another approach to the horrors of history. Its promise is to hear and respond to the suffering cries. In apocalyptic, God does not act through historical processes but interrupts them to intervene, judge, and bring to resolution. Often, it is the powerless, who have given up on history and are looking for extra-historical means of dealing with historical processes, who turn to apocalyptic, although the powerful also appropriate it for their own uses. The powerless are seeking rescue from beyond the history of suffering. In apocalyptic, God does not act through historical processes but interrupts them to intervene, judge, and bring to resolution. Apocalyptic emphasizes the discontinuity in history. In that way, it allows for rupture.

Apocalyptic is often hyper-dualistic in its approach. It makes the actions of God absolute. Good and evil are clearly delineated and demarcated and even given cosmic status. Hope is reserved for those who are aligned with the good. It is directed toward and fed by God's intervention. While there are clear problems with an apocalyptic approach, it does offer an alternative to linear views of history.

The strands of apocalyptic present in the New Testament writing maintain eschatological tension by invoking God's promised future as imminent. They emphasize how little time is left. Hope is not to be deferred, but practiced in the here and now since God may appear at any moment. The Gospel of Mark's repeated use of the term "immediately" conveys this tensive, heightened expectation. The warnings about preparedness and the judgment to come underscore the tension.

The biblical book of Revelation, also referred to as the Apocalypse, contains a full narrative of apocalyptic expectation and imagination. That narrative reveals both the appeal of apocalyptic thought for resolving history but also the dangers it holds. The evocation of a power greater than any earthly power can provide hope to the downtrodden and persecuted, but promises of resolution via divine intervention do not give due recognition to the persistence of rupture and injuries that cannot be repaired. In the end, apocalyptic thought leaves history behind.

The broad appeal of apocalyptic in popular Christian culture is motivated by the possibilities the genre offers both to ignore history and to read into it dramatic versions of power plays. The signs of the times may then be named and used by the powerful to put forward their own agenda for time. Dispensationalists are particularly prone to this: historical events are evaluated by how much they move us toward or away from the desired rapture. In the end, neither history nor earth matter, however, so our accountability is not toward history or creation, but only toward God and faith in God's power.

There are theologians, however, who offer alternative readings of apocalyptic and find there hope for the marginalized who are trying to claim power, for those who suffer and have suffered in history, and even for the increasingly threatened earth. Johann Baptist Metz is one such theologian. Metz, a German, Roman Catholic political theologian, turns to the tones of apocalyptic, though not its imagery, to respond to what he sees as the crises and catastrophes of contemporary history, especially the Holocaust and the poverty of Two Thirds world countries. In contrast to most strains of apocalyptic thought, however, Metz continues to look for hope in history. History and the world are the places where God is working out salvation.

The question we should then consider is: how is God working out salvation? Models of salvation history, which assume a resolution and suggest that all is accomplished, do not attend to the process of history itself. Metz uses a German folktale about a race between a hedgehog and a hare to illustrate this point. In the folktale, the hedgehog "wins" because he positions his wife, similarly dressed, at the end of the course. The race is then over before it begins. The outcome is predetermined, and the race itself is never really run. Metz points out that Christian claims about redemption, such as that the final victory is already won, negate the process of history. They imply that what happens in history is not really significant. Metz wants to keep redemption—and the threats to it—as fully historical. He wants the race to be run.

At the same time, Metz argues against identifying God's redemptive action with any historical movement and with western approaches to time and history. Modernity tends to make time timeless and continuous. Evolutionary progress "rolls" over the disasters and catastrophes of history in an endless progression toward the future that holds no surprises or ultimate obstacles. The victims of the past are "sacrificed" to progress. Achievements in history negate or cancel out what has been suffered in history. No time is given to mourning. Feelings are numbed. Christian churches are essentially service providers that do not ask for any commitment. Hope is reduced to desire and wish fulfillment or empty longing. Postmodern approaches to time are also problematic. They make time "timeless" by denying that it, history, and even subjectivity have any ultimate reality.

In the place of such approaches to time, Metz draws upon apocalyptic tones to argue that the time we have is limited. Such an apocalyptic view of time neither collapses the course of history, nor sees it as endless, nor points to fulfillment in history. Time is not just empty waiting or a void or ongoing progress, but eager longing and hopeful expectation for an end that will come.

This approach conveys urgency because the time is shortened. The shorter the time, the greater the danger, according to Metz. Danger is a motivator; it carries hope and promise and possibility. It grounds graced resistance. Metz is not trying to use scare tactics but to issue a wake-up call. He wants the middle class, those whose lives are characterized by complacency, to be aroused from their apathy and enter more fully into responsible and engaged historical action in faith. His use of apocalyptic language is toward that end.

In his book *Faith in History and Society: Toward a Practical Fundamental Theology*, Metz argues for a Christianity of imminent expectation, which in turn is fueled and driven by "dangerous memories" of faith that can erupt into our lives and interrupt the status quo.[7] The Christian story and Christian faith, as "dangerous memory," remind us that the way things are is not the way they ought to be. They recall us to the promises and visions of faith. Dangerous memories also honor suffering and struggle and point to God as the source of grace that enables us to have life. For Metz, that quality of interruption is what makes memories potentially dangerous and salvific. With danger comes grace and possible rescue and redemption.

Thus apocalyptic maintains historical tension. Time is limited. The outcome of history is not given, though it is promised. For Metz, those promises are transmitted by the Christian tradition, including its dogmas, which he understands to be vehicles of dangerous memory. That tradition provides a counter-story, which can disrupt the hegemony of the narratives of the historical dominants and offer judgment on history's easy resolutions. The emphasis on memory foregrounds past suffering. It reminds us that any future accomplishments do not answer the cries of those who have suffered and died because of historical injustice. The march of so-called progress cannot erase their demands.

There would seem to be possible correlations between Metz's approach and some of the themes and ideas that are emerging from trauma studies. Metz recognizes discontinuity and seeks to remember the sufferings of the past and to preserve what has been lost. Although Metz tries to give due honor to suffering and losses in history, he still expects that suffering is meaningful. His God ultimately acts—read "rescues"—from outside history. Metz's program is primarily one of historical interruption and judgment. History and memory belong to God, who remains fully in charge of history. Metz's apocalyptic outlook stresses the discontinuous, interruptive, and episodic nature of history in a way that judges history, but does not provide much direction for acting in history.

In the end, Metz's theology cannot accomplish what he wants it to because he reads history as a morality play in which, in the end, the good necessarily wins out. Apocalyptic thinking works for him because it both judges history and its pseudo-solutions but also provides a final resolution. Metz has not embraced a tragic approach or accepted the ambiguity attending any hoped for resolution. Despite all his emphasis on interruption and danger, there is not enough room here for the ambiguity and provisionality that seem to be the lot of those who deal with trauma. One reason for that is Metz pays scant attention to place. Because the world is more the realm of judgment and possibility and because redemption continues to be seen as rescue, Metz's theology is not concrete enough in the way it thinks about either place or time. We are after all, in the end, passing through. While Metz wants to make sure we pass through with care and especially with attention to all who suffer, the story ends elsewhere.

Feminist theologian Catherine Keller offers not so much an alternative but a critical reading of apocalyptic. In *Apocalypse Now and Then: A Feminist Guide to the End of the World*, which she refers to as her counter-Apocalypse, she engages the text of the book of Revelation in the context of late modern/postmodern American society.[8] Writing at the turn of the millennium, Keller argues that apocalyptic language displays both desire and deferral. It reads history as determined by its finality. In that way, it privileges the end as the be-all and end-all of time and life. Keller seeks to move away from "endism" to a more spirit-centered spirituality that values the present, as both time and place, and that privileges life itself.

Keller is highly critical of the ways in which apocalyptic and eschatological Christian thinking not only have shaped western views of history and time, but also have produced practices that devalue life and the earth. Keller is motivated by all that has been suffered and lost in history: the ongoing violence that leaves so much in its wake, including the slow destruction of the earth. Such violence is not simply accidental, but is, in part, the product of the kinds of eschatological and apocalyptic ideas that infect western thought.

Keller sees the core of such thinking as moral dualism, the absolute separation of good and evil. Other dualisms are connected to this fundamental moral dualism, including those of we/they, time/place, spirit/flesh, and male/female. Apocalyptic thought feeds on dualism as its lifeblood. Present life, with all its suffering and limitations, is not true life. True life, the really real, is elsewhere or nowhere/utopian. Its presence requires total transformation. The old adage, adopted from Augustine, that Christians are in but not of the world is reflective of dualism. Such dualism breeds what Keller names as dissociative strategies.

Keller's use of the term *dissociation* is different from the psychological mechanism of dissociation described above, but there are significant connections and perhaps shared rooting. Both practices of dissociation lead to disconnection and fragmentation. Both feed off moral dualism. Dissociation, in either form, results from the inability to stay connected with what is happening in one's life. In the case of trauma, the disconnection is the result of terror and suffering that assaults the self. It is used as defense strategy. In apocalyptic thought, dissociative strategies may also be viewed as defensive. Apocalyptic offers the powerless a way to disconnect from the powers that be and to render them ultimately ineffective. In both cases, what dissociation costs persons are relation and connection, integrity and grounding.

Keller is not focusing on psychological processes but social and theological ones. Her counter-apocalyptic "antidote" to the dissociation, dualism, and endism of apocalyptic consists of attention to the rhythms of time; to the materiality of history, including its struggles; to finitude; and to time and space as relations.[9] In other words, the opposite of dissociation, and the remedy for it, is location in a web of relations that are bound by limits and present to the rhythms of life. These rhythms of life are endless in the sense that they are not directed toward a *terminus*; they are ongoing. Living without dissociation means embracing multiplicity and complexity and ambiguity and even paradox. There is no rescue nor escape, no postponement or deferral, not even acquiescence—which is to say there is no final resolution or solution. Some suffering remains irredeemable. Yet, as Keller, using an earthy metaphor, concludes: "almost everything" is "composted."[10] Hope, for Keller, is in and through the living and the composting.

Connecting Places

These theological voices, attending to tragedy and apocalyptic, offer helpful and different insights into fractured time. Keller and Sands step out of a traditional Christian time frame in a way that Farley and Metz do not. Farley and Metz remain passionately focused on the pain and suffering that are endured in history by those who seem to be its victims. They are searching for a way to tell the story of faith that honors the suffering of those victimized and without theological insensitivity and further abuse. Their focus remains, however, more on the suffering than on the living.

Keller and Sands seek to find a different way to claim life. For both of them, that requires a refusal of moral dualism. Sands comes to that refusal through the category of the tragic. Keller comes to it through an analysis of the uses and abuses of Christian eschatological thought. Both seek to revalue place and location.

What all four do, along with other theologians dealing with suffering and tragedy, is unmask the illusions of time as simply sequential and progressive. They also challenge, albeit not always successfully, any notion of time coming to an end, a culmination or fulfillment, in a way that elides over what remains in history as challenge and demand. Some things are finally unable to be redeemed or resolved. At best, to use Keller's metaphor, they may be composted. But maybe they are not even compost material. Maybe they will not break down enough to allow for any transformation to occur.

That seems to be the message coming from those who attend to trauma. The question then becomes how to honor the undigested and yet claim life and live it with integrity and commitment. How do we live with black holes? There is an old adage: time heals all wounds. Those attending to trauma and tragedy question that saying. Some wounds remain open and even fester, not only personally, but also socially, and for generations to come. If we can try not to solve or "heal" time and its wounds and if we do not cover them over with worn narratives as bandages, then the fractured time sense of the traumatized may serve to correct traditional, linear views.

Another old adage—good wins out in the end—may not be true as well, at least not always. Suspicions about the potential of good to prevail fuel the tones of apocalyptic as desires for power and triumph are projected onto the coming end. Apocalyptic offers assurance that suffering has purpose in a grander scheme of history and time, albeit in distorted and fantastical ways. It suggests that the sufferings of the present age are not the last word. In that way, apocalyptic manages to preserve a comedic ending. But—and this remains the lure of apocalyptic—it also highlights the sense that history cannot be resolved within itself. Good may not often win out in history. Rather, history leaves promises outstanding.

In an essay entitled "Theses on the Philosophy of History," the literary critic and historical theorist Walter Benjamin, a German Jew who committed suicide in 1940 as he was trying to leave Europe, offered a series of short, cryptic, and provocative paragraphs meant to challenge our thinking about time. In one of these "theses," Benjamin describes Paul Klee's painting *Angelus Novus*. The painting depicts an angel who is looking backward but being propelled forward by a violent wind. The implication is that the angel has no choice but to move forward or, more accurately, to be pushed forward, by forces outside itself. Yet the angel's attention is focused on what is left behind, which is a growing pile of debris. For Benjamin, the wind propelling the angel is progress, and the debris is all that is left, and seemingly lost, in its wake. Benjamin writes: "The angel would like to stay, awaken the dead, and make whole what has been smashed. But a storm is blowing from Paradise; it has got caught in his wings with such violence that the angel can no longer close them."[11]

Benjamin's notes and commentary on the painting have been important to a number of theologians, among them Johann Baptist Metz, who draw upon Benjamin's essay for their own critique of progress. For Metz, the painting portrays the losses that are inevitable in any march to the future and the fact that we will not see these losses if we are only looking ahead. Along with the angel, we need to look back. We need to attend to the past and hold it in memory, if we are to know what is left behind and how much is lost in the movement ahead. When we do pay attention to what is suffered or lost in history, we are not led astray by Christian triumphalism and its power-play resolutions.

In Benjamin's commentary, the storm propelling the angel forward is coming from "Paradise," which suggests that the future arises from an idealized state of origin. If the storm blowing the angel forward originates in Paradise, can it be bad or wrong to be carried along? Is this dynamic part of the dilemma of the linear narrative?

Benjamin ends his essay with a discussion of the Jewish sense of remembrance and of "Messianic time." Such Messianic time is not to be understood so much as future, as ever potentially present: "For every second of time was the strait gate through which the Messiah might enter."[12] Time then is about expectation: what is yet to come and may come now. Messianic time is focused on the now, as perhaps the moment of the Messiah's entry. It is neither about the past (what has already happened), nor the future (as the moment of fulfillment). Moreover, in this aphoristic ending, Benjamin points to the importance of attending not only to time but also to place. The Messiah's entry into time is *placed*. The image of the gate is a physical entry point. History is not only about time but place.

I began this chapter by talking about dislocation and displacement, which is the language of place more than time. Along the way, we have come to see that part of the problem that haunts Christian theologies of hope and history is a splitting of space and time. I refer to this as Christianity's incarnational aversion. Christianity has tended to put too much emphasis on transcendence, and leaving earth behind, as the way to redemption. Finitude, which is a characteristic of space (despite images of an endless universe), is seen as a problem related to sin, rather than a given of creation and life. When coupled with the moral dualism that haunts Christianity, finitude finds itself most often on the side of what is deemed evil. Such Christianity seems to offer few resources for those whose lives carry imprints of finitude: bodies maimed, homes left behind, families torn apart, and dreams lost to the wind. Though these marks may be the effects of evil and of someone's sin, those living with them are not helped by such judgments. Rather, life ongoing requires acceptance of the limitations and brokenness of life.

The place Christianity has traditionally offered to those who suffer is the cross. But the cross is a problematic location. It has most often been viewed as a site of sin, rather than of suffering and trauma and terror. Jesus died because of sin. Christianity claims his death was for our sins. Johann Baptist Metz, in concert with many theologians concerned with those who suffer in history, has sought to correct and expand how the cross is understood. The victimized are encouraged to come to the cross for solace and strength and to find place for their sufferings with those of Jesus. The implication is that the cross can hold the suffering of all. Jesus suffers with suffering humanity so no one need be alone in suffering. In solidarity with Jesus, those who suffer can find meaning in and through the cross.

There are two fundamental problems with such a perspective on the cross. One is semiotic: to suggest that the symbol of the cross, which has been so identified with sin and judgment against humanity, can be so easily "redeemed" and reinterpreted is to pay insufficient attention to the power of symbols and their historical location and formation. The other is that to give meaning to suffering through the cross tends to make suffering good and even redemptive. The experience of those who have suffered the most in history indicts such uses of suffering. Suffering violence at the hands of others ought not to be, nor is it meaningful or good.

Yet, again and again in the history of Christian thought, the story of the cross has been told in a way that makes suffering the means of redemption. I want to propose that this need for suffering to be meaningful and redemptive is connected, at least in part, to a desire to maintain that God is in control and that history has a *telos*, that there is eschatological closure and fulfillment. Rethinking eschatological closure requires displacement and reinterpretations of the cross as well.

Another site that Christianity offers those who suffer is heaven, the location of eschatological fulfillment. In his final discourse in the Gospel of John, Jesus states: "In my Father's house there are many dwelling places" (14:2). This verse, often read at funeral services, is assurance that there will be room for those whom God brings into the heavenly realm. The promise is not only of space but also of rest and peace. The remedy for suffering is repose in heaven. Such a remedy does nothing to address the suffering in history. It only promises an end to it and a restoration at the end of time. In so doing it shifts attention away from history to eternity. This may be a tempting option for those whose historical lives are so shot through with suffering, but it leaves history and the losses behind.

Also left behind are the messy questions. What does it mean to attend to history when it seems to be a pile of debris? How can we remain historically rooted when history seems to offer only brokenness and lack? Perhaps we need to back up from the finality of the cross to a Messiah who has yet to come, who may enter any minute, through a strait gate we can barely perceive. Maybe we need to forgo heaven, to find home on earth.

A home on earth offers up its own set of questions. What do we do with debris and clutter that is more than the ordinary messes of living? How do we deal when the roof caves in or we have a home invasion? Or what if our primary experience is of homelessness, of dislocation, of lack of a safe place? What if our existence seems to disappear into a black hole? And what effect do all these possibilities have on the metaphor of housekeeping?

We know that traumatic events inflict great injury—physically, emotionally, psychically—on persons. The harm and suffering caused in history by traumatic injuries can produce tidal waves of historical and personal impacts and implications. At the very least, we ought not add to the harm by telling time's tale in a way that overlooks and minimizes the damage. At the very least, we should acknowledge the existence of black holes.

For Further Reading

There is a growing body of literature on trauma and victimization by psychologists and psychiatrists as well as social and literary theorists. These works discuss both the nature of trauma and the effects of traumatic injury. Some key texts include Cathy Caruth, *Unclaimed Experience: Trauma, Narrative, and History* (Baltimore: Johns Hopkins University Press, 1996); Cathy Caruth, ed., *Trauma: Explorations in Memory* (Baltimore: Johns Hopkins University Press, 1995); Shoshana Felman and Dori Laub, eds., *Testimony: Crises of Witnessing Literature, Psychoanalysis, and History* (New York: Routledge, 1992); Judith Herman, *Trauma and Recovery* (New York: Basic Books, 1992); Dominick LaCapra, *History and Memory after Auschwitz* (Ithaca: Cornell University Press, 1998) and *Writing History, Writing Trauma* (Baltimore: Johns Hopkins University Press, 2001); Lawrence Langer, *Holocaust Testimonies: The Ruins of Memory* (New Haven: Yale University Press, 1991); and Michael Roth, *The Ironist's Cage: Memory, Trauma, and the Construction of History* (New York: Columbia University Press, 1995). See also Jeffrey C. Alexander, Ron Eyerman et al., *Cultural Trauma and Collective Identity* (Berkeley: University of California Press, 2004); Paul Antze and Michael Lambek, eds., *Tense Past: Cultural Essays in Trauma and Memory* (New York: Routledge, 1996); Susan Brison, *Aftermath: Violence and the Remaking of a Self* (Princeton: Princeton University Press, 2003); Yael Danieli, ed., *International Handbook of Multigenerational Legacies of Trauma* (New York: Plenum Press, 1998); and Jenny Edkins, *Trauma and the Politics of Memory* (Cambridge, UK: Cambridge University Press, 2003). In my own published works, I discuss victimization and trauma in *Redeeming Memories* (Nashville: Abingdon Press, 2000) and "Witnessing Trauma: Dorothee Soelle's Theology of Suffering in a World of Victimization," in *The Theology of Dorothee Soelle*, edited by Sarah K. Pinnock (Harrisburg: Trinity Press International, 2003). For perspectives on victimization and trauma from a Christian perspective, see *Proverbs of Ashes* by Rita Nakashima Brock and Rebecca Parker (Boston: Beacon Press, 2001) and J. Jeffrey Means, *Trauma and Evil* (Minneapolis: Fortress Press, 2000).

In addition to the theologians and texts discussed in this chapter, namely, Kathleen Sands, "Tragedy, Theology, and Feminism in the Time after Time," in *New Literary History* 35:1 (2004) and *Escape from Paradise* (Minneapolis: Fortress Press, 1994); Wendy Farley, *Tragic Vision and Divine Compassion: A Contemporary Theodicy* (Louisville: Westminster/John Knox Press, 1990); Johann Baptist Metz, *Faith in History and Society: Toward a Practical Fundamental Theology* (trans. David Smith; New York: Seabury Press, 1980); and Catherine Keller, *Apocalypse Now and Then: A Feminist Guide to the End of the World* (Boston: Beacon Press, 1996), readers might also turn to Catherine Keller's more recent *God and Power: Counter-Apocalyptic Journeys* (Minneapolis: Fortress Press, 2005) and her *Face of the Deep: A Theology of Becoming* (New York: Routledge, 2003). Selected essays by Johann Baptist Metz may be found in *Love's Strategy: The Political Theology of Johann Baptist Metz*, edited by John K. Downey (Harrisburg, PA: Trinity Press International, 1999). For further reading discussion of Metz's theology, James Matthew Ashley's *Interruptions: Mysticism, Politics, and Theology in the Work of Johann Baptist Metz* (Studies in Spirituality and Theology 4; Notre Dame, IN: University of Notre Dame Press, 1998) provides an overview and sets Metz's theology in context.

Notes

1. Kathleen Sands, "Tragedy, Theology, and Feminism in the Time after Time," *New Literary History* 35:1 (2004): 43. See also, Kathleen Sands, *Escape from Paradise* (Minneapolis: Fortress Press, 1994).

2. Sands, "Tragedy, Theology, and Feminism," 42.

3. Ibid.

4. Wendy Farley, *Tragic Vision and Divine Compassion: A Contemporary Theodicy* (Louisville: Westminster/John Knox Press, 1990), 59.

5. Ibid., 65.

6. Ibid., 29.

7. Johann Baptist Metz, *Faith in History and Society: Toward a Practical Fundamental Theology* (trans. David Smith; New York: Seabury Press, 1980), 171.

8. Catherine Keller, *Apocalypse Now and Then: A Feminist Guide to the End of the World* (Boston: Beacon Press, 1996).

9. Ibid., 130–33.

10. Ibid., 310.

11. Walter Benjamin, "Theses on the Philosophy of History," in *Illuminations* (ed. Hannah Arendt; trans. Harry Zohn; New York: Shocken Books, 1968), 257–58.

12. Ibid., 264.

5

HERE AND NOW

Moments in the Hallowing of Time

When my grandmother moved through our house at sunset on Saturday with smoking incense, she was not only welcoming the Sabbath but also hallowing time. She was paying attention to time and its passage. There was nothing dramatic or extraordinary about her practice. It was actually quite ordinary: a regular, weekly act. And yet her action held great import. It welcomed and honored the time of the coming of the Sabbath. Her attention and intention made the Sabbath holy. This Sabbath eve practice of burning incense was but one of the rituals in which my grandmother engaged. She also prayed regularly and often. Each day she stood by her bed, with hands outstretched before her, and said her prayers. At meals, she crossed herself and said grace. Thus she lived her days and weeks.

My grandmother's actions were embodied. When she welcomed the Sabbath, she made her way from room to room while carrying the incense. In doing so, my grandmother was not only preparing for the Sabbath, but also blessing the space in which we lived. She was recognizing and dedicating our embodied lives and the places that contained them. All the while she was chanting and praying, thereby giving voice to her actions and filling the air not only with scented smoke but also with sound and sight as well. Her rituals involved movement and the use of her body. They were fully sensual. Their effect was so powerful that they have stayed with me all these years.

So far we have looked at Christianity's preoccupation with the end as future fulfillment and resolution. We have also looked at the hold of the past, not because of an allegiance to tradition, but because the past contains trauma, suffering, and loss, as well as outstanding promises, that render history as unresolved and lacking closure. The hold of the past fractures time and disrupts linear narratives. Whether our attention is directed toward the future and its fulfillment or toward the past and its potential for interruption, we are pulled away from the present moment. The value of the present becomes primarily derivative; it is as consequence of the past or anticipation of the future. In this chapter, in contrast, I explore what it means to be centered in the moment and in the rhythms of life, not in a way that excludes the future or the past, but that focuses our attention in the now and on our manner of living.

My exploration will draw on several movements in our society whose practices and attitudes are pointing to different ways to think about and practice time. These expressions speak of the present moment and of cycles that constitute the rhythms of our lives, on a daily basis and over lifetimes. Among them are feminist theology's attention to embodiment and the cycles of life; the ecological movement's concern for the earth and its rhythms; Hispanic American spirituality with its distinctive rituals and its attention to the "everydayness" of life; the Buddhist teachings of Thich Nhat Hanh; and Christian liturgical and ritual traditions. I will briefly look at each of these expressions to see what they might reveal about time and the present. Albeit in different ways, they seem to challenge the western focus on historical, linear time and progress or movement in history. In turn, these expressions have sometimes been criticized for not paying sufficient attention to history and devaluing historical commitments to social change and justice. However, I do not see them so much as leaving history behind as opening up further dimensions of what it means to live in time.

There are two common emphases that emerge from these expressions. One is a recognition of finitude, more so than we have heretofore encountered. Such finitude is not a dimension of sin or a consequence of evil or even an aspect of human limitation. It is not primarily a problem but a necessary affirmation. It is a given of the human condition that ought to be embraced. Finitude is then not opposed to transcendence but is a way to transcendence. The second emphasis is attending to and valuing embodiment and space. In fact, for these ways of being in time, time abstracted from space is part of the problem. When we deny the materiality and concreteness of existence, we, in a way, "displace" human problems and so ignore them. Therefore, we need to recognize that we do not simply live in time but also in space. Our lives are located; they are placed. One way to remind ourselves of our concrete existence is by attending to bodies and to the earth. Another is through ritual practice.

Feminist Theology's Embrace of the Body

In the early days of the second wave of feminism, anthropologist Sherry Ortner wrote an article entitled "Is Female to Male as Nature is to Culture."[1] Ortner pointed out that, in modern western cultures, males are associated with history and culture that are, in turn, privileged and valued. Females are associated with nature and the body, which then are devalued and indeed seen as less good. Feminist theologian Rosemary Ruether extended and elaborated on Ortner's ideas by outlining operative dualisms that associate the male with mind, rationality, and transcendence and the female with emotion and body, irrationality, and immanence. In concert with Ortner, she also argued that whatever was associated with the female was devalued and regarded as lesser in western thought.

At first, most feminist theorists responded to such analyses in one of two ways. Either they sought to claim the realms of culture and history for women and so to establish women's intellectual and political contributions to history and culture. In other words, they argued that women were as engaged in history and as culturally productive as men were, especially given the restrictions placed on women in male-dominated spheres. Or feminist theorists emphasized and embraced women's association with body and nature. By celebrating women's sexuality and their birthing/nurturing abilities, feminist theorists argued that nature and body were good, not bad. In other words, what was devalued in patriarchal terms was now to be honored and seen as valuable.

Both of these responses were problematic to the extent that they were reactive. They were trying to take definitions of male and female—

definitions women had not participated in fashioning and which tended to be proscriptive—and to make them work on behalf of women. Neither perspective called into question or was critical enough of the originally premised dualism of culture and nature. As feminist theory and theology matured, Ortner's argument and her categories were challenged and criticized: nature and culture could not be so cleanly opposed or even separated. However, the need to pay attention to and value embodiment and to recognize our fundamental connections with nature remained in place. The affirmations of embodiment and connectedness became key contributions of feminist thought and feminist theology.

Women's embodiment embeds them in the processes and cycles of nature. As early feminists argued, because women's bodies are more intimately involved in the processes of life, women are closer to nature. Women carry new life and give birth; they nurse their offspring and help them grow; all women, whether they are mothers or not, bleed regularly during their child-bearing years and follow the rhythms of moons and tides when they do so. Yet women's bodies, able to bleed and not die, to grow in size to accommodate a fetus and then stretch open to deliver a baby and to produce milk to feed the baby, have been devalued. They have been so devalued that menstruation, pregnancy, birthing, and lactating have been considered unimportant, even though they are necessary to make life go on, to make the future possible. And even worse, these natural processes have been considered bad, sinful, and unclean.

Early feminist attention, directed toward celebrating women's bodies, shifted over time to a growing recognition of the violence perpetrated against women and of women's bodies as the site of violence. Awareness of the physical and sexual abuse of women seemed to provide further evidence that women's bodies were considered to be of little worth. Men have claimed ownership of women and their bodies in ways that allowed them to control and harm, beat and rape. As feminists explored all these dimensions of women's embodiment—either to celebrate women's bodies or to condemn the abuses women endure—they came to recognize embodiment as a valuable, important, and necessary dimension of what it means to be human, to be alive.

Feminist theology added further significance to embodiment by examining the relationship of the divine to nature. Feminist theologians have argued that the natural order and everything in it, including bodies, are not only created by God but are also the location of revelation and of God's presence. Therefore, feminist theologians have claimed that God is manifest and known through women's experiences, including women's bodily experiences. All women, through their embodied experiences, are God bearers. Given that embodiment and a valuing of the natural order have been so overlooked in the dominant theological traditions, women's experiences contribute new revelation and new awareness of God's presence and God's being. Women have been changing what we know about God. Embodiment is a source of wisdom.

Much of women's bodily life, especially anything having to do with conception and birth, occurs in cycles. Menstruation is governed by cycles and indeed is even referred to as women's cycles. Giving birth also has a cyclical character, though this seems less evident in the modern world. The time of pregnancy and the duration of lactation provide a rhythm that effects a kind of birth regulation. Women's life cycle is also centered around these processes: coming to maturity is defined by the onset of menses and menopause signals entry into a new life stage. In some expressions of spirituality, these stages are referred to as the threefold expressions of maiden, mother, and crone. The maiden is characterized by the potential for giving birth and producing life, the mother by the act of giving birth and providing nurture, and the crone by the wisdom that comes from maturity and life experiences.

The God who comes to be known through these processes and through embodiment is more immanent. This God not only created the universe but is also involved in the natural world. The character of that involvement is intimate and ongoing. Nature, as well as history, is the arena of God's saving actions. Theologian Sallie McFague offers a model of God in which the universe is God's body, in order to highlight the intimate relationship of God and creation. God inhabits creation. Creation is God's body. The transcendence of God is not opposed to God's immanent presence.

It would be problematic and false to reduce God to the universe or women to their cycles and processes. I am not suggesting that women are only, or primarily, birth givers and milk providers. However, as we give more attention to women's experiences, including women's bodily experiences, we will find ourselves rethinking the ways we understand ourselves in the world. Along with feminist theorists and feminist theologians, we will realize that these women's experiences call attention to certain aspects of our lives that have been overlooked in western, linear, time-centered, end-focused thought. Here I would point to four important dimensions of human life that have all too often been ignored in the modern West.

One is that our lives are shaped by cycles and rhythms, and it is precisely these cycles that are, quite literally, life producing and life giving. The time of our lives is not lived in the linear fashion we have imagined it in the West. What grounds us in life are the rhythms of life: the daily rising and setting of the sun, the monthly waxing and waning of the moon, the yearly turn of seasons. These correspond to human life processes: the need for days to contain activity and rest; the monthly cycles of menstruation to mark women's reproductive lives; the turning of years in which new life issues forth and the old die. Such cycles are not abstracted from the earth; they do not make death a bad thing, the result of sin. Rather, birth, growth, maturation, and death are all necessary if life is to go on. Women tend to be more in tune with these cycles not because women are more "natural," but because society has relegated women to be the ones who tend to the young and the old, who are keepers of hearth and home. As a result, women experience these natural cycles more closely and so may be more attentive to life rhythms.

Recognition of the cycles of birth and death and awareness of embodiment deepen an appreciation of finitude and limitation. Finitude is not the opposite of our yearning for infinity and, therefore, a negative or at best a grudgingly accepted reality. Rather finitude is a given, natural aspect of what it means to be human, to be embodied. Bodies are by nature not infinite; they are limited. Finitude is actually "ordinary"; it simply is a dimension of what it means to be human. It is important to embrace such finitude as given and good.

In fact, finitude is what makes it possible for life to go on. That may sound like a contradictory statement, but only if we view life from the perspective of an individual, autonomous subject. If I am aware of myself as part of a whole, then what is ongoing is the whole, and for the whole to keep going on, I will need to "get out of the way" when the time comes. My finiteness, my ending, is necessary for the life of the whole to continue.

With its emphasis on embodiment, feminist theology is also calling our attention to the importance of space. Bodies take up space; they are placed. And, if the universe is God's body, then God is manifest not only in time but also in space. This emphasis on space is an important corrective to western thinking that has devalued materiality and concrete, physical existence. If we begin to value space and materiality differently, then we are likely to pay more attention to the ways in which we treat bodies and the earth. The violence we perpetrate on bodies and against the earth becomes a primary ethical concern. But attention to space is more than a matter of ethics. It is important that we inhabit our spaces well, that the character of our living be appreciative and joyful.

This brings us to the last affirmation: relationality. As embodied beings who inhabit space, we come to realize that, at the heart of reality, is relation. Recognition of the importance of relationality and connection is arguably the primary contribution of feminist theology. We are beings in relation. Human persons cannot exist without relationships. Such relationships not only connect us to one another and to all of creation, but also constitute who we are in fundamental ways. The world is a web of relations, and life is in and through the connections.

Because we are all connected, we are interdependent, and what happens to one happens to all in creation. Our fundamental interconnection suggests a deep intimacy that intends joy. We are meant to enjoy creation and life itself in all its variety and beauty. Such enjoyment is based on living embodied, finite, located lives, attentive to life's rhythms and cycles.

The Ecological Movement's Call to Simple Living

These four affirmations, central to feminist theology, are also found in the ecological movement, especially among eco-feminists. The ecological movement's primary goal is to maintain the health of our planet and promote sustainable life. This movement is sounding an alarm bell to warn us of the ways in which we are destroying the earth and its resources. If we human beings, especially those of us in industrialized countries, continue to treat the earth as we have been, we will make life on earth no longer viable for most living things. Already there are species and varieties of vegetation that are dying out because of changes in the earth's ecology.

Creation—the universe, the earth, and all that exists on the earth—constitutes a wondrous, interconnected system with built-in processes and mechanisms to maintain and balance itself. That system contains abundance enough for all to sustain life, but we are bankrupting its resources. Our lifestyles and activities interfere with ecosystems in ways that may not be immediately discernible but are slowly, but surely, destroying the earth's balance and ability to restore itself. Each and every day we lose more and more capacity for life. We are causing whole species to become extinct; forests to be destroyed; the atmosphere to be polluted; the ozone layer to be pierced; and many other eco-systems to be fatally compromised. New strains of viruses appear regularly and threaten destruction of human life. Our actions are resulting in system failure; the processes built in to restore balance are breaking down.

"Live simply that others may simply live," one of the slogans of environmentalists, underscores a key and basic message. It is important that we pay attention to how we live here and now, in order for there to be life for others. While it may seem that much of the rhetoric of the ecological movement is directed toward the future, toward guaranteeing life in and for the future, its strategic focus is more on the present and what we are and are not doing now. Unless we, especially those of us in the industrialized West who consume a disproportionate amount of the earth's resources and whose practices produce harmful effects, change our present behaviors and habits, we will destroy any possible future for the majority of the earth's inhabitants: human, animal, vegetable, and mineral. Unless we learn to live more simply, others will simply not be able to live.

In their quest to change thinking and behavior, ecologists and ecology-minded theologians point to certain important dimensions of ecological consciousness. One is paying attention to nature and the created order itself. That may seem to be stating the obvious, but it is not often practiced in today's world. We human beings, especially in industrialized settings, do not attend to the natural world. We do not live our lives by its rhythms or acknowledge our dependence on creation. We live abstracted lives, which is to say that we act as if we are not part of nature. We approach the natural world as something available for aesthetic enjoyment, such as taking a ride into the country to see the fall colors or going hiking in the spring as trees and flowers come into bloom. Or we notice nature only when it gets in the way of our lives and our plans, whether that interference be due to rain on a day that we planned to be outside or a hurricane that batters our homes or illness that cuts short our lives.

Technological advances contribute to this abstracted and detached way of living. They allow us to distance ourselves and ignore natural processes and the natural order. For example, the discovery of electricity and the invention of the light bulb made it possible to have twenty-four hours of light and thus to ignore the daily rising and setting of the sun. The light bulb made it viable for factory work to proceed around the clock. God may have divided the day and the night, but industrialists make no such distinctions. The seasons also come to be less meaningful as modern transportation makes it possible to import "summer" fruit from warmer regions and have it available for consumption year round.

Most ecologists, who criticize the ways in which we are ignoring and harming creation, are not suggesting a romantic return to nature and an earlier age. They are not asking us to give up electricity and use only candles and oil lamps; nor to abstain from the use of computers and airplanes. They recognize the benefits of technology as well as its limitations. Rather, ecologists are arguing for a change of consciousness and practice, away from seeing the earth solely as a resource provided for our benefit and use. Such a change in our thinking and acting would require us to shift from an anthropocentric focus toward an ecological or more cosmocentric focus. Such a move would literally "decenter" us as human beings and locate us more within creation, not over creation or over against it. We would then not measure creation's bounty by its usefulness to us or its desirability. Value would be assessed by the good of the whole. A species that may be of little worth to us may, however, perform a crucial role in keeping the earth alive and balanced.

If we begin to shift our consciousness and change how we behave, a number of other things begin to move more into perspective. As we come to understand ourselves to be part of creation, we will become more attuned to its rhythms. Time will no longer be viewed only in linear fashion but in cycles. We will become more aware of the changing seasons. The seasonal cycle brings us back to where we began in endless repetition: winter, spring, summer, and fall. This repetition is not to be devalued or criticized for lack of progress. Rather, the cycles are what keep life going. There is a necessity and purpose to the rhythms and the changes of season. Each season has its purpose and contributes to the life of the whole.

This cycle of the seasons is but one of the multitude of cycles to be found in creation. Every species has its own inner rhythm that governs its existence. Snakes molt their skin and grow new skin; dogs grow fur and shed; trees blossom and bloom and lose their leaves; fish lay eggs that hatch to produce baby fish. The list is seemingly endless.

But endless is not a word we can apply to creation. The created order is finite; it is limited. Things—the tiniest of species and the grandest of stars—can and do come to their end. There are not boundless resources; there is no endless wilderness or universe. This recognition of limitation is precisely the point of the ecologists' alarm. Because we do not pay attention to the finiteness of the earth and its resources, we are coming to the end much more rapidly and "unnaturally" than if the created order were to run its own course. Living in harmony with creation requires that we live with awareness of its limits and within its rhythms.

If we attend to creation and the natural world, then we will come to appreciate finitude rather than see it as a problem, as has been characteristic of Christian thought. Finitude is not only a given aspect of the created order, it is a necessary one. Some things must come to an end in order that others may come to be. If flowers did not die back, then nothing else would be able to bloom alongside them. If species kept reproducing endlessly, they would upset the balance of relationships and make living impossible for other species.

Accompanying this appreciation of finitude is an awareness of space as finite. Even though physicists talk about endless space, our daily lives make us aware that space is limited, and we have to share the space we have. This is true for the vines that take over our gardens, and it is true for human beings living in close quarters. The less space we have, the more careful we need to be. The ecological message is that we are running out of space. In fact, we are wasting the space we do have and so lessening its availability.

As we pay attention to creation and its rhythms and cycles, as we become more appreciative of finitude and seek to honor space, we will begin to see the intricate beauty and interrelatedness of creation. At the heart of the created order are relationships, multiple interconnections that form a sustaining web of life. Naturalists have been pointing to this web of life for a long time, but those of us who live abstracted from nature rarely notice it. We also pretend we are not part of it. We not only ignore the interconnections, but we also interfere with them. Living ecologically demands that we see and stay in our place in life's web, that we honor the connections and relationships.

In all these ways, an ecological consciousness is pointing out that history is not separate from creation. By destroying creation, we are jeopardizing history. We are threatening time. We cannot claim progress when we are endangering species along the way and compromising the very air we breathe. For ecologists and ecological theologians, these are all present concerns. The future is now in the sense that if we do not begin to change our ways, there will be no future to come. But even more than changing for the sake of the future, we need to appreciate and value the present and to give due recognition to the cyclical nature of time and creation. We need to become more aware of our place as human beings in the intricate web of life. Our sense of place needs to include respect for everyone and everything with which we share the earth. Everything together, in balance, is what makes life possible, now and in the future.

The Everyday and Mystical Time of "Fiesta" in Hispanic American Spirituality

Hispanic Americans are a rapidly growing portion of the American population. In some parts of the country, such as the southwest, they will soon be the majority. Whatever the numbers, however, the southwest reflects this Hispanic—especially Mexican—presence. Mexican sensibilities are present in the regional food, in cultural patterns and customs, and in local celebrations, including religious ones. Mexican religious practices reflect layers of ethnic and cultural influences, from the ancient expressions of Mayan- and Nahuatl-speaking cultures to those of the conquering Spanish Catholics. Mexican folk religion has blended, rather than rejected, these various influences to produce its own unique religious practices and attitudes. As the Hispanic American population has embraced its differences and reflected on its distinctiveness, it has birthed its own theologians who are giving theological expression to these religious practices and attitudes. Some of the key themes emerging from Hispanic theology have to do with time, as well as place, and the nature of relationships in time.

Despite the stereotypical expression *mañana*, meaning tomorrow, that is often used to describe Hispanic attitudes toward time, Hispanic theologians are pointing out that Hispanic life is focused on the every-dayness of the present. *Lo cotidiano*, daily living, offers a critical perspective on the dominant Anglo abstraction from the materiality and rhythms of life. Orlando O. Espin defines *lo cotidiano* as "that which occurs and recurs daily. It is everyday reality—with its routines and its surprises, its mysterious depths and its pedestrian quality."[2] This emphasis on everyday life suggests that ideas and potentially abstract principles, such as justice, can be encountered and known only in the concrete, in the real-life, everyday settings of the people. Justice is what happens each day; it is not an ideal or a future goal. Hispanic culture and spirituality are grounded in such everydayness.

Because the native peoples of Mexico and Central and South America were oppressed and disenfranchised by the conquering colonizers, they were neither able to practice freely their own native religions nor to have power in the colonial system. Therefore, they developed alternative, folk religious practices, which, theologians argue, are more reflective of a popular Hispanic religiosity than the practices imposed by the *conquistadores*. The concept of time in the grand narratives of history might be under the control of those in power, but the indigenous populations were able to exercise some influence and control over the ordinary and daily routines of life. Since many of these practices of popular religion took place in the home and in familial settings, they eluded the notice of those in charge of the official religions. Because they involved seemingly unimportant matters of the daily and everyday, they did not seem to compete with the grand religious rites of the church. Such practices included home altars devoted to favorite saints, who functioned as folk heroes, and the use of alternative approaches to healing and spirituality.

Sometimes, the church and the practitioners of popular spirituality did find themselves in competition or at odds. Sometimes there would be struggles for control of particular religious expressions and practices. Often, symbols and practices would hold multiple meanings in an ambiguous space between the church's Christianity and the indigenous religions. An example is Our Lady of Guadalupe: according to the church's teaching, the female figure who was encountered by the poor peasant Juan Diego on Tepeyac hill in sixteenth-century Mexico was an apparition of Mary; for some, it was a manifestation of an ancient Aztec goddess; for many, it probably was some combination of both. Our Lady of Guadalupe continues to be many things for those who find meaning in the symbol.

These popular religious beliefs and practices and their sense of the everydayness of time seem to share particular characteristics. They tend to promote celebratory times of *fiesta*. Fiesta is usually characterized by commemoration and by communal relationships. One never celebrates alone. A fiesta draws people together and engages them in the "confluence of play *and* work."[3] It is always a present celebration, but catches the past and/or future in its wake and so is reminiscent and/or anticipatory. Fiesta is commemoration in which the community through its celebration receives and responds to life as gift. The future is made present through desire and the imagining of possibilities. The imagined future as fiesta confirms and strengthens the community in the present. As an action of the community, fiesta constitutes the community and informs its identity. Fiesta also affirms the goodness of life and so is ultimately a celebration, a rejoicing in life. While it may seem that the time of fiesta is not everyday time, that it is a special celebration, fiesta is actually of the everyday. It happens in and through ordinary time and gives that time a particular character and quality.

Times of celebration are meant to be expressions of beauty. The tendency in Hispanic culture toward exuberant decoration is a manifestation of this desire for beauty. Such beauty is understood to reflect the divine and to celebrate humanity made in the divine image. Hispanic culture, as some Hispanic theologians such as Roberto Goizueta and Alex Garcia-Rivera argue, is characterized more by an aesthetic than an ethical or historical sensibility. Because beauty is not time-bound, the presence of beauty evokes and suggests the fluidity of time as past, present, and future.

A specific example of this fluid sense of time can be found in the Mexican celebrations of the *Dia de los Muertos* or "Day of the Dead." The Day (or Days) of the Dead coincides with All Saints and All Souls days on the Christian liturgical calendar. Both commemorations are focused on the dead, but the two cannot be equated. The Day of the Dead is a longer festival, lasting at least two to three days, and sometimes longer, and its origins pre-date the Roman Catholic Christian presence in Mexico. The purposes of both the Christian and pre-Christian versions are, however, to remember, honor, and connect with the dead.

In Mexican tradition, this is done in a variety of ways. Elaborate home altars are constructed that are then decorated with pictures of the deceased, as well as with flowers, candles, incense, candies, and various foods. Among the offerings on the altar are objects the deceased might desire to have, including clothing, cigarettes, and liquor, and foods they might enjoy. This altar remains in the home for a number of days, and the family spends time with the deceased by attending to it and gathering around it. Different days may be devoted to various "categories" of the deceased: a day to remember children that died usually precedes the day on which adults are remembered. Offerings are prepared as well for those who died without families, so that no one is forgotten.

Families visit with the dead not only at their home altars, but also at the graves of the departed. The gravesites are decorated with flowers and other objects, and family members bring offerings of what the deceased might desire and food for their own feasting. Families may spend all night long at gravesites: eating, drinking, telling stories, and being present with the dead.

This celebration of the Day of the Dead is based on the premise that on these days a type of connection with the departed is possible that may not be available at other times. The dead are understood to be truly present. Family members do not gather at the altars simply to remember the dead, but to welcome them and provide for them and be with them. In some places in Mexico, church bells are rung to announce the arrival of the dead and subsequently their departure. The dead are understood to partake of the offerings provided for them, and these "provisions" ease their way through death. Such partaking is not literal, but consists of extracting the essence of the foods and gifts. Folk tales suggest that those families who do not prepare for and honor the dead will experience negative consequences in this life.

Decorations for the Day of the Dead feature images of skeletons, *calaveras*. Special breads, cookies, and candies for the day are decorated with skeletal shapes. One of the candies produced especially for the festival is in the shape of skulls made out of sugar. These skeletal figures are not grotesque or frightening, but playful and even comical. The candy skulls are smiling. The skeletons are engaged in activities, including joyful ones, that are part of living. Common images are of a band of skeletons playing music or a skeleton riding a bicycle. The skeletons may be clothed in appropriate dress and costume.

These images suggest that the dead are not simply dead and gone but are very much engaged with life. There is, however, no denial of death here. The figures are clearly skeletons. Nor is death ignored. Rather, it is given a particular type of intensified attention as images of life and death are so vividly presented, occupying the same space and time and even the same body! The skeletal images playing instruments and performing tasks seem to suggest a fluidity not only of time and space but also of what it means to be embodied and living.

It would be easy to dismiss these folk practices as superstitions or as signs of immature religiosity, especially if they seem foreign and even grotesque to our sensibilities. However, such dismissals would overlook the sophisticated and complex understanding of time and space reflected in these practices. On the Day of the Dead, the living and the dead, the past and the present and even the future, this world and other worlds are all in relationship in such a way that the boundaries between them are seen as permeable. This makes for seemingly surprising juxtapositions. The past is not only past: the dead still want to smoke. Gravesites are not just places for mourning and remembrance but for feasting as families celebrate the ongoing connections with those who have died. Generations are bonded together in different ways as the young learn about those who died before they were born. Favorite relatives are remembered along with all the times that were shared together. Problematic family members, dead and alive, are also present, so there is recognition of concerns that remain outstanding, wounds that have not healed. These familial connections also engender hope for the future and a continuing solidarity of relationships.

These events attend not only to time, but also to space and place. The home altars and the gathering at the gravesite are all about making space and marking place. The altars literally take up space in the home and so remind families of the presence, the being present, of their deceased loved ones. The dead, in that way, have place among the living. The concrete materiality of the altars acknowledges the need for celebrations to be embodied. The decorations and foods are further evidence of that. They suggest that the dead can still enjoy dimensions of embodiment: the pleasures of food and beauty.

Indeed, it is from such placed embodiedness that the aesthetic sensibility Hispanic theologians point to arises. As Roberto Goizueta suggests, the purpose of life is "to be," and being is witnessed to by enjoyment, celebration, and play that are rooted in bodiliness.[4] In this world, life is an end in and of itself. Such life, however, does not exist only in the time and space dimension of those still alive. It encompasses all the living—past, present, and future—in a fluid embrace of relationality. It recognizes the cycle of life and death that constitutes human existence. That cycle also contains the unresolved past and the desired future. In the moment of celebration, thankfulness and sorrow, pleasure and pain, may converge. The smiling skulls stand as symbols of such juxtapositions and convergences.

Especially in the southwest United States, where the presence and influence of Mexican culture are so vivid, in the last decade or so the Day of the Dead has been gaining popularity as a practice not only among Hispanics, but non-Hispanics as well. While the adoption of this cultural religious practice by those outside the Hispanic community raises questions of cultural appropriation, it also points to the need felt by many to treat time differently, especially in relation to those who have died. The people who construct altars in their homes for the Day of the Dead want to remember and connect with the dead in a way that allows them to be more present. These non-Hispanic practitioners of the Day of the Dead also seem to be seeking a relationship with time that steps out of a simple linear and sequential flow of past to present to future.

Buddhist Mindfulness

In the last several decades, as Americans have broadened their search for meaningful spiritual and religious practices, many of them have also found rich resources in Buddhist traditions. Leaders and teachers of those religions have achieved public prominence, probably none so much as the Dalai Lama, the exiled leader of Tibetan Buddhism, but also the Vietnamese Buddhist monk, peace activist, and poet Thich Nhat Hanh.

I was sitting very close to the front of the hall as Thich Nhat Hanh addressed hundreds of people who had gathered to hear him on a summer night in Providence, Rhode Island. This monk, exiled from Vietnam for his protests against the war there, had relocated to Europe and America, founded monasteries on both continents, and continued to teach and write. He was speaking that night about mindfulness, the state of being present to oneself and what one is doing. He was also talking about the relationship between mindfulness and peace, not only in ourselves, but also in the world. I marveled at Thich Nhat Hanh's ability to talk so deliberately and for so long, over an hour, without a piece of paper or any notes, in English, a language that was not his own.

At one point in his talk, he paused to drink some water. He stopped speaking. Then slowly and deliberately, he picked up the pitcher that had been placed next to him. He poured water into the cup that rested by the pitcher, and put the pitcher down. He then picked up the cup, held it cradled between his hands, and brought it to his mouth. There he drank slowly and attentively. I could see him swallow each sip. All the people present in the audience were quiet and still. Everyone's attention seemed to be on the act of drinking water.

For Thich Nhat Hanh, there is much similarity between drinking water and working for peace in a world of war. Both call for mindfulness, an attention that requires all of one's self, not only one's mind, but also one's will and one's emotions, and one's body, all focused and intentional. The act of drinking water is not only about quenching thirst but also about living. Being aware of the actions of pouring and lifting, sipping and swallowing affects not only the experience of drinking, but also one's sense of self and even one's place in the universe. It is as important to be mindful of drinking water as it is to be a bearer of peace. Indeed, the two are so intimately related that drinking water without mindfulness displays a type of violence.

The many hundreds of people who gathered to hear Thich Nhat Hanh that summer evening are evidence of the appeal of his message. The program began with one of the monks leading the audience through a breathing meditation. Breathing in, we were told to say to ourselves that we were breathing in. Breathing out, we were told to say to ourselves that we were breathing out. The message was that everything comes down to breathing. Breathe, be still, breathe, be empty, breathe, let go, breathe, be mindful with a clear mind, breathe. Breathe deeply, slowly, deliberatively. It all comes down to the breath. Breathe.

It seems we are all learning to breathe. Eastern religious practices, especially Buddhist and Hindu ones, are becoming so widespread in American society that they are now almost taken for granted. Yoga, once a seemingly esoteric practice of the few, has become a part of the exercise and relaxation programs of many women, men, and even children. Buddhist and other forms of meditation are taught widely. Whether for stress reduction or enlightenment, people are practicing breathing and all that comes from the breath.

Breathing and practicing mindfulness focus time in the present moment. All that exists is the moment. All that is is in the moment's breath. This affirmation, however, is not so much an intensification of time as a way of having time not be determinative. There is, so to speak, a falling away of time, as there is of space. Even though attending to one's breath, doing yoga, and meditating are practices of the body, their purpose is more about connection with a reality that exists in neither time nor space. The goal is enlightenment and union and transformation. While there is, in these approaches, a notion of progressing along a spiritual path toward such transformation, those who engage in these practices do not understand time linearly. What is important is the moment and one's mindfulness or devotion in the present.

As Thich Nhat Hanh points out, the present "is the only moment available to us."[5] We cannot be in the past or the future. We can only be in the present. Thich Nhat Hanh states: ". . . the teaching of the Buddha is that you can be happy right here, right now. The conditions for your well-being and happiness can be found in the here and the now. This is the teaching of living happily in the present moment."[6] Being in the here and now breaks down the distinctions of sequential time and the separation of mind and body, time and space.

Buddhism and Hinduism are not religions that talk about God's actions in history, as do the western religious traditions. The narratives and religious literature of these great eastern religious traditions are characterized more as myth and philosophy. Time is a wheel, ever turning. Life is a cycle of return, again and again. What we do within the time of the present helps determine the turning of the wheel. Western critics have often argued that these eastern emphases result in a devaluing of progress and of change. Eastern ideas of cyclical time and of reincarnation are said to foster a type of passivity in the face of suffering and a fatalism about life. Such criticisms, however, tend to simplify these alternative perspectives.

Viewing time as cyclical, coupled with attending to the present, tends more to focus time than to render it endless. The goal is to have time not be determinative. Contradictory as it may sound, by being wholly present in the moment and fully attentive, we let go of time's hold. We embrace change as the condition of existence.

Indeed, change is a constant factor. For Thich Nhat Hanh, life is characterized by impermanence; time is the marker of change: "impermanence . . . is the expression of reality from the viewpoint of time."[7] Moreover, as physicists have also been pointing out, time and space are not separate. All that we know and are, all time and space, is the realm of change and impermanence.

Everything that has existence is also interconnected or, to use Thich Nhat Hanh's term, "inter-is." "Interbeing," the connectedness of all, is the true reality. Everything is dynamic energy in connection. Relationship is not a matter of connecting separate entities. Rather, everything that is is present in and with everything else; it "inter-is." Again, there seem to be connections between Thich Nhat Hanh's teachings and the findings of quantum physics. Thich Nhat Hanh even uses concepts, such as indeterminacy and energy, which are often found in the language of physics.

Thich Nhat Hanh's teachings offer further evidence for the idea that what we know of time is the narrative we tell about it. The Buddhist narrative focuses on everything as impermanent and on the present as the moment of being. The goal is not to "escape" from change but to become one with the energy of life. Eternity is in the here and now, in and through focused attention.

When one is practicing mindfulness or being in the here and now, time is experienced both as more focused and more fluid. Time that seems to have to do more with the world of desire and illusion than of truth and enlightenment is held lightly. Yet mindfulness also inten-sifies time. Everything and all time is in the present moment. Spiritualities of mindfulness suggest that western narratives about time are not only limited but also distorted. These spiritualities are offering a corrective. For Thich Nhat Hanh, western thinking focuses too much on the future, in a way that forgets the here and now. It is also too goal-oriented and too much about hope in the future. Such attention to future goals and future hope can "overlook" all that is available in the present. Hope can get in the way of finding joy and peace in the present.[8] In contrast, mindfulness is not goal-oriented. It is sense-oriented and be-ing oriented. Its intent is to attend to and enjoy what is.

Such ideas may sound strange, and perhaps even wrong, to western ears. Thich Nhat Hanh is well aware of such reactions and the challenges his teachings pose. The words may be provocative, but he is not so much arguing against hope as he is offering an alternative understanding of the character of hope that embraces what is. Embracing does not, however, mean acquiescing. Thich Nhat Hanh refers to his practice as engaged Buddhism: "Mindfulness must be engaged. Once there is seeing, there must be acting."[9] For example, we engage in transforming violence and suffering through active mindfulness and compassion. As the title of one of Thich Nhat Hanh's books points out, "peace is every step." The way to peace is through our steps, our acting. Thich Nhat Hanh concludes: "We don't need the future. We can smile and relax. Everything we want is right here in the present moment."[10] All we have to do is breathe and be.

Hallowing Time

So far in this chapter, I have explored four different movements and spiritualities that understand time to be, in varying degrees and ways, cyclical and fluid. Buddhist thought concentrates attention in the present moment; feminist, ecological, and Hispanic approaches tend to focus more on the cycles themselves and their rhythms, as well as on everyday life. All four share a concern for mindfulness, for paying attention to the way in which we inhabit the world. They also have in common a sense of the deep connections and interrelatedness that permeate all that exists. Mindfulness and interrelatedness are expressive of an aesthetic sensibility.

Often, as I have suggested, cyclical views of time are defined in opposition to or in distinction from what are considered more historical and political perspectives. In other words, if we focus attention on the present or on the rhythms of life, then we are perceived to be disregarding history. The aesthetic sensibility that seems to characterize these present-centered and cyclical approaches also lends itself to such an interpretation. History and historical change are the realms of moral commitments. Justice is in and for history. Aesthetics transcends history. It has become commonplace to say that western religions that focus on history are concerned with justice; eastern religions, popular, indigenous religious movements, and more "nature"-based approaches are concerned with beauty and being, but not with justice *per se*.

Such characterizations employ rather simplistic ideas of justice; in a sense, they beg the question. Each of the movements and expressions explored in this chapter has an ethical dimension. Each incorporates a concern for justice. Whether it be the Buddhist ethics of compassion or the ecological movement's ethics of interdependent living, these movements and practices embody vital commitments to justice. Indeed, Thich Nhat Hanh is known for his devoted work for peace; he was even nominated for the Nobel Peace prize. Justice, however, is imagined differently precisely because these perspectives do not view time or justice in linear, progressive, and teleological ways. Justice is not an accomplishment or a goal; it is a practice. Justice as right relation is embodied in connections and interrelationships again and again.

In Christianity, one place where a more aesthetic sensibility and different sense of time are enacted is in ritual and liturgy. Just as my grandmother's weekly ritual of moving through our home with incense on the eve of the Sabbath was a way of both attending to and hallowing time, liturgy intensifies time through its cyclical character and focused concentration. The liturgical calendar, with its seasons, narrates the "linear" Christian story in an annual cycle. Every year the events of Jesus' birth, life, death, and resurrection are remembered, rehearsed, and reenacted. The different seasons offer distinct tones and moods through a variety of practices, appropriate to the purpose. Whatever the practice, the intent is to intensify the mood and the experience. So, for example, the fasting of Lent is meant to create hunger and desire in order to receive more fully and deeply the feast of Easter. The waiting and anticipation of Advent heightens the gift of Christmas joy. The practices are intended to enable participants to feel and experience the difference between deprivation and abundance, between death and life.

The Christian year moves from anticipation and celebration of Jesus' birth through the rehearsing not only of his story but also that of the church. The events of Jesus' life are the focus of the year from Christmas through Epiphany and Lent to Easter season and Pentecost. Then the long Pentecost season attends to the life of the church community and of salvation history, culminating in the strongly eschatological tones of the triumphal return and reign of Christ.

We might think this narrative structure, ending as it does with the final reign of Christ, reflects the linear and teleological model that developed into the dominant western historical view. However, the liturgical narrative is not so simply or neatly linear. The final triumph is not just an ending but also a beginning, as Advent comes upon the heels of the eschatological finale. Advent takes the Christian community back to the beginning of the story and starts again the annual cycle. It also anticipates return. In Advent the Christian community waits not only for the birth of the Christ child but also for Christ's coming again that itself inaugurates the new age. Thus, beginning and end are forever intertwined. The nature of hope, textured by these movements, is more than a combination of linear and cyclical views of time. It is an interplay of past, present, and future in ways that defy easy patterning. Hope is not so much in time as through time, throughout time.

Such dynamics of time are also present in liturgical celebrations and most especially in the liturgy of the Eucharist. Each celebration of the Eucharist is a reenactment of salvation history. The prayers rehearse God's actions in creation and in history; they tell of the saving event of Christ, culminating in resurrection and eternal life. In those Protestant denominations that celebrate the Lord's Supper as a memorial meal, and which view the sharing of the bread and cup primarily as an act of remembrance, there is perhaps less emphasis on the intensification and confluence of time. But even there, the memorial is a recalling of the past in a present celebration that is a promise for the future. Meanwhile, for those Christian churches that do not speak only of memorial but of the real presence of Christ or of an anticipatory banquet or of communal transformation, the intensity is heightened.

Something happens in the moment of the ritual that involves time in and through all its dimensions. In the celebration of the Eucharist, the past is made present as is the future. Even as the past actions of God are recounted and rehearsed, the future promises are being made manifest not simply through anticipation and narration, but through participation. A foretaste of the heavenly banquet is offered in the bread and wine of the Eucharist.

The Eucharistic narrative and the actions of the community enable the intensification and confluence of time. The "presence" of Christ in the liturgy, in the community, and in the bread and wine is a sign of that intensification. Community members do more than gather at the same table to share a meal together; they are joined together in a mystical communion. They are connected with the holy, with one another, and with those in all times and places who have engaged in the same ritual actions. The Eucharist is thus an enactment of connection and communion across time and place.

The Eucharist is not meant to take participants out of the world and history. Indeed, the celebration of communion is an act of the world that God creates and redeems. The commemoration is of history, shot through with God's redeeming presence and action. Participants are fed and nurtured for the work of God in and for the world. The bread and wine are fruits of creation, reminding us of the elemental interconnection of all. Being in right relation with one another is a prerequisite for authentic communion; making right relation in and with the world is a sign of the Eucharist's ongoing efficacy and power.

The Eucharist is also an embodied practice. The materiality of the bread and wine—their concreteness—grounds the ritual in the everyday experience of eating and drinking. In the Eucharist, time is hallowed, and so are the ordinary elements of bread and wine and of bodies. Each is offered and transformed through the ritual. In one of the Eucharist prayers in the Episcopal Book of Common Prayer, the celebrant says: ". . . we offer and present . . . our souls and bodies. . . ." The celebration of the sacrament is fully participatory. Communicants bring their whole selves to the ceremony. They place their bodies into the moment of liturgical action, for the purpose of being transformed. Then they take those bodies out into the world in order to engage in the work of transformation.

Through the performance of the Eucharist, all time and space are made present in the here and now. The past and future come together in the moment of celebration, not only as warrant and promise but also to reveal that God's time transcends linearity and sequence. All time is centered in that moment beyond temporality. The barriers of space dissolve as well. The world is there on the table, present in the bread and wine. The interconnectedness of all reality is made manifest. Thus are time and space hallowed in the here and now, in the moment, in place. God's time and our times, God's realm and the earth, all of life, present and eternal, here, now, in the hallowed moment.

The several expressions of hallowing time surveyed in this chapter open up ways of viewing time as cyclical patterns, as rhythms of life, as moments of being/interbeing, as intensification and fluidity converging. They direct us toward the present as the only moment in which we truly exist. They also de-center time itself. Ironically, by intensifying time—either by emphasizing finitude or by mindfulness in the present or by liturgical celebration—time tends to fall away as the container of our lives. Time is not necessary as the measure of our lives, nor of change, nor of the actions of the divine. Indeed time, as we "know" it, no longer exists. And thus freed, we may find that the dead, those who lived in the past, are here with the living. The future is now, and that which is past returns again and again. Even more amazingly, through our attending to time, we may find intimations, not of immortality, but of life that is not bound by our narratives of time. A common thread weaving its way through the accounts of feminist theology, of ecological thought, of Hispanic spirituality, of Buddhist spirituality, and of liturgical theology is that each one is centered on life, on preserving and honoring life. Deep and abiding concerns for the care of the earth, for the welfare of the world and all its inhabitants, for justice and peace in history, are in essence concerns for life and living. Each of these expressions, in its own way, is about living well as embodied, breathing, creating, desiring persons.

The space that opens up in these approaches to time is one that claims life as something to be honored, enjoyed, and practiced with intention and intensity. There is no way to live fully without recognizing that we all exist in a web of relations, of interbeing, with all living things. Hope is found in the interconnections, throbbing with life.

In the end, our habitation, our home, is life itself. It is important to maintain it as a living environment. But that is not sufficient. It is not enough to do the work of housekeeping and home repair, to rebuild the ruins when necessary, and to make and keep life habitable. Life is more than staying alive and keeping going. The quality of our lives matters. There needs to be room for all to live and live well. There needs to be beauty and purpose, meaning and companionship, play and joy. The voices expressed in this chapter remind us to pay attention to the content and contours of our lives, interdependent, embodied, filled with desire and appreciation for life.

The incense that filled my childhood home each Saturday eve carried such prayers of desire and appreciation. Sabbath rest reminds us that we and all creation need time, time that is not about doing or making or producing, but time for being and remembering and feasting and abiding. As the smoke of the incense moved into and occupied the spaces of our house, our house was infused, in that moment, with the promise of life.

For Further Reading

In the last several decades, feminist theologians have produced a large and growing corpus of works. Particularly relevant for the contributions highlighted in this chapter are Rita Nakashima Brock, *Journeys by Heart: A Christology of Erotic Power* (New York: Crossroad, 1988); Carol P. Christ, *She Who Changes: Re-Imagining the Divine in the World* (New York: Palgrave, 2003); Catherine Keller, *From a Broken Web: Sexism, Separation and Self* (Boston: Beacon Press, 1986); and Rosemary Ruether, especially *Sexism and God-Talk* and *Gaia and God*, which have already been cited. Among the collections of essays available, *Horizons in Feminist Theology: Identity, Tradition, and Norms*, edited by Rebecca S. Chopp and Sheila Greeve Davaney (Minneapolis: Fortress Press, 1997) and *Weaving the Visions: Patterns in Feminist Spirituality*, edited by Judith Plaskow and Carol P. Christ (San Francisco: Harper & Row, 1989) contain useful articles. For further reading on violence against women, readers might turn to *Proverbs of*

Ashes by Rita Nakashima Brock and Rebecca Parker, previously cited, and two collections of essays, (1) *Christianity, Patriarchy, and Abuse: A Feminist Critique*, edited by Joanne Carlson Brown and Carole R. Bohn (New York: Pilgrim Press, 1989) and (2) *Violence against Women and Children: A Christian Theological Sourcebook*, edited by Carol J. Adams and Marie M. Fortune (New York: Continuum, 1995). For global perspectives, see *Women Resisting Violence: Spirituality for Life*, edited by Mary John Mananzan, Mercy Ambe Oduyoye, et al. (Maryknoll, NY: Orbis Books, 1996).

There is also a growing body of theological works dealing with issues of ecology, the natural world, and the fate of the earth, as well as a vast array of literature from scientists, ethicists, and others. For theological approaches, see the works of Sallie McFague already cited, as well as her *Super, Natural Christians: How We Should Love Nature* (Minneapolis: Fortress Press, 1997), and the works of Carol P. Christ, Catherine Keller, and Rosemary Ruether. See also Thomas Berry, *The Great Work: Our Way into the Future* (New York: Bell Tower, 2000); Ivone Gebara, *Longing for Running Water: Ecofeminism and Liberation* (trans. David Molineaux; Minneapolis: Fortress Press, 1999); and Larry L. Rasmussen, *Earth Community, Earth Ethics* (Maryknoll, NY: Orbis Books, 1996). *Christianity and Ecology: Seeking the Well-being of Earth and Humans*, edited by Dieter T. Hessel and Rosemary Radford Ruether (Cambridge, MA: Harvard University Center for the Study of World Religions, 2000) offers a collection of articles from a variety of perspectives. For inspirational, as well as informative reading, I suggest the collection of essays, *Small Wonder*, by Barbara Kingsolver (New York: HarperCollins, 2002).

For Hispanic spirituality and religiosity, I would direct readers to the following collections of essays: *From the Heart of Our People: Latino/a Explorations in Catholic Systematic Theology*, edited by Orlando O. Espín and Miguel H. Díaz (Maryknoll, NY: Orbis Books, 1999); *Hispanic/Latino Theology: Challenge and Promise*, edited by Ada María Isasi-Díaz and Fernando F. Segovia (Minneapolis: Fortress Press, 1996); *Mestizo Christianity: Theology from the Latino Perspective*, edited by Artura J. Bañuelas (Maryknoll, NY: Orbis Books, 1995). See also Roberto Goizueta, *Caminemos con Jesús: Toward a Hispanic/Latino Theology of Accompaniment* (Maryknoll, NY: Orbis Books, 1995). For more information on the Day of the Dead, turn to Elizabeth

Carmichael and Chloë Sayer, *The Skeleton at the Feast: The Day of the Dead in Mexico* (Austin: University of Texas Press, 1992) and Juanita Garciagodoy, *Digging the Days of the Dead: A Reading of Mexico's Dias de Muertos* (Niwot, CO: University Press of Colorado, 1998).

Thich Nhat Hanh is a prolific writer. Along with *The Path of Emancipation* (Berkeley: Parallax Press, 2000) and *Peace Is Every Step*, edited by Arnold Kotler (New York: Bantam Books, 1991), readers might find his books listed with and available from Parallax Press in Berkeley, California.

For liturgical spirituality and ritual, see Herbert Anderson and Edward Foley, *Might Stories, Dangerous Rituals: Weaving Together the Human and the Divine* (San Francisco: Jossey-Bass Publishers, 1998); Tom F. Driver, *The Magic of Ritual: Our Need for Liberating Rites that Transform Our Lives & Our Communities* (San Francisco: HarperSanFrancisco, 1992) and Don E. Saliers, *Worship as Theology: Foretaste of Divine Glory* (Nashville: Abingdon Press, 1994).

Notes

1. The article was originally published in 1972. It can be found in Sherry Ortner, *Gender: The Politics and Erotics of Culture* (Boston: Beacon Press, 1996).

2. Orlando O. Espin, "An Exploration into the Theology of Grace and Sin," in *From the Heart of Our People: Latino/a Explorations in Catholic Systematic Theology* (eds. Orlando O. Espin and Miguel H. Diaz; Maryknoll, NY: Orbis Books, 1999), 125.

3. Roberto S. Goizueta, "Fiesta," in *From the Heart of Our People*, 94. This discussion of fiesta draws heavily on Goizueta's article.

4. Ibid.

5. Thich Nhat Hanh, *The Path of Emancipation* (Berkeley: Parallax Press, 2000), 118.

6. Ibid., 23.

7. Ibid., 170.

8. See Thich Nhat Hanh, *Peace Is Every Step* (ed. Arnold Kotler; New York: Bantam Books, 1991), 41–42.

9. Ibid., 91.

10. Ibid., 42.

6

THE HABITATION OF TIME

Contours of Hope

In the preceding chapters, I explored a number of approaches to time and the telling of time. I indicated that the dominant western and modern narrative of time as linear, progressive, and teleological is being challenged by modernity itself. This narrative's portrayal of history as a morality play whose outcome is determined and given, either by God's action or by human action, has been revealed for both its hubris and its naiveté. The overwhelming presence of tragedy and trauma in history provides ongoing evidence of rupture that disturbs, if not destroys, any sense of continuity. Tragedy and trauma tell a story of pain and suffering that remain, unanswered by any future resolution. They present a narrative of loss, lament, and lack of closure in which the past is present, demanding recognition. There are yet other tales of time, found in patterns of thought and practice neglected in the West, as well as in non-western traditions. Such tales focus attention on the rhythms of life, in the moment and ongoing. They draw upon an aesthetic sensibility of appreciation, awareness, and wonder.

How are we to understand these different narratives, these different modes of telling time, in relation to one another? How are we to find among them pathways to hope? In other words, how are we to inhabit time with hope today? The ways in which many of us in the modern West are used to living in history and time are not able to yield fruit in our present context. These modes of living and thinking seem only to reproduce the same crop, increasingly shriveled and lacking in the nutrients necessary for abundant life.

Meanwhile, the heralds of both modernity and postmodernity have claimed that we live in a time like no other. These claims to uniqueness underscore the need to attune ourselves to the particularities of our historical location. We cannot assume an easy fit between our situation and the lives of those in other times and places. Nor can we boast that our perspectives apply to them. It is simply our own lives that we are seeking to inhabit with due recognition of the limitations of any perspective. What might be true and work for us today is not true for others, and may not even be true for us tomorrow. But that does not make it any less life-giving today. This is the first operating assumption that undergirds what is offered here.

A second operating assumption is that we cannot escape contradictions. In his poem, "Song of Myself," Walt Whitman wrote: "Do I contradict myself? Very well then I contradict myself, (I am large, I contain multitudes)."[1] I have quoted this line often, precisely because it seems to capture our human condition. Over the years, as I have become more deeply aware of the complexities of life and the abiding fissures that form the landscape around us, I have come to find these words to be profoundly true. Walt Whitman allows us to understand that the world we inhabit and our very selves are large and contain multitudes, often in contradiction. He points us toward the insight that growth in wisdom is accompanied by a greater capacity for ambiguity and the practice of a generosity that allows difference and even contradiction, both within and around us. Life is full of contradictions; so are time and history. It is better to live with the contradictions than to fight them or try to resolve them.

A third operating assumption is that we do not really know what we are talking about. That may be a surprising and odd—and contradictory—claim to make, especially as I intend to spell out the implications of all that has been explored and discussed. But it is true. And it is important to state if we are to be clear and honest. Ultimately, the aim of this book is to help us to live differently, to imagine hope anew. I do not assume that process will be easy.

Those of us schooled for so long in the dominant western and modern model will find it a particularly difficult challenge. Imagining hope anew means nothing less than changing our lives, fundamentally.

It requires us to examine and shift the ways in which we think, the operating assumptions that shape us. Such a transformation does not happen overnight, nor does it happen without intentional effort.

Shimon Malin, in his book about quantum physics, *Nature Loves to Hide*, helps us to understand the nature of such change. He points out that, even though we know the new science, even though the paradigm has shifted, we still live out of the old one of materiality and Newtonian physics.[2] We are so habituated to Newtonian ways of thinking and living in the world that we continue to practice them even though we know that they no longer apply or work. We know that energy and dynamism are what drive the universe, but we hold onto static materiality as what is real. The same can be said for those of us who think of time as linear and progressive and future-oriented. We may claim to know that time is not linear, or even that time does not really exist, but we continue to think of it as linear, sequential, and directional. We think that our sense of chronology is what is real time. The language and models we have available to use reflect and reinforce such an understanding of time.

The truth is that we not only inhabit time, but it inhabits us; or more accurately, our narratives of time inhabit us. Such habitation forms us and shapes us not only as persons but also as cultures. As a result, we are habituated to a certain way of understanding time (whether we like it or not), which means we live in the world in a certain way. We cannot change this by a simple snap of the fingers or by rearranging the furniture. What we need is not only a paradigm shift, but also different practices, new habits. We need to change our habitation of time.

In this chapter, I will begin to outline the contours of what it would mean to think and live differently in time, to inhabit time differently. The ideas presented here are the fruit of the exploration of the preceding chapters. They will provide guideposts, so to speak, to help us move into new territory, into a different habitat. In the next chapter, I will suggest some habits that we might cultivate to help us "rehabituate" ourselves and live differently.

Which Story to Tell

Should the story we tell about history and our lives be comedic? Or is it tragic? Or is it ironic? Is it a fable? Or even a tale of magical realism in which different worlds connect in unexpected ways? Yet again, is it an epic or a never-ending saga or a romance?

Perhaps the question really should be: must we choose? Must it be one or the other? As we have seen, the emplotment of the classical Christian story is relentlessly comedic: all's well that ends well for the redeemed. And all will end well because God is in charge. Such a plot effectively and rather emphatically excludes the tragic or anything other than a story line that moves inevitably toward a resolution in which what is deemed good, right, and true prevails. We have also seen that there are alternative story lines that both challenge such an assumed comedic ending and offer different ways to name and participate in the events of history. These also begin to suggest that there may be no supreme plot, no meta-narrative, no singular story of everything. Rather we live in and among a number of plot lines; we do not know how the story will end.

In some ways, modern Christian thinking about time has been a battle between these challengers and linear, progressive, teleological thought. Again and again, modern Christianity defined itself over against cyclical ways of understanding time and eschewed the tragic as fundamentally contrary to Christian understandings of God's sovereignty and goodness. Modern Christian thought also tended to dismiss any view of time that did not plant itself fully and squarely in history. More spiritual and mystical and even liturgical understandings were seen as having a dangerous potential for ethical passivity.

Thus the stage was set for inevitable and ongoing battles between narrative modes that ultimately twisted and distorted the narratives themselves. I myself find none of the narrative structures sufficient in and of themselves. Sometimes life seems mostly a comedy, other times primarily a tragedy. Still other times we are overwhelmed by the epic dimensions of what is happening all around us. Any major historical event will contain all these plots, all these narratives. The December 2004 tsunami that resulted in the death of over 200,000 people in the islands and lands of South Asia had an epic feel. The event seemed to surpass what we could imagine. The losses sustained, with both immediate and long-term impact, defied any easy classification as tragic. Alongside these realities were arrayed all the stories of generosity and courage, of care and aid. In this one event, ironically, history was changed forever, but not in any absolute way. In 100,000 years from now, or even 100 years from now, will the event be only a mention in history books or will it be mentioned at all? Will its geological impact be acknowledged or widely known?

Perhaps, for this reason alone, I would choose irony from among the available narrative alternatives. Irony allows for differences in perception and even contradictions. It includes incongruity. Irony also seems the most modest of the choices, mainly because there is so much we do not know, so much that we cannot see. Everything is affected by everything else. And ultimately it is the play of those effects that moves and changes history. We cannot control the play, we cannot even necessarily see it, but we do experience its outcomes. And here is part of the irony: we are not simply bystanders and witnesses in the play; we are actors. We participate in it. History is neither something that just happens to us, nor is history something we can make happen in an anthropocentric mimicry of the God of classical theism, effecting the divine will through historical actions and intervention. We cannot opt out or pretend we are simply bystanders to history, living our own lives, nor are we in control.

Another way of saying this is: we cannot escape time in its narrative, historical mode. We are participants whether we want to be or not. Obviously, this is true of our individual lives as we are born and grow, age and die. But it is true of our corporate lives as well. There is no bystander role, and there may be no director's role, but we are all actors, playing our part, alone and together, in this drama that is life. The comedic, tragic, romantic, epic, and ironic are all dimensions of this drama. The tale we tell and need to tell is a complicated and intricate one that we improvise as we go along.

And so does God. The God of history, the God who created and entered into time, took on the uncertainty and complexity that comes with sharing power and inviting participation. Otherwise time and history would not really matter.

The classical Christian stance, focused as it was on God's being and sovereignty, approached these matters somewhat differently. It took God out of time. The God of classical theism is beyond time, as is the finality of God's action. The work of salvation is ultimately in eternity, which is by definition not endless time but not time, not in time.

The more emphasis that was put on God's sovereignty and God's power, the more the work of redemption was understood to be already determined. The drama of history then had no real impact on God and God's plan, except perhaps to reinforce and demonstrate the need for God to make things right, to bring human struggle to resolution or to reveal God's power. In this theological approach, the resolution was outside time and history, even though God acted within history. Redemption was outside time, in eternity.

Ever since the dawn of the modern era and its embrace of history and the world, it has become more difficult theologically to maintain this view of redemption, without eschewing modern thought. Thus, adherents of classical theism tend to oppose many of the strains of modern and postmodern thought, or they try to find aspects of such thought that are more compatible with preserving a God who is fundamentally other than the world God created. Such a God relates to us human beings and to creation but is not in time with us. Ultimately, our relation with God is not in time either but in eternity.

Oddly, this notion of eternity also makes history ironic, because what happens in history is finally of no consequence. Yet God is still claimed as the author of history. This seeming contradiction in Christian thought between a God who is the God of history and a God who is outside of time and history has been there from the beginning. It is a key dynamic in the tension between biblical views of God and those views that draw more upon Greek philosophical ways of thinking. The former tends to emphasize God's actions, the person of God, and the latter, God's being, the nature of God.

Christianity has never resolved these differences, though in theological thought the God of the philosophers won the day more often and received more attention. In fact, a considerable amount of theological energy has been spent to preserve and justify the goodness and sovereignty of the God of the philosophers, given the evidence of history.

Enter from Stage Left (Or Is It Right?)
Post-Newtonian Physics

To further add to the ironies of time, contemporary physicists, from Einstein on, if not before Einstein, have been telling us that there is no such *thing* as time. Time is not a thing. It does not exist. It is a construct, an idea. And it is infinitely relative. In fact, time is so relative that scientists have imagined time travel that can take us back in time to the past. They have also imagined parallel universes, two times existing simultaneously, if you will. There is no time's arrow, moving in one direction. Nor is the measure of time set.

However, at around the same time (if you will) that physicists were beginning to challenge the fixed universe of Newtonian physics, other scientists were producing technology, in the service of industry and development, to fix time universally. The need to coordinate the railroads and railroad schedules resulted in the time zones and universal clocks that we still use today. For these scientists, time was fixed, or, more accurately, they were fixing it.

Herein lies yet another irony. While theoretical physicists were challenging any notions of the fixity of time, other scientists and engineers were finding ways to measure and regulate it more exactly. We are more influenced by the latter than the former. All of us know what it means to live by a schedule. We wake up to alarm clocks. School children move from class to class at the sound of a bell. We race to get to the bus on time. We check watches and clocks to make sure we are going to be on time for meetings and events. Otherwise, we know chaos would reign. We would miss appointments, classes, and meetings. Trains would not arrive on time. They would collide as two trains found themselves on the same track at the same time. But the ordering of time, for there to be order in our lives, is a construct. The minutes, hours, days, and years we count are simply conventions. We have agreed to them to make our lives easier and more workable. But they have no reality beyond that.

The truth is that chaos is more real than time, or perhaps not chaos, *per se*, but what we perceive as chaos, because it is other than the order we know. We have created for ourselves an island of time. We live on this island as if it were the whole of reality. Even though we know there is more, we do not step off the island for fear of the danger and potential chaos we may encounter. Perhaps like those who, upon first being told the earth was round, rather than flat, felt it a great risk to sail toward the horizon, we are reluctant to let go of our long-held habits of thought and behavior.

Embracing Indeterminacy

In the Newtonian universe, the building blocks of life and reality were material; they had substance. Newtonian physics served well for the technological advances of the last centuries. But Einstein and others challenged and changed all that. The Einsteinian revolution not only told us that all is relative, but it is also energy, the opposite of material, of mass. What is most real in the universe is energy, which has no substance in and of itself. Such energy is motion. It cannot be located, which is to say it cannot be determined or fixed.

The universe, and everything in it, is indeterminate and dynamic. What we know as material bodies are convergences of energy or whatever it is that makes up the universe. While there is evidence of an ordering to such convergences, it is not set or predetermined. Rather the order emerges in the process of interaction and interplay. It comes from the process itself. Nothing is lost in this process, but it is not fixed either.

If the universe is energy, then is not the divine itself energy, a constant dynamism, present in and with all of creation? From this viewpoint, the divine is most fundamentally the life force that animates the universe. It enables, engages, and sustains life.

There is a wildness and even chaotic dimension to such energy. This is the divine wind that blows where and when it will. That wreaks destruction, as well as offering comfort. That is in the whirlwind poetry of Job. The power of such divine energy is for life, but life itself is conflictual. At the heart of the divine and of life is ambiguity and conflict, multiplicity and change.

This is a very different image of the divine than the monarchial God, enthroned in heaven, directing the universe. It is also different from the loving God as ever-present comfort and source of order and security. This is a universe of potentiality but not determinacy—of constant change but not of absolute givens.

Every Which Way

In this universe, time's arrow does not move in one direction. Indeed time does not have direction as we imagine it; it is not linear. Even though there is a chronology and linearity to our lives, which is to say that we age and our aging progresses toward death, that is only one mode of perceiving time.

Nor is time an endless cycle, the eternal wheel of life, that seems ever to turn and return. Life contains many cycles. There is a cyclical quality to our experience of time, but time is not in itself cyclical. This cyclical quality is about renewal and restoration. The metaphor of housekeeping works to remind us of the need to maintain the environments, in all the meanings of that word, in which we live. The process of living creates its own messes and its own disorders that need to be cleaned up and fixed if life is to be lived and lived well. The purpose of housekeeping is to enable and enhance the living. It is not an end in itself; it is a part of life.

Ruptures in time may be absolute in the sense that they cannot be undone. But they are not ultimate. They do not rend the fabric of life in such a way that it cannot be worn, cannot continue. What seems like a fundamental tear becomes, from a broader perspective, a nick, a pull, a small hole. Indeed this material metaphor is insufficient for the ongoing energy for life of the universe that honors the breaks and ruptures, yet finds a way through or around them in order to sustain life, on and on. Ruptures may then affect the flow, but they do not stop it. Having let go of the need for directionality, energy for life can find its way—*a* way—whatever that may be.

The narratives of time that honor and intensify the present may find it easier to come into rhythm with such a universe of energy. Breathing, for example, is itself about energy and life. Yet time cannot be only in the present mode; it is not contained or confined to the moment. The vibrancy of the wild movement of life defies any such bounds. Future and past are not collapsed into present. Rather all three are freed from fixed relationality into indeterminacy.

The closest we may come to these senses of time—multiple, converging, holding different meanings, and conveying different qualities—in the available narratives and practices is that of liturgical time. In liturgy, time is not so much indeterminate as intensified. Past, present, and future come together and coalesce in a hint of eternity, of breakthrough to another mode of being. The sense of liturgical time does not, however, obliterate past, present, and future, so much as illuminate them as conventions of understanding. In and through ritual action, we find ourselves potentially transformed and transposed into an alternative universe, a parallel realm, if you will, of transcendent relationality.

What is gone from this universe is any notion that what happens in life is once and for all. If nothing is fixed, then the idea that any historical accomplishment, any human achievement, is given forever becomes illusory. There is a provisionality to everything, a sense that all is potentially momentary, that nothing is final. Such provisionality is different from a pattern of return, an endless turning of a wheel. It is also different from any sense of the futility of time. I am not suggesting that there is nothing new under the sun, nor that all is vanity because it will pass away. Rather, I am proposing that we cannot take anything for granted. What is accomplished can be undone. There is no fixed movement, no change that moves only in one direction, no set horizon.

The Non/Sense of an Ending[3]

As we have seen, a linear model of time was wedded in Christianity and in western thought with the idea of an ending, not simply as *terminus*, as end, but as *telos*, as goal, realization, and fulfillment. This Christian affirmation that God has already written the ending, that God is working out God's purposes in history and will bring history and even creation to completion, assumes that time and history have purpose and goals that are under God's direction. We have examined different versions of this basic affirmation. In an apocalyptic view, the fulfillment happens through a direct and dramatic intervention by God breaking into and interrupting history. In other eschatological views, the movement is more evolutionary and the fulfillment happens in and through historical processes or at the end of history when God brings it to closure. Whatever the approach, God is the one in charge and directing the movement to its God-given end.

In the modern West, these perspectives were secularized and made fully historical. The *telos* came to be understood as a goal in history, whether it be total justice and freedom or total domination. History was measured by progress toward that goal. The future end shaped and determined the present and all movement in history.

Such focusing on the end has shaped our thinking about time being purposeful, about historical change moving in only one direction, and about change being once and for all. We assume progress. Anything else surprises us and seems an intrusion, an aberration. We expect good to win out, the future to be better than the past. Indeed, such expectations characterize our understanding of hope: hope for better tomorrows, for more justice and freedom, prosperity, and peace in the world. Our sights are set on the end goal. To suggest letting go of the end, of a *telos*, in any fixed sense, may seem blasphemous.

Yet this is precisely what I am suggesting: we can imagine the future as open-ended, in time that is undetermined and ongoing. There is no given or known outcome. There is no fixed direction. Tomorrow could bring injustice into our world as easily as it brings justice. In fact, if recent historical events are any indication, more often that not injustice seems to prevail. In the last years of the twentieth century and the opening years of the twenty-first, many of the gains in social programs and legislation for justice that were put in place in the twentieth century have been eroded. Totalitarian communism may have died, but resurrected in its stead are forms of fundamentalist totalitarianism that sponsor even more repressive and oppressive regimes. Rather than progress, history seems replete with fits and starts toward and away from justice and peace. Accomplishments are fleeting; nothing is guaranteed.

If time and history are open-ended, then there is no predetermined closure or resolution. To suggest otherwise is to imply that history is, in effect, over because its end is known. In post-Enlightenment theological thinking, there has been much debate about how much the outcome of time is given. Those theologians who want to affirm the historicity of God's actions suggest that the outcome cannot be assumed, that God's redemptive work is not already fully accomplished, that what happens in history matters and makes a difference in the outcome, in the end. Others continue to affirm God as the one in charge of a process that God is bringing to completion in a way that has already been determined. This debate is over whether the race or battle has already been won, which is to say whether redemption is already accomplished. If not, then we are still in the race and the winner is not yet known. If so, then what happens in history is just aftermath. In the latter scenario, the nature of hope is primarily about whether we are included in the outcome, whether we, too, are among the saved. In the former, hope has to do with whether God ultimately prevails. However, either way, what matters, what makes the difference is the end, the outcome. God's ends will be accomplished, one way or the other. In other words, the point of running the race is reaching the goal where all attention is focused.

In addition, the racecourse has already been laid out. And it can be run only in a particular direction. What I propose is the need to imagine a different kind of course—that is not a racetrack on which runners move in one direction toward a goal, but an open field with multiple activities happening simultaneously, both separately and in relation. As we observe such a field there is no one place to direct our attention. There is no finish line to focus on. On this playing field, we are not simply observers; we are participants. We are on the field itself. We are aware of our own participation and of some of what is happening around us, but we cannot take it all in. There is no center and no end point. Rather there is multiplicity and simultaneity.

In this scenario, what is important is the playing, not the outcome. The outcome is not given and cannot be known. There is no goal that is obscured and yet to be revealed. Our attention and energy are focused on the action and the process. Within that process, there are definitely desired values we seek to realize: justice, peace, freedom, harmony, well-being, abundance of life, and even redemption. But these are not separate from the process and the activity. We do not, for example, run the race in order to achieve peace. Rather, we run the race peacefully, and in the running, we become peace and we nurture peace. As Thich Nhat Hanh says, "Peace is every step." Such peace is not the end goal, a thing won or accomplished, but a value practiced, step by step.

To say that we need to imagine time and history as open-ended does not mean that we think of it as infinite. History will end, as will the finite universe. But there is no guarantee that such an end will be a fulfillment or a completion. We cannot assume a *telos* or a resolution, especially one that is guaranteed.

Thus the end is no longer determined or determinative. There is no end toward which all is moving inexorably. We cannot count on such closure or resolution. Instead, we need to find value and meaning in the process itself, rather than in its outcomes. We need to learn to live with and embrace ambiguity and uncertainty that leave outcomes open and our lives de-centered. God's sovereignty may then be re-imagined as God's energy, present and active, in history, rather than God's absolute and determinative dominion over the outcome.

Finding Room for Excess

This is not an easy way to live. We human beings want answers. We look for someone or something to be in charge, directing the action. We want the things that happen to us to make sense, to fit into neat patterns, rather than present as a crazy quilt of odd and surprising juxtapositions. We want these things, but such wants create their own problems. A crazy quilt can incorporate all available material. The quilt maker sets the pieces of cloth and the patterns and colors they carry into some relation to one another, but there is no necessity of a unifying and repetitive theme. However, if the quilt maker is creating a singularly patterned quilt, then only certain materials can be used; other pieces of cloth will either be the wrong color or the wrong pattern and will be excluded.

We western human beings would prefer to live in history and time as if life were an orderly, patterned quilt. But then, in order to tell a coherent story, a unified narrative, we find ourselves unable to include all the available pieces. They remain as excess: the pieces that do not match or work in the pattern. Because there is no place for the excess, because we cannot easily fit certain events, certain experiences, into the story line or the pattern of the quilt, they are either forced to fit or more often than not, they are excluded and discarded.

The excess does not, however, disappear. Freud would tell us the things that do not have place make up the worlds of repression and fantasy. Trauma theorists would suggest they form traumatic memory. Marx might tell us they lead to revolution. Theologians might name them as sin and/or evil. Because human beings did not obey God, did not follow the pattern laid out by God, did not stay in their assigned place, they no longer neatly fit the prescribed pattern.

Too often in the history of thought, such excess has been made the problem, the cause of difficulties, rather than the result of limitations or problems with the dominant modes of thinking and acting. Marginalized people—women, the colonized, the poor—know this. They have been deemed sinful and evil, not because of what they do but who they are. They have been the "other," the repository of fears and of fantasies, and the object of hatred for being different. They are the excess, that which does not fit the pattern.

These are precisely the ones who, as we have seen, are often calling into question the pattern. They are motivated by the experience of exclusion and rejection. Sometimes, however, their goal is to be included in the established pattern. This is too modest a goal and may even be an erroneous and dangerous one. Inclusion is a strategy that will not ultimately work. The fabric cannot hold the contradictions, the ambiguities, the conflicts. It will tear.

Such rupture might be transformative if it could be embraced, if excess could be a source of joy rather than fear, celebration rather than exclusion. Then the torn pieces could be worked together into a crazy quilt, full of diversity and multiple patterns. More often than not, however, rupturing causes the opposite reaction. Those invested in the pattern are all the more determined to maintain it at all costs. The problem is not the pattern, they contend, but the excess. Anything that does not fit is rejected. What would it mean, however, if instead we changed the pattern, or got rid of it entirely, and opened ourselves to new possibilities?

Imagination Gone Wild

In order to let go of the pattern, we need to imagine our lives differently. We need to imagine life itself differently. In order to do that, our imaginations need exercise: they need to bend and stretch and exert themselves in new ways. The alternative ways of thinking about time and history and hope that we are exploring are attempts at such exercise. I know it has stretched my thinking and imagination to wade into the murky and turgid waters of these questions and topics. And that is just the beginning of a long, slow, and difficult process of transformation.

What would happen if we let our imaginations go wild? What if we stepped outside the bounds of conventional thinking and into uncharted territories? There are hints in this book, and especially in this chapter, about some of the characteristics of the space into which we might step. It would be wild territory, not only because it is unknown and unexplored, but because it lacks the type of order and pattern to which we are accustomed. While largely unknown, we have caught glimpses of its characteristics, including ambiguity and a certain chaos, provisionality and a lack of set direction, multiplicity and contradiction, complexity and irony.

These characteristics make maneuvering and finding our way feel treacherous. They are not the type of guideposts to which we are accustomed. We do not generally go looking for chaos or contradictions or even complexity and multiplicity. So we need to develop some new skills in order to recognize these things as guides and not threats, as welcome indicators and not foreboding warnings. They can help us see the path that we would miss were we looking only for straight and clear roads, leading toward a defined goal. They will show us ways to move in and through a path and will teach us to discern differently. Ultimately, we will find ourselves more at home and able to live more easily in this wild terrain.

Along the way, we also need to attune our vision, to keep in sight the values we seek to embody: justice and community, peace and freedom, goodness and care, beauty and truth. These no longer function as goals at the end of a road, the outcome of the journey. Nor do they, in and of themselves, define the nature of God or the purpose of history. They are not givens or prescribed ends. Rather they are values and commitments, those things that we choose to identify as important and necessary in our lives. They guide our way. They are what we hold dear and that offer texture and purpose to our lives. Indeed, justice, peace, and goodness are what we risk our lives for, with no guarantees, no promise of final or full realization.

Place Setting

The metaphors I have been using in the preceding paragraphs are primarily spatial ones. This is no accident. Because western thought has tended to privilege time over space/place, the over-emphasis on time needs correction. As human beings, we live our lives in particular places; we are located beings. We position ourselves in relation to the spaces we inhabit. Those spaces set our horizons that, in turn, define our locations. The contours of those places shape us; our locations form our habitations. The places we inhabit define the resources we have available for living.

Thus, who we are, the way we are, is a function of our place in the world. Such place, understood literally as geographical location, or more figuratively, as class standing or ethnic identity, gives our lives their character and, in a way, their content. We identify ourselves by our locations. We are American or, more specifically, a Texan or a

New Yorker. Such identifications are not fully fixed or determinative. They can change, just as spaces can change. But they cannot be disregarded and dismissed. As a version of an old saying goes, you can take someone out of New York, but you cannot take New York out of the person.

Taking place more seriously slows us down; it tends to keep us in place. We are not simply pilgrim people, moving through the world and life, as a milieu but not a habitation. To be sure, we can change location. In our ever-mobile society, many of us move numerous times during our lives. Yet, in each location, we need to locate ourselves, find our way, set down some roots, however shallow. We make home wherever we find ourselves, even if it is the hotel room we inhabit for few nights. We may still, even in that setting, put a child's picture by the bed or arrange our toiletries the way we always do. We bring our routines and habits, that which is familiar and makes us comfortable, with us.

There is something about us human beings that seems to want the familiarity of place. St. Benedict, the founder of the Benedictine order and much of western monasticism, asked of his monks not only promises of poverty, chastity, and obedience, but of stability. They were to attach themselves to one monastery and not move during their lifetimes. Benedict lived at a time when western society was falling into ruin and the known civilized orders were crumbling as a result of invasion and war, as well as implosion. Stability seemed like a good thing, a wise way to resist the dissolution and to preserve some order and continuity.

In Benedict's world, order and stability were more valued than they are today. Change was seen as a bad thing, a threat to a God-given and static universe. We live today in a radically different world, but Benedict's wisdom may still apply in our own context, not in any absolute way, but as a pointer to the importance of stability for the nurture of grounded selves.

Grounding may be an apt word for the value of place. Being located, standing in place, grounds us. Without such grounding, we lose our balance and get disoriented. The place we stand orients us to the world around us and positions us in relation to that world. Being grounded is characterized by limits. Both sensory deprivation and sensory overload are problems. Knowing where we stand helps prevent both.

The advocates of globalization claim that it dissolves boundaries. The whole world is now potentially connected. We are citizens not only of the localities in which we reside but of the world. Globalization is also eroding the particularities of place. Companies such as McDonald's and Coca-Cola serve as icons for the erosion of boundaries and differences. Everywhere we go, we are able to encounter the golden arches and familiar logos.

Globalization breaks down other barriers as well. We no longer have to actually change our own location in order to experience another one. Satellites and the Internet allow us instant connection with any place or any event, anywhere on the globe. Companies can have employees all around the world. Some laud such developments as the benefits of globalization; others decry them.

Is globalization changing our experience of place or even the nature of place? I would suggest that it is, but not in a way that fundamentally alters our need for grounding in the particularities of who, what, and where we are. When we go to places such as Paris or Yerevan or Beijing and can easily find Coca-Cola, our experience of those places is affected, including whether and how we encounter them as different. Ironically, however, at the same time that globalization seems to be taking over the world, so to speak, more and more people are claiming identities defined by differences and particularities. Many of the conflicts in places all around the world are fights over identity and borders and territory. Might this widespread phenomenon be evidence of a refusal of the homogeneity of globalization?

The more we rub up against each other, the more the boundaries among us shift and change, the more movement there is within and among societies and culture, two opposite trends seem to be emerging. On the one hand, there is evidence pointing to increased intermingling and blending, to what has been termed the hybridization of identities and cultures. In other words, with fluid boundaries, cultures mix easily and produce new and mixed identities, new modes of being. On the other hand, we see people asserting the difference of their particular identities and making claims for the importance of maintaining purity and uniqueness and for the absolute value of certain principles and ways of living. The fundamentalism that seems increasingly to define many religious identities today is but one example of this phenomenon. Fundamentalism is characterized precisely by a refusal to change, accompanied by an assertion of absolute rightness and truth. It draws the boundaries in ways that exclude difference.

In the end, globalization does not so much negate place as shift the ways in which we define place. The same is true when we consider the Internet and virtual reality. The Internet allows us to create webs of connection all over the globe, across time as well as space. Virtual reality simulates places and puts us into new spaces without our having to leave the ones we are in. Even though both phenomena defy boundaries and seem to shrink distances, they, at the same time, point to the importance of location: real, imagined, or virtual.

We human beings need to be located. Therefore, along with celebrating worldwide webbing and the possibilities of virtual reality, we need reminders of limits, of their importance and necessity. In our human experience, we understand place as concrete. Because we are enfleshed, embodied beings, there is always a material dimension to our experience. The Christian doctrine of incarnation reinforces and strengthens the value of concrete and material existence, as does the affirmation that God created the universe and it is good. How do we hold together the importance and necessity of concrete, material existence with what we know about space as flexible, fluid, and relative?

This is one of the challenges we face today. But whether real or imagined, concrete or virtual, space is a dimension of our lives. However we imagine the space we inhabit, setting ourselves in place is a value. Placement is necessary for balance, orientation, and vision. At the same time, we must recognize that such placement is not set absolutely. We do not stand upon eternal rock but upon shifting sands. We both need to be located and know that any given location is provisional.

Space/Time Continuum

Physicists have taught us that space and time are not ultimately separate from one another. They are one phenomenon, one reality. It is more accurate to speak about a space/time continuum than of two separate dimensions, and to understand space and time as relative to one another. Physicists have also introduced into our thinking the related idea of indeterminacy. Neither space nor time is fixed.

In order to demonstrate these characteristics of space/time, physicists, along with science fiction writers, have written about such things as time travel and transporters. In the series *Star Trek*, Captain Kirk and his crew would be "beamed up" from one location to another. Movies such as *Back to the Future* offer stories of travel back and forth in time. The sequencing of time from past to future and the materiality of bodies, things we take for granted, are no longer givens. These phenomena change the way we think about the universe and what we term as reality. If we allow them to leave the pages of fiction and begin to entertain them as real possibilities, then some of our assumptions about the nature of reality will be challenged. This can be very unsettling.

What might help in the process is giving full rein to our imaginations and letting go of the strictures we have placed on them. As an example of such an effort from a theological perspective, let us imagine what it might mean to revisit and reinterpret the Christian affirmation of the resurrection of Christ from the perspective of a space/time continuum and an indeterminate universe.

Belief in the resurrection is a central tenet of Christian thought. Indeed for some, it is the linchpin of faith. God's ability to resurrect Jesus from the dead is evidence of God's power and sovereignty. God's promise through Jesus Christ is of resurrection from the dead for human persons as well. Salvation is understood to be such resurrection into eternal life.

Many Christians understand the resurrection to be a concrete historical event, a fact in history, which defies the laws of nature and, therefore, is a miracle. Enlightenment thinking challenged precisely this claim about the miraculous nature of the resurrection. Enlightenment rationalists and empiricists argued that such a miracle could not be literally or scientifically true. Meanwhile, defenders of traditional Christian teaching continued to assert the resurrection as a miracle, a concrete event that provides evidence of God's ability to change even the most given aspect of the natural world—death. Other theologians, looking for ways to respond to and account for Enlightenment challenges, offered alternative interpretations: the resurrection was not something miraculous that happened to the person of Jesus, but it was what happened to individual believers and/or the community around Jesus. For example, existential theologian Rudolph Bultmann argued that the resurrection was experienced in and by the faithful. The "miracle" was the change that occurred in the person of faith as a result of the encounter that led to new insight and commitment. Battles have been waged among theologians on the differing sides of these debates. One of the most famous of these was between Rudolph Bultmann and Karl Barth, two major figures in twentieth-century Christian theology. Barth insisted the resurrection was historical fact; Bultmann understood it more as existential encounter.

Such arguments about the nature of the resurrection event are based on the physics of a material universe with set laws, the universe that Newtonian physics reflected. If we let our imaginations enter the world of quantum physics, then the resurrection story can be understood in a different light, as the transformation of matter into energy. The resurrection is about the life force that moves the universe being manifest in the resurrected Christ and among Christ's followers. The resurrection appearances are the configuration of the energy of Christ in that moment.

Time and again, in the resurrection appearances, Jesus' followers do not initially recognize him in the risen state. He is not concretely the same. In the biblical accounts, the resurrection is never portrayed as a simple reappearance, but as a transformation into a form that can walk through walls (Gospel of John) and appear along a road miles from Jerusalem (Gospel of Luke). Only after an encounter are Jesus' followers able to recognize the one who is with them as the resurrected Christ. Perhaps what happens in these encounters and appearances is that through the exchange that enables their faith, the followers of Jesus are able to see beyond materiality to the dynamic, interconnected, and interconnecting energy that constitutes space and time. Recognition happens when they let go of the known universe.

The "miracle" is this vision, the being able to see differently, which then changes what had been deemed reality. In the resurrection, God's power breaks through as life energy, the power of transformation. Just as in concrete form, a child's transformer toy is able to change shape and become something else, the energy that was the person Jesus is transformed and in turn transforms Jesus' followers. Such an interpretation of the resurrection might allow us to reimagine it from a scientific viewpoint, without eliminating the power of the event or of God's action.

What Hi/Story?

But there is more to consider when it comes to the resurrection event. Those who argue that the resurrection "really" happened also often insist on its historicity. For them, it is necessary that the resurrection be an historical event, which is to say something that happened in time and space, in the chronology of events that happened to the person of Jesus. The language and images of quantum physics would seem to leave history behind. Rather than telling a historical tale, those images speak of the cosmos. They move us out of the time and space we seem to inhabit in our ordinary existence and into a cosmos of dynamic energy that is not bounded.

What happens to history in this move? What happens to our historicity as human beings, living in narratives of time and locations of space? Is history ultimately not real, which is to say that what happens in history does not really matter or is of no enduring consequence?

This is the rub for me, the core questions around which so much of what I have been trying to work through in this book swirls. An easy out, it seems, might be to leave history behind and embrace a more cosmocentric worldview. Christianity in its classical formulations did that; it did not pay much attention to history at all. Rather, classical Christianity cast its lot with cosmology, even if its cosmology was the tiered universe and static world of Platonic philosophy that recoiled from change as something abhorrent. Once Christian thought wedded itself to Greek philosophy, Christianity had trouble embracing its Jewish roots, which put the emphasis on God's actions in history. In classical Christianity, God was still affirmed as being "in charge" of history, but what happened in history was ultimately of little consequence for understanding God or God's work of redemption.

In modernity Christianity became more worldly, which is to say that what happened in history, in this world, was understood to reveal the presence of God. But such an embrace of history brought with it a whole set of problems. If, as in classical thought, redemption was seen to be outside of time—in eternity—then what happened in history might still be accounted for somehow, at the end. Ultimately, God's will would be accomplished; healing and fulfillment would be realized, not in time, but in eternity. It was the end, the *telos*, that mattered. Moving the work of redemption into history, however, and seeing redemption also as a historical process complicate the picture. They make what happens in history matter.

As we have seen, political and liberation theologians wrestle with this problem, as do those theologians who are trying to redefine the ways in which the time of history is envisioned. All these theologians want to maintain history as the realm of God's saving work, but also to give due attention to the problems of history. They do not want to fall into any easy optimism about what may or may not be possible in history. They eschew any simple linear and progressive model of history, and yet, they do not want to take redemption out of history, out of time.

How then do we deal with historical time in relation to a cosmological apprehension of time and space? Is history what is real, the only reality we can know? Or is it ultimately just an idle tale or a fantasy? Is history a mere fiction or myth, having no true reality?

History is story; it is narrative. History *is* the tales we tell about the lives we live. But such tales are anything but idle. As we have seen, they form and shape our existence. They set the horizons and character of our living. They define the known world. We understand and interpret our lives in their light. What lies in the shadows is excluded from what we do or how we do it. These shadows often fall outside our imaginations, except for those among us who are visionaries and explorers, those who dare to venture beyond the known world. Also in the shadows are the marginalized, who live at the peripheries of power and so have less stake in the world as it is. The explorers' charting of new territory ultimately changes the narratives and how we live in history. The raised voices of the marginalized also affect the stories we tell. These all redefine the known. Exploring, challenging, and redefining are ongoing processes. History is not static; it is an ever-changing narrative.

Thus history, the narrative of our lives, is crucially important for how we live. But the story line is not set; the outcome is not known. The characters may change, as may the plot. Even time cannot be understood to be continuous. As we have seen, postmodern thought (as well as science fiction and fantasy fiction) offers alternative perspectives on time as something other than linear, sequential, and one-directional. We often find these perspectives disorienting, which indeed they are in the most fundamental meaning of the word. They challenge and change our orientation. They undermine our sense of stability; they put us off balance. They transform us.

The Character of Change

The closest we get to a given in this world, the most we can approximate a fixed narrative, is to assert that change is constant and that nothing is fixed. History is the narrative of change; it is our ongoing attempt to tell a story of what we are experiencing, of what is happening in our lives.

We human beings both want change and do not want it. Sometimes we resist it mightily, especially if it is unwelcome and not of our choosing. But even when a change is something we want, there always seems to be a loss attached. We may want to birth children, but we do not want our loved ones to die, whatever their age, in the unrelenting turn of generations. We want to advance in our careers and look for new opportunities, but we mourn what is left behind in any move. If the changes are unwelcome and unwanted, the losses may be felt even more acutely. Sometimes change is on a personal scale, and sometimes it is on a grand scale that impacts the world in which we live. Whatever the source of the changes, it seems we are in a constant state of making adjustments, of losing and regaining our balance.

Such changes will not go away. In fact, futurists have argued that the rate of change is increasing. We are experiencing more changes in our lifetime than have previous generations. In this book's introduction, I narrated my own experience of such changes and their unrelenting and confusing character, leaving me dizzy and sometimes unable to get my bearings.

Change is constant and it is difficult. We make it more difficult when we resist it or try to turn our back on it and pretend it away. We increase the feelings of loss when we think we can stop change, which is to say when we think we have more control than we do.

We also increase the problems attendant to change when we do not accept the finitude of existence and so find ourselves surprised again and again by the passing of life or the limitations in our lives. One of the ironies of life is that while change is constant and anything is possible, not everything will or can change. Change implies choices that preclude other choices, at least temporarily. That is the nature of fini-tude and one of the reasons why life is experienced as tragic.

Change is not necessarily in one direction; it can take us in any direction. Perhaps even to speak of direction is inaccurate. Rather, change is random. It is purposeful in the sense that change has specific effects, but not in the sense that it always follows a set pattern or is moving toward any end goal. In other words, while there is order in the universe, it is not ultimate or unchanging itself. Life is unpre-dictable. It includes chaos.

The biblical accounts depict God as the one for whom all things are possible. This affirmation has most often been interpreted to be about God's power. God is in charge of everything and can do any-thing. Therefore, there is order in the universe; all is determined by God. Might we, however, read this affirmation differently, as a state-ment about God and change? Then God, as the one for whom all things are possible, would be ever changing, ever bringing into realiza-tion the possible. God would be energy, dynamic, potential, and even indeterminate.

Believing Is Seeing

If what I have outlined is a depiction of the universe and of life and of God that we choose to live by, what would be the implications for faith and for our fundamental commitments? Can we even speak of hope in this world of constant change and indeterminacy? If so, what is its nature? Might hope be an attitude toward life and a commitment to living it, without knowing the outcome, without seeing the end?

"Seeing is believing" is a familiar saying. Those who believe in progress ascribe to this point of view. They direct our attention to all the ways in which the world is changing and changing for the better. Those who are critical of such easy optimism also argue that seeing is believing. They, however, lift up all the evil and injustice in the world to make their point. Dispensationalists, those who see the end in sight, offer a more extreme version of this same approach. They draw up lists of signs pointing to the end in order to predict what God is doing and when.

Most people of faith, however, suggest that the reverse is true, that believing is seeing. Faith means that we see the world and life through lenses that allow us to commit to life and its value, whatever else may be encountered along the way. God is on the side of life, forever. The biblical tradition affirms this faith again and again. Contrary to the evidence and signs, God is present, making life happen.

The Bible also asserts that without a vision the people perish. Our lives, our living, are guided by our vision. Our vision consists of the values, commitments, and beliefs that shape who we are and what we do, that inform the way in which we live our lives. Our vision is what gives our lives meaning and purpose and even direction. It forms our desires. Just as dancers or ice skaters fix their eyes on one point in order to keep balanced when spinning, our vision is where we fix our gaze in the whirlwind of our lives.

However, we get in trouble when we think that our vision, our desires, and our expectations will be realized in any once-and-for-all way. We begin to lose hope when we assume that vision is the end goal toward which all is moving. The vision then comes to be about the goal and not the process, about the ends of life and not life itself.

Vision is what gives us direction and purpose, but only so long as it remains vision, something in front of us upon which we focus in order to keep moving, to stay balanced. If we turn our gaze, we get off balance and fall down. Without the guiding vision, we lose our way. And we lose our pacing if we think we can rush ahead or reach ahead to somehow capture the vision.

The Process Is the Thing

We are an ends-driven society. Phrases like "what's the bottom line" reveal not only our capitalist orientation, but our obsession with outcomes. We determine value by results and productivity. Our energy is focused almost entirely on the end product. We evaluate success, whether our own or that of others, by achievements such as our career advancement, salary and standard of living, and even our families.

Life, however, is about the living of it. Life is process and movement. How we live is ultimately more important than what our living produces. The character of our lives, the values we embrace, the meanings we contemplate, the relationships we nurture and enjoy, the work we engage in, all of these contribute to and constitute our living. They are what it means to be alive, to live fully.

The value of such living cannot be measured by its products. We have little control over what our living produces, but we can commit wholeheartedly to the living itself. What our living produces is so often the result of chance and luck, of factors not of our choosing or making: where and when we were born, how we were nurtured, and what opportunities we were afforded as a result of the accidents of our lives. Where and when we live also impacts greatly what we are able to do and how. For example, when I graduated from college, in the state in which I resided I was able to take a state exam and as a result of my score on that exam, I was offered a position as a social worker in public housing projects. The only qualifications I needed were a Bachelor's degree in any field and a good score on the exam. The job was a wonderful experience for me. However, if I had graduated from college just six or so years later, I would no longer have qualified for the very same job, no matter how well I did on the exam. By then, the requirements had been changed, and applicants needed to have a Bachelor of Social Work degree even to be considered. An opportunity that was easily available at one time was no longer a possibility for me.

There was much chance in what happened to me. In my interactions with the residents of the public housing project, I also learned that many of the people I served, the residents of the projects, did not have the same type of options that I had, not because of their character or abilities, but by virtue of certain circumstances of their lives that they could not change. Many were ill or disabled or elderly. Others, due to family circumstances and available work, could not get out of poverty no matter how hard they tried. If these people were to measure the value of their lives by their accomplishments and successes, by what their lives produced, they might be deemed lesser. Yet, if they were judged by how they lived, they might well be regarded as caring, loving, and able people, doing the best possible in difficult circumstances.

Life is a process. How we live is what is important. In this production- and ends-driven society, we need to remind ourselves of that again and again. We need to live into believing it.

Embracing Values Rather than Goals

Judaism and Christianity claim that God's activity is on behalf of justice and peace, freedom and harmony. These things constitute the ends toward which God's work is directed. Visions of the kingdom of God or of the divine Shalom or of the transfigured cosmos reveal a fulfillment of these ends. As we have seen, modern views of God's activity move these ends more into the domain of history itself and argue for them as historical accomplishments. The work of Jews and of Christians in the world is to be about mending the world (for Jews) and establishing God's reign of justice and harmony on earth (for Christians). And as we have seen, such optimistic and progressive views of history are precisely what are challenged by historical realities and by other contending understandings of time.

What, however, happens to these goals? Are justice, peace, and freedom no longer what we should set our sights on? Sometimes those who draw us toward more cyclical and present-centered views of time or underscore the tragic suggest that focusing on historical accomplishments is a vanity. They then opt for an aesthetics of living or an existentialist or determinist view of life that may seem like a settling and giving in. So they, in turn, are accused of quietism and of not taking history and what happens in history seriously enough.

What I have been suggesting, which I see to be truer to the biblical understanding, is to understand justice and peace, freedom and harmony not as ends, but as values, guiding values that direct our lives. They constitute the vision on which we are fixed and which keeps us in balance. Without these core values, we would be wandering aimlessly in life or be dissolved in a heap, dizzy from the spinning of life.

As values, they inform and shape the process of our living. They are guideposts for the choices we make and for assessing our lives. We do not measure our lives, however, by how much justice or peace or freedom has been established, but by whether we have lived justly, peacefully, and with freedom, for ourselves and others. The well-known verse from Micah states: "What does the Lord require of you but to do justice, and to love kindness, and to walk humbly with your God?" (Micah 6: 8). The emphasis is on the doing, the acting, the moving, the process.

If we commit to these historical "goals" as values, then we do not expect our accomplishments to be once and for all, nor do we anticipate a time when our work will be done. Rather, as long as there is a living creation and as long as the divine enlivens the universe, living with commitment and faith will mean embracing and living by these values.

To the extent that we are able to see justice and peace, care and freedom as values and not ends, then we will live more and more into life as a process. Even though we will care passionately about peace in the world and we will work diligently to create just societies, we will not live for the ends we may or may not accomplish. The world may be ever changing, but our commitments and values and faith remain constant. Our faith is in the process of living. The divine promise is of such life—ongoing. We take history seriously, because it is the context of our living, but we do not view it from the perspective of a *telos*. Nor do we view it from the viewpoint of an original perfection and a fall. The only beginning or end is life itself, and life is its own justification. The divine is the one who animates our living. In that sense, God is working out God's purposes. Those purposes are life and the living of it.

Re-imagining Hope

I have been hinting, along the way, how we might understand the nature of hope in today's world. Hope is about commitment to life as ongoing. In that sense hope is directed toward the future but not as an end. Hope is living with vision as the values we give our lives to and that guide our living. An attitude and a value itself, the content of hope is not specific. We do not know the needs of life of another place and another time. Our vision is limited; our finitude sets boundaries on our living. So we cannot specify the content of hope for all times and all places. We can name it only for our own context. Nor is hope utopian. A modesty of hope does not make hope any less compelling, any less necessary. Indeed, it has the opposite effect. Our hope is quite intensified in the moment, whichever moment, in which we live.

The early New Testament witness, with its sense of imminent expectation, narrated such intensity. That witness, however, focused on the ending of time (or so it has been interpreted), rather than time's intensity. I am suggesting that the intensity itself, the sense that the present moment potentially contains all of time, is what fuels hope.

Hope is about embracing this intensity in a way that allows it to shape, but not over-determine, our lives. In a real sense, this is what it means to take history seriously, to ground who we are and what we do in history. Often a sense of imminent expectation is interpreted as a devaluing of history. It is yoked with an understanding of redemption as rescue from outside of history, from some place other than the time and place in which we live. I am suggesting, however, that this need not be the case. A sense of imminent expectation does not have to portend apocalyptic rescue and resolution. Indeed, if our focus is on the process and not the end, then we would not even be looking for resolution or finality.

Our hope would have the character of Advent anticipation. We would be on tiptoe, so to speak, yearning and straining for what lies before us, but the resolution would remain open-ended, unfixed. Hope would be in and through the anticipatory tension of the future, which is fed by the past, with its fulfillments, terrors, and losses. But the living would be in and for the present, as the meeting place of desire and fear, birth and death, of all the living.

Such hope would also be placed and grounded in life and in what is life giving. It would recognize the concreteness of creation, the materiality of existence, with all its limitations and finitude, as well as its renewing capacities, as the location of life, now and forever. That materiality is, however, fundamentally energy. Finitude is both given and pliable; existence is dynamic.

On the one hand, change is bound by location, so that the future may contain the new but not in a way that negates the present or the past. On the other hand, such boundedness does not constrain the possibility of the new, the emergence of the surprising. Hope lies in dancing amid these seemingly contradictory affirmations.

Thus, hope is a process and an attitude. Fundamentally, it is a practice. In the next chapter, I will consider some habits we need to cultivate in order to enter into and deepen hope. Before turning to that task, however, there are a few other implications of this view I would point to.

Beyond Moral Dualism

The moral dualism that runs throughout the history of Christian thought, which banished from the divine realm whatever was deemed evil or negative and relegated it to the satanic or to human will and behavior, is not compatible with the nature of hope as outlined above. If nothing is fixed, if the outcome is not given, indeed, if the concept of outcomes is itself problematic, then the absoluteness of dualistic categories of good and evil cannot be sustained.

We have also observed that when chaos is part of creation, rather than that which is overcome in the process of creation, and when indeterminacy is built into existence, moral dualism cannot hold. Rather, the universe is a throbbing, pulsing dynamism of powers that manifest in manifold and conflicting ways. Such energy cannot be categorized easily or consistently.

In this universe, God is power for life, which we deem good, but which is not first and last moral in the way in which we human beings have come to understand such things. We can find such a God of life in some non-dominant strains of the biblical witness. For example, the book of Job presents a somewhat different image of God. This God of Job speaks out of the whirlwind with raw power. This God questions the categories that both God's defenders and challengers have used. The long poem, toward the end of the book of Job, tells a story of creation that emphasizes not goodness but life. As we saw in chapter 1, Job's response to the God of the whirlwind, which has so often been translated as "I despise myself and repent in dust and ashes," can also be translated: "I despise and repent of dust and ashes." The first translation portrays Job as submitting to the moral superiority of God. It presents the "moral" of the book of Job as one of submission and dependence on the goodness and power of God. If we follow the second translation, however, we end up with a very different "moral." Job's words are a bold assertion of life, even in the midst of loss, even as he sits on a dunghill. This claiming of life is a resurrection moment. Job refuses to give in to the death that surrounds him. He is upheld by the God of life, ever on the side of the living.

The Good, True, and Beautiful

In chapter 1, when I described the modern worldview that understands God to be in charge of time, which moves in linear fashion toward fulfillment and resolution, I suggested that this worldview privileges the moral in a way that marginalizes or excludes the true and the beautiful. My project of re-imagining is motivated in part by a desire to reclaim the true and the beautiful, along with the moral, and not to privilege any one perspective or sensibility over the others.

In the history of western thought, as I have indicated, dedication to truth invited contemplative knowing and wisdom. Such contemplation rested in honoring what is and searching its reality. The goal was to be in the divine presence. In classical Christian theology, contemplation of God was the intended end for human beings. Thomas Aquinas, for one, named this the beatific vision.

If we give truth its due, not only would we be drawn into the realms of divine contemplation, but there might also be enduring place in our understanding of life for that which is not good or beautiful, for the terrors and traumas of our lives. These are true, though we do not often want them to be. Indeed, it seems to me that those who live with traumatic pasts struggle a great deal to find a way to reconcile what happened to them with belief in a moral universe where goodness ultimately reigns. They wonder how their experience could be true if the world is good, if the driving force of the universe is moral goodness working out the divine purpose.

To name something as true is to grant it existence and validity. If these survivors see their horrific experiences as true, then they are suggesting that perhaps goodness is not the final word. Granting the truth of terrors and traumas means accepting a past that cannot be accounted for or made "good." Such truth invites a type of knowing that gives due honor to the victimized.

Overemphasizing the moral also tended to exclude the value of beauty for its own sake. In the modern West, aesthetics was subordinated to morality or it was instrumentalized. Beauty was not an end or value in itself; it was judged by its use value, either for its contribution to the good or as a means to an economic, technological, or political end. Hispanic spirituality, however, is one movement reminding us of the importance of beauty for its own sake. Revaluing beauty will cultivate in us an appreciation for life and its richness. Beauty makes our living worthwhile and enjoyable. As we pay more attention to beauty and cultivate an aesthetic sensibility, we will find ourselves living more fully and deeply. We will locate ourselves in the present, in the moment we inhabit.

The Westminster catechism used by the Presbyterian Church states that the purpose of life is "to know God and enjoy him [*sic*] forever." Such knowledge and joy are nurtured by contemplating truth and appreciating beauty, as well as working for the good. Because the world in which many of us live has privileged the moral, it is important to recall to ourselves truth and beauty. As we do so, they will transform us. This process would be enhanced if we understood the good, the true, and the beautiful more as values to be practiced, than ends or goals to be achieved. It is in and through our contemplating, appreciating, and doing that we will come to know God and live fully.

Telling Time Differently

In this chapter, I have surveyed the broad, complex, and perhaps even contradictory implications of what it means to hope and to tell time in the world we live in today. I have indicated that we need to learn to tell time differently. Clearly, telling time is no longer simply a matter of counting: minutes, hours, days, months, years, centuries, and millennia. Such chronologies of time tell only partial tales that cannot help us live in the time that is our lives. Spiritual teachers speak of discernment, of being able to read the signs of the times and of the heart's desire. In this book, in the telling of time I have put forth here, I have tried to discern the structure and shape, language and content of a narrative of time for hope today.

Such a narrative is a complex telling, holding together various narrative strands that seem at times to be in conflict and not resting comfortably with one another. This narrative does not begin "once upon a time." Nor does it end "and they lived happily ever after." The God of this narrative does not claim to be the Alpha and the Omega. Although we may yearn for fairy-tale endings and linear plot lines and even though we may project that yearning onto our religious desires, the story we live is not so simple or comedic, linear or complete.

Perhaps the subplots of intrigue and thwarted desires, of confusions and mistakes, of terrors and tragedies, as well as of pleasure and delight, play and pretend, appreciation and contemplation, may help us move toward a more ironic mode of narrative. Irony seems better suited for helping us hold together the contradictions and live through the conflicts.

Not only do we need to tell a new and more complex story, but we also need to cultivate new practices of living. The next chapter will outline such practices, as habits to cultivate that might in turn help us to inhabit time differently. The character of our hope will be shaped by these practices and habits. We will find ourselves telling time differently and living differently. Hope will flourish in us as we are able to engage in this process of transformation.

For Further Reading

Since this chapter pulled together and applied many of the ideas introduced in the preceding chapters, I would direct readers to the texts on physics, history, narrative, and time already cited. Additionally, readers might explore essays in Roger Friedland and Deirdre Boden, eds., *NowHere: Space, Time and Modernity* (Berkeley: University of California Press, 1994) and Eviatar Zerubavel, *Time Maps: Collective Memory and the Social Shape of the Past* (Chicago: University of Chicago Press, 2003). For further reading about chaos theory and its implications for life in the world, see F. David Peat and John Briggs, *Turbulent Mirror: An Illustrated Guide to Chaos Theory and the Science of Wholeness* (New York: HarperCollins, 1990) and Ilya Prigogine and Isabelle Stengers, *Order out of Chaos: Man's New Dialogue with Nature* (New York: Bantam Books, 1984). Related theological resources include Sheila Davaney, *Pragmatic Historicism: Theology for the Twenty-First Century* (Albany: State University of New York Press, 2000); Edward Farley, *Faith and Beauty: A Theological Aesthetic* (Aldershot, UK: Ashgate, 2001) and Gordon Kaufman, *In Face of Mystery: A Constructive Theology* (Cambridge: Harvard University Press, 2004). I have found the work of sociologist Peter Marris helpful for understanding the dynamics of change. See his *Loss and Change* (New York: Pantheon Books, 1974) and *The Politics of Uncertainty: Attachment in Private and Public Life* (London: Routledge, 1996).

Notes

1. Walt Whitman, "Song of Myself," in *Leaves of Grass* (New York: MetroBooks, 2001), 76.

2. See Shimon Malin, *Nature Loves to Hide* (Oxford: Oxford University Press, 2001).

3. This section title is a play on Frank Kermode, *The Sense of an Ending: Studies in the Theory of Fiction* (New York: Oxford University Press, 1967).

7

PRACTICES OF HABITATION

Hope for Life

Many years ago, I attended a lecture on the topic of hope by the German political theologian Dorothee Soelle. Even though I am no longer able to recall the exact words she used, what she said has remained with me all these years. She likened the character of hope to a baby beginning to walk. It is in and through getting up on her feet and taking the steps that a baby learns to walk. Similarly with hope, we will learn to hope anew as we practice hope. The practice of hope is a process. It requires risk as well as boldness. Indeed, there is a miraculous quality to it, not unlike the miracle of a baby learning to walk or talk or laugh. The miracle of hope is experienced in the practice of it, not in absolute guarantees. Just as babies gain confidence in walking as they take more and more steps and manage to stay on their feet more often than they fall, we will gain confidence in hope as we enter more deeply into the practices of hope. The word *confidence* means "with faith." To hope is an act of faith and a trust in life. It means "believing is seeing": learning to live by and with the vision that guides us.

In this chapter, I survey habits, practices, and attitudes that are important to the process of learning to tell time differently and so learning to hope anew. All of these practices are meant to contribute to the *process* of hope. They neither define the particular content of our hope nor promise any given outcomes. Rather, they teach ways to hope. The vision and desire underlying them is for life, for living fully and deeply, with faith and commitment.

I trust that by now the reader is well aware that life in this world is characterized by provisionality, which is to say that life is improvisation. The dance of life does not follow a set choreography with intricately detailed and patterned movements producing a pre-determined effect. Rather we are making up the dance of life as we go. We are constantly improvising as new and changing circumstances force themselves upon us or as we seek and welcome the new and different into our lives.

Improvisation is not, however, a free-for-all. The ability to improvise requires practice and training and technique. In order to improvise, dancers must also be acutely attuned to one another and to the flow of energy, to the dynamics of the interactions among them. What is true of dance is also true of acting and music. Improvisational theater happens among and through the players engaged in it. Improvisational music, such as jazz, takes considerable training, practice, and skill, not only in playing instruments but in listening to one another and sensing the movement of the music.

In improvisation, the players and dancers share a commitment to some fundamental elements of the genre and to certain guidelines for the interplay. But there is no set outcome, no cookie-cutter product. Rather, the dance or the play or the music emerges out of the process. So it is with hope. Hope emerges out of the process of hoping, shaped by practices.

Habit/ation

Hope is nurtured, fed, and shaped by habits, which in turn grow out of and are formed by practices. Habits are ways of being and acting that, because of repetition and reinforcement, because of practice, have become part of who we are. They are characteristic of us and, in that sense, define us.

When we say we are habituated to something, we mean that we do something without choosing it each time. For example, most of us are habituated to brushing our teeth before we go to bed. We do not ask ourselves each night: shall I brush my teeth tonight or not? Perhaps, on those nights when we are particularly tired and just want to crawl right into bed, we may choose to skip the brushing or, at least, "force" ourselves to do it. But most nights, we just brush our teeth as part of our bedtime routine. When we were children, our parents made sure we developed this practice into a habit. Each evening, they would tell us to brush our teeth before we went to bed. Our parents and probably our dentist showed us the proper way to do so and impressed upon us the importance of this practice. As we grew up, we formed the habit of brushing our teeth without reminders from adult authority.

Brushing our teeth is a good habit, something that contributes to our well-being. Many of us also form bad habits that are harmful to us. For many years, I smoked cigarettes. I considered myself habituated and not addicted, because I was able to choose not to smoke fairly easily. When I stopped smoking, I did not experience my body as craving the nicotine, but rather found myself missing the habit of lighting up after dinner or sharing a cigarette with a friend. There are crucial differences between addictions and habituation. Habits can be altered by changes in behavior and cognition. Addictions are resistant to such change; they require a different type of process and practice. They necessitate a deeper transformation because they are by definition behaviors over which we do not have control.

Habits are more amenable to our wills, though the process of habit formation is not necessarily a conscious and active one. We habituate ourselves and become habituated to good and bad ways of being in the world throughout the course of our lives. We pick up helpful and harmful, healthy and unhealthy habits. Some habits may not necessarily be bad or unhealthy in themselves, but are harmful because of what they cause to happen. For example, there is not anything intrinsically bad about smoking, but cigarettes harm our health. Or we may develop a habit of hesitance in our speech, saying "um" or "uh" or "like" after every other word. That behavior is not a bad thing in and of itself, but it gets in the way of people being able to listen to us and to take what we are saying seriously.

So "bad" habits may either be harmful to our lives and well-being or they may get in the way of our living as well or as fully as we would like to live. Throughout this book, I have been arguing that some of our habits of telling time—the ways we think about time, history, and hope—are inadequate, unhelpful, and even harmful for us in our current context. We have been habituated into particular narratives about time and hope and even God that are not able to tell a fully life-giving story. We need to develop different and better habits of telling time. The practices I am proposing in this chapter are meant to help us cultivate such habits. These good habits will, in turn, enhance our hope and our living. As we engage in these practices and develop different ways of being and doing, we will not only become habituated to hope, we will also inhabit our world differently. We will change our lives.

Indeed, my youthful desire to change the world still remains strong, but the changes I envision are of a different character and order. I no longer have expectations that everything will always change for the better or that any of us can guarantee the future. Rather, as we live our lives with confidence and hope, we will stay true to our fundamental values and desires for renewing the world.

Habits of Hope

The practices suggested here and the habits they might cultivate are for this time and place in history. I see them both as correcting some of the bad habits of our time, as well as helping us to form good habits. These practices will give us tools for improvisation, to help us live with hope in the world today.

The survey of practices and habits that I present below is meant to be suggestive rather than exhaustive, which is to say, these practices and habits are not the only ones that might be helpful. Since readers will bring their own energy and perspectives to this process, I expect readers will take and use what seems useful and add to or alter the practices as they engage in their own improvisation.

Our practices reveal our values. Values are defined as those things we hold dear and cherish. They are guideposts for our living. A stated value is not true unless it is acted upon and practiced in an ongoing way. These practices are intended to form habits that demonstrate values of hope and living fully and well with one another and the earth.

There are five habits or modes of habitation that I propose we need to cultivate: honoring time, moving in place, imagining creatively, participating in interrelation, and living in wild wonder. Each of them includes practices that will enable the process of habit formation.

Honoring Time

Much of what I have written in this book has been about paying attention to time and honoring it in ways that have been overlooked or neglected. To honor time is to recognize the present as the time in which we live and from which we regard the past and future. Honoring time does not require us to disregard linearity but to understand a linear view of time as just that; it is but one perspective. Indeed, if we are to give time due honor, then we need to change our perspectives on time.

Ironically, to honor time is also to realize that there is no such "thing" as time. The challenge of the habit of honoring time is to give time its due and also to see time for what it ultimately is/is not. This is a difficult attitude and habit to cultivate. We need to keep reminding ourselves that anything we claim to know and say about time is a narrative. The practices for honoring time are about expanding and changing the dominant western narrative so that we might live in time differently.

The first practice of honoring time is to "take time." So many spiritual practices are about stopping and stepping outside the normal rhythms of life. They involve breathing and paying attention to one's breath. Such practices are meant to help us take time and, paradoxically, both to recognize ourselves as beings in time and to let time fall away. We rarely take time in our lives; we do not stop. One of the ironies of life in the western world today is that rather than having more leisure, as futurists predicted a generation or so ago, we have less. So the first step is to stop: to take time to pay attention to time.

When we take time, we can begin to engage in practices of appreciation and thankfulness, as well as reverence and wonder. We inhabit a wondrous universe. The moon rises in the sky. If we notice it, how can we but wonder in awe? When we are loved unconditionally, how can we not respond with thankfulness? These are spontaneous reactions.

We can also actively cultivate practices of appreciation and reverence. At their core, these practices emerge from an attitude of receptivity, a recognition that life is ultimately a gift. So much of what constitutes our lives is simply given to us in and by the world, if we are able to accept and receive what is offered. We will become more attune to this dimension of life, if we take time to practice thankfulness and reverence; we will then deepen our sense of appreciation and wonder.

Sometimes we may feel reverence and wonder but not appreciation. This is especially true when the wonders of creation seem to result in harm. Earthquakes and tsunamis, tornadoes and hurricanes are amazing events, full of great power, that are more often than not destructive to human and natural life. Although it may be grotesque to talk about gratitude in such instances, there is a place for receptivity and wonder at the power of the universe. Such wonder causes us to feel both the insignificance of our particular lives in the vast universe and the importance of respecting and remembering each and every life.

Remembering is another practice that contributes to our honoring of time. The act of remembering may help deepen our practice of reverence in the present, but it is primarily a practice about the past. When we remember the past, we recall all of it—the good and the bad of it. The good is easier to remember. We comfortably recall the past joys of our lives and fall into nostalgic reminiscence. Anniversaries lend themselves to such practices. We get out pictures of our weddings or our children's births or their graduations and recall all the joy and promise those events contained. When we do so we bring that past along with us into the present and keep the past incorporated in our ongoing narrative. Remembering past joys is another way to practice appreciation and reverence.

The practice of remembering also makes it possible to pay attention to the bad and harmful things of the past. Remembering can give recognition to the traumas and losses of our lives and so preserve what was lost, at least in memory. Remembering, therefore, honors the traumas and losses in time by not allowing the march of time to leave the past behind. Memorials are often intended for this purpose. The Vietnam War memorial lists in stone the name of each and every American soldier who died in that war. As long as that memorial stands, those soldiers are remembered.

Many of us do not want to remember the traumas of the past. In fact, one of the dynamics of trauma, as we have observed, is a forgetting, a splitting off of memory. Sigmund Freud taught us that melancholic repetition is not about remembering, but its opposite. Trauma resists remembrance. This makes it all the more important to find ways to bring past trauma into living memory.

Remembering is a practice not only for those who have experienced the trauma or loss, but also for those who are or were witness to it. Trauma survivors are often helped in their remembering by having their experience recognized and acknowledged by witnesses. The Vietnam War memorial serves that purpose. The nature of that memorial, whose design was considered quite controversial, has affected the way that war is remembered, including the traumatic experiences of soldiers. The memorial does not glorify war; it acknowledges loss.

Remembering the past invites us into grieving. Traumatic losses especially need to be grieved, but the remembrance of the joys of the past also contains elements of loss. Even as we rejoice in our children's growth, we mourn the passing of their childhood. The grieving that accompanies life's transitions is balanced by the joy. The grieving of traumatic loss contains no such balance. Remembering trauma produces overwhelming and sometimes seemingly unrelenting grief. No wonder the survivors of trauma resist entering into the memories that would require such mourning.

Our culture allows little time or space for grieving. We are culturally untutored in mourning. As a result, many of us are not practiced at it. If we are going to remember the losses of the past in a way that honors time, we need to learn how to grieve and to take grieving seriously. The work of mourning takes time. We cannot mourn if we do not stop and give ourselves over to the feelings and disorientation that characterize the experience of acute grief.

Given the many changes that we undergo in a lifetime, over which we have little control and each of which has loss attached to it, many of us live with losses left behind and unmourned. Instead of turning toward the past to revisit and work through these losses, we have been trained to cast our attention forward and hope for a final resolution that will put everything in place. I have argued that such hope is false.

We will learn to hope anew as we find ways to practice remembering and mourning. We can glean lessons about such practices from those who attend to the dynamics of trauma. We can also learn from those among us who have preserved ways to honor the dead and to remember loss. The Mexican custom of marking the Day of the Dead is one example of a practice that is able to combine mourning for loss and rejoicing in connection. It is about making time to remember, as well as negotiating the dynamics of attachments in the past and the present. As an annual event, the Day of the Dead ceremonies make clear that the process of remembering, mourning, and incorporating the losses of the past is ongoing. Honoring time is a repetitive and yet ever-changing and developing practice.

Moving in Place

A second habit of hope we need to cultivate pays attention to place and to embodiment and physicality. An emphasis on concrete existence is foundational to Judaism and Christianity. God's act of creation not only inaugurated history, it also brought the earth and the universe into being. Creation thus marked the beginning of time and of place. As the narrative of the biblical creation story tells us, God created a garden and placed human creatures, as well as other created things, there. Being human, being creatures, means being located, specifically and concretely. We human beings are our bodies, and our bodies are always placed.

Because our bodies take up space, that space is unavailable to other bodies. Space, as we experience it, is a limited commodity. Our bodies are also characterized by their limits: how far we can reach, how fast we can run. Given modern and postmodern cultural trends and ways of thinking that have tended to abstract human beings from both our embodiment and our placement, we often do not pay sufficient attention to this dimension of our lives. We pretend there are no limits and that growth and expansion can be unlimited. We forget that we take up space and that the earth has only so much space, so many resources. We ignore the concreteness of our locatedness and our finitude. The habit of moving in place recognizes the need for growth and development, but also pays attention to available space and resources.

To develop this habit of moving in place, which means taking our concrete embodiment seriously, we need to practice setting limits. In order to set limits we have to recognize sufficiency, which, in turn, means being able to assess what we need. This is not so easy for many of us in the West. The technological, capitalist worldview, which many of us inhabit, is all about unlimited expansion and infinite growth. The late capitalist economy that drives this worldview requires unchecked consumption and industrial and corporate expansion. This means that people do not buy what they need, but what they think they want or need, as those are defined for them by advertising and by the market. As a result, those of us who live in affluent western societies no longer are in touch with our needs or even our real wants. We are not practiced at sensing sufficiency and knowing how to set limits.

The measuring meters we might use do not work. This is true on every level of our living. We do not practice setting limits in terms of our bodies. Many of us overeat (or we develop eating disorders) and overwork; we do not sleep enough and are not attuned to our bodies' needs. We rely on medication to correct what gets out of balance as a result of our bad habits. Nor do we practice sufficiency in relation to our lifestyle. Many Americans carry immense amounts of personal debt. We buy beyond our means and our needs, having succumbed to what advertising and a sense of competition tell us we need. There seems no end to our spending or our acquiring. There is always a larger house or a newer car or another luxury item beckoning us.

Our government does no better; its behavior reflects and reinforces our bad habits. The national debt is staggering. A mentality of infinite expansion drives the economy. We assume the world and the universe is ours for the taking. There seems to be no limit to our country's sense of power.

On every level, our society needs to become more practiced at sufficiency, setting limits, and honoring them. Practicing sufficiency will help us to inhabit our lives and our bodies better. This requires relearning our desires. We are often out of touch with what we really want. We get distracted by whatever is presented to us and what seems readily available. In other words, we respond to outside stimuli—the new car being advertised on TV or the chocolate candies sitting in the break room at work—rather than being attuned to our internal needs and wants. We let those stimuli direct our desires.

We also confuse hope with wish fulfillment. We may wish we had a bigger house or a more powerful car. Then we let those wishes define our hopes: we hope for such things. When we do so, we tend to get even more confused between what is necessary and sufficient for the good life and what constitutes our consuming desires. Learning to practice sufficiency requires that we sort out such confusions.

There is a long spiritual and theological tradition about desire and the way in which sin or, to use an old-fashioned term, concupiscence, affects our desires. Concupiscence is, in fact, misdirected desire. We struggle both with misdirected desires and with desires that know no bounds.

As we learn to recognize limits, to know what enough means, our desires will become better directed. One set of practices that might help us re-train ourselves may be drawn from spiritual traditions and their disciplines. Earlier, I wrote about St. Benedict's fourth vow of stability and the disciplined life he outlined for his monks. Stability and discipline set external boundaries; they regulate behavior. Their purpose, however, is to enable monks and nuns to develop an internal life, to become more in touch with who they are and what they truly want. In monastic traditions, disciplines are about training and directing the monks' and nuns' desires and spirits toward the divine or toward truth. The disciplines are not meant to be ends in themselves but means toward enlightenment or deepening love and service or union with the divine.

Many spiritual traditions require their practitioners, especially the novice ones, to step outside their "normal" lives and withdraw for a period of time. Whether for the purpose of retreat or to undergo initiation, such withdrawal involves eliminating outside distractions in order to focus energy and attention. Quite often such withdrawal is accompanied by some form of fasting or, at least, disciplined eating and drinking, and includes following a prescribed schedule of activities, whether of prayer, meditation, or other spiritual practices. Among these may be ascetical practices that focus on disciplining the body as well as the spirit.

Unfortunately, we find in the histories of Christian spirituality and of other traditions numerous examples, such as self-flagellation, of such disciplines being distorted and used harmfully. They then function to deny limits and embodiment rather than to cultivate healthy practices. Despite these distortions, however, we can continue to glean wisdom from these traditions in order to become more in tune with our real needs and with the desires we are seeking to serve.

Withdrawing from outside stimuli is a valuable practice. When we stop running around busily in our over-scheduled lives and eliminate such things as watching television and surfing the Internet, we are engaging in a type of fasting. Such withdrawal, when we first attempt it, may be very difficult. We may well feel as if we are struggling with an addiction. We will want a "fix"; we will crave outside stimuli. If we can get through those feelings, however, we will come to a different level of awareness. We may sleep more or notice what is around us in a different way. We will begin to appreciate being and not only doing. But most importantly, we will begin to get back in touch with ourselves and our desires. Once that happens, we can slowly begin to assess what it is we really want and need, and contemplate what is enough and sufficient for us. We may also develop an appreciation for and a valuing of what we do have.

Developing such attitudes will not be easy or quick. They are so counter to many of our cultural messages that we will meet resistance, both external and internal, at every step of the way. Such resistance can best be dealt with not by fighting against it, but by recognizing its power and moving out of the way. We can draw wisdom here from some of the Asian martial arts traditions that "fight" by yielding and moving in such a way that the aggressor is thrown off balance and the attack is rendered ineffective. Moving in place may mean learning to get out of the way in order to protect ourselves from harm.

Another practice that would help us learn to move in place is patience. I myself am a very impatient person. I hate to wait. Therefore, I have no illusions about how difficult it is to be patient, to allow the necessary time. But I also know that so much of what happens in life happens *to* us, without our inviting it or wanting it. None of us wants to get cancer, but many of us do. None of us wants to lose loved ones, but not one of us can prevent death. These realities are part of our finitude; they are givens of life.

Patience may seem more a practice of honoring time than embracing embodiment. Waiting is, after all, in time. I have chosen, however, to include patience as a practice of embodiment because it is ultimately about finitude and about not being in control of our environment. We become impatient when we cannot get what we want when we want it. Or we react negatively when we have things, such as cancer, that we do not want. Such moments remind us of the limits of our abilities; they are indicators of our finitude. We cannot make everything happen when we want it, any more than we can cure a cancer overnight.

Patience means taking things as they come. It entails recognizing that everything has its time and place. Oddly, there is considerable similarity between being patient and being a patient. When we are sick, we are made acutely aware of the limitations of our bodies and the reality that we do not have full control over them and what happens to them. Both being a patient and being patient require a certain giving over (but not giving up) and allowing what needs to happen, to happen.

Practices of withdrawal and patience will help us develop a habit of dynamic embodiment or moving in place. Taking location seriously and placing ourselves concretely does not mean that our lives are static or that the limits of our embodiment are absolute. Valuing stability is not the same as being static. Finitude is not constriction. Patience is not passivity.

As we learn to inhabit our bodies fully and explore the habitation of place, we will discern that the dynamics of place are complex and even contradictory. We have been so trained to fear finitude that it may be difficult to see that it actually breeds possibility. Limits offer a type of security: a stability that engenders exploration and experimentation. Finitude implies provisionality and ambiguity. Since we have no absolute vantage point or destination, anything we know or do is subject to change and to the effects of powers we cannot see or fully determine. There is risk in any movement. Our vision is partial. Therefore, there is always the need to adjust and to improvise.

In the history of Christian theological thought, as we have seen, finitude was most often opposed to freedom. Human beings were understood to be pulled between freedom and finitude. Their dilemma was that the two could not be reconciled. Human beings yearned for freedom but were "caught" by finitude, due either to their nature as creatures or because of their sin. As long as freedom and finitude remain opposed, finitude will be seen as problematic, or else freedom will be deemed a temptation rather than a true desire. If finitude implies provisionality, however, then freedom becomes necessary to finitude and finitude to freedom. Freedom keeps finitude from being constricting. Finitude teaches freedom sufficiency. Freedom is most fully realized not in opposition to finitude but in relation to it. Another practice then of embodiment is keeping freedom and finitude in relation.

To the extent that we do so, we will also practice authenticity. We will be true to ourselves as provisional, located beings. Our integrity comes through recognizing our contingency and our creaturely embodiment, as does our creativity. We are not to stand in place, but to move, to dance, to be in dynamic interaction. We are our bodies, in space and time, but our bodies are essentially energy and dynamism. We are always on the move, even in our most still moments. Being able to live in and with that reality is what the habit of moving in place is all about.

Imagining Creatively

Yet another habit of hope is that of imagining creatively. This habit requires that we free up and exercise our imaginations. Without the capacity to imagine, it would be difficult to speak of hope. The more we imagine, the more hope will grow. A habit of creative and free imagining is then crucial for living in hope.

Unfortunately, our imaginations have become constricted. They have been colonized by the onslaughts of the media, by the dynamics of late capitalist economics, by a culture of fear that serves the interests of the dominant powers, and by a traditionalist ethos that is bent on preserving what is, rather than imagining what might be. In all these ways, our imaginations have become preoccupied with the *status quo*. As a result, they have atrophied. In order to develop a habit of imagining creatively, we need to exercise and train our imaginations.

Imagination is rooted in desire and yearning for the righting of wrongs, for the realization of growth, for the fulfillment of promises. The biblical witness is shot through with such desire and yearning: the blind will see, the deaf will hear, captives will be released, and the poor will be fed. And there is more: deserts will bloom and lions will lie down with lambs. There will be peace and harmony and justice. For the biblical writers, these things are imagined and portrayed as God's promises.

They represent not only God's promises but also God's passion. God's deepest desire is for the life of the created order and all that is in it. This divine passion forms us and abides in our hearts. It is the source of our imaginative energy. Imagination begins then in passion, in the practice of passion.

As we learn the contours of our own desires that are not distorted or directed by external lures and temptations, we will begin to feed our passion. Passion lives in the utmost core of our beings. It is the energy of our hearts giving us life and breath. Our passion enables us to feel and be alive, fully alive.

Passion as energy is wild and powerful. It is a driving force in all that we do. The power of such energy can be dangerous and potentially harmful. Our passion can blind us or carry us off to oblivion. Just as desires need discipline, so does passion. We need to pay attention to how and what we feed our passion in order to practice it with care. We need to direct it into creativity.

Passion provides the power for our imagining. It is the organic energy source that moves us not to settle for what is, but to dare to envision something other and different. For centuries, the word *passion* has been used in Christianity to name and describe the suffering of Jesus on the cross. Actually, the word has several meanings: desire, suffering, and zeal. These meanings suggest that desire and zeal and suffering are related, which is to say that we may suffer for the things we care about and give ourselves to. The "outcome" of passion is, therefore, not necessarily success but devotion. It was Jesus' desire and zeal, his devotion to what he understood to be his mission. that resulted in his death on the cross.

In the practice of passion, we need not only to find our way through its dangers but also to test the capacity of our devotion. The depth of our passion is measured by that devotion and by what we are willing to live for and give our lives to. Such passion takes form and finds expression in imagination and envisioning.

To imagine is to dream. It is to dare, as the Bible suggests, to dream dreams and see visions. When we dream, we channel our passion, our energy of desire, into form and expression. The power and role of imagination is to give voice and content to our heart's desire. The practice of dreaming helps to connect our desires with our imagination.

Often our dreams, especially of change and transformation, grow out of our discontent and our thwarted desire. We want to make justice in the face of injustice and establish freedom in the place of tyranny. But our dreams also emerge from our creativity and our yearning for goodness and beauty and truth. We imagine ways to wholeness. We envision lush and colorful landscapes, nurturing and joyous households, and realms of justice. Both discontent and creativity are important and necessary sources for our dreams. Being able to envision change in our present circumstances and to imagine a different and better life are fundamental to being able to hope.

Hope, however, in its joy and wild power goes further. It not only imagines the righting of wrongs and the betterment of what is, but it also brings into conception what never existed and may never have even been entertained in thought. The word "conceive" means both to begin the process of coming to birth and to think or to bring into thought. Our imagining is a process of birthing, of bringing into being and life what has not existed until now.

Often, it is the orators and revolutionaries, artists and inventors—those we name as visionaries—that lead the way in our imagining. Who would have imagined, we might say, that Pablo Picasso could evoke so much expression through abstract shapes or that scientists could take human beings to the moon? Who would have predicted the world of computers we now take for granted? Where would this country be without the words of Martin Luther King Jr. and the vision of justice and equality he created for us all? How different would women's lives be today if the early feminists had not dared to imagine themselves in places—such as pulpits and executive offices—from which women had been excluded or if they had not begun to listen seriously to women's stories of abuse and harm and dreamt of safe shelters where women and children might find refuge? So much of what we value in our world is there because of those who dared to dream dreams and those who worked to make those dreams reality.

These visionaries may be our most grand dreamers, but all of us are capable of using our imaginations. Imagining creatively is not only a habit of hope; it is also essential to our being human. The ability to imagine helps to make us human. We human beings have the capacity to see beyond the immediate. We are able to dream of and envision what is not concretely in existence. This ability to imagine, cultivated into a habit, is fundamental to our fullness of life.

As I have suggested, we need to practice dreaming and to exercise our imaginations. There are a number of conditions that would help us in our regiment of exercise. One such condition is having time and space, set aside, when we are not too distracted and busy with the demands of everyday life. Case in point: Virginia Woolf, in *A Room of One's Own*, argues that for there to be more women novelists, women need to have rooms of their own. They need to be able to get away from others and the needs and wants of others and to focus their attention, which is to say, they need to be able to devote their passion.

Another condition that would aid our imagining is freedom, especially in the sense of being unoccupied. To be free then is to be unencumbered by other obligations. We say to our friends: "Yes, I am free to come to dinner on Saturday. I am otherwise unoccupied." Being free also means not being preoccupied, which so many of us are. Our preoccupations, in the form of worries and fears and anxieties, block our imaginations.

These preoccupations are often produced by cultural colonization. As I have indicated, we are colonized, or occupied, by cultural
definitions and controls that restrict and constrict us. We literally
cannot imagine other possibilities when we have so internalized cultural messages that tell us who we are, what we want, and what we can
and cannot do. Some of these messages are easier to see and name
than others. African Americans have been claiming for decades that
American culture is replete with images and ideas that equate white
with good and black with bad or evil. The women's movement has
raised questions about cultural definitions of femininity that restrict
women's options.

It is not enough to unveil these distorted ideas. The point of colonization is that these ideas have been internalized. African
Americans and women and the colonized have to come to terms
with the fact that they themselves believe these things and so need to
challenge the power and control of these perceptions. In this culture,
all of us experience colonization, albeit not all in the same ways or
with the same intensity. As a result, none of us is fully free from occu-
pation. Freeing ourselves is an ongoing practice and a necessary condition for creative imagining.

What we imagine, dream, and desire will shape our hope and give
it content. In passionate devotion, we will seek to realize our hopes
and actualize what we imagine. We will not only dream of a society in
which all are equal, but we will also work to make that happen. We will
not only imagine a world in which more powerful nations do not
bully and impoverish smaller, struggling countries, but we will also
find ways to put in place international guidelines and standards that
would effectively hold nations to account.

In other words, we will actively participate in making our dreams
come true. We will work hard to turn possibilities into realities. Just as
we cannot claim something as a value unless we act on it, we cannot
say we are passionate about justice or peace or health care or public
education or arts in the schools or community centers for the elderly
unless we commit ourselves fully to making such things happen.

However, and this is key, if the power of our hope and the purpose
of our imagining are defined by the success of such actions, then our
hope will quickly evaporate. Hope needs to be in and through the
commitments we hold and the dreams we embrace, whatever may be

the outcome of our work. In that sense, the habit of creative and free imagining is an end in and of itself. The act of imagining strengthens our hope. In turn, our imagining is strengthened as we work to accomplish what we imagine. We are to find value and joy in the process, at the same time that we give our all to making our dreams come true and accomplishing our desired outcomes. This means we do not invest ourselves too much in those results. We do not depend too much on their realization even as we devote ourselves fully to that realization. This is a difficult and different way to be in the world—one is which we are not sufficiently practiced. Knowing we are not alone in this process will help us become more adept.

Participating in Interrelation

We do not hope alone; nor can we cultivate these habits by ourselves. We need the support of others in order to engage in the practice of hope, and we need to support others in their practice. Hope is ultimately a social habit, not simply a personal and spiritual one. If our practices are to produce social change, then it is important to attend to their communal and institutional dimensions. Such attention begins with the recognition that everything and everyone is interconnected. This recognition results in, but is also dependent upon, practicing interconnection and interrelation.

In numerous fields of study today, more and more attention is being given to relationship and interconnection. Scientists are seeing webs of relation as essential to life, on the smallest and grandest scales. Thich Nhat Hanh uses the term *interbeing* to ground his ethics of connection. All being is interrelated, and, therefore, everything we do affects everything else. Feminist thinkers have also been reacquainting us with the importance and necessity of relation. As cultural values of separation and autonomy are challenged, our sensibilities and practices are beginning to shift.

As I narrated in the introduction, I grew up in a family and an ethnic milieu that began with the whole and moved to the parts rather than *vice versa*. The family and the ethnic group were central and determining. My personhood existed within and among those connections. Independence and autonomy were not valued; in fact, they were seen as threats. My familial/ethnic milieu clashed with the prevailing ethos of American culture that I was learning through my public school education. The ethos of that dominant culture seemed to value independent action, autonomy, and individuality. Adulthood and maturity were defined by separation and independence; success was measured by individual achievement. Sometimes I was embarrassed and confused by these differences between my familial and ethnic values and what I experienced at school, but mostly I was caught in their crossfire and had a difficult time choosing one over the other. Even though, on the surface, I "left home," I carried with me the sense of fundamental relatedness.

The connectedness of my Armenian family had a particular character. It was not about being committed to one another as a moral virtue or even an act of love. Nor was it about recognizing the importance of family and social groupings. Rather, the connectedness was characterized by participation. If the whole precedes the parts, then our position is always one of participating, of being part of the whole. Ideas such as "interbeing" or the web of life reflect a similar perspective that is not just connection across difference but being part of one another, part of all that is.

In order to foster such participation, we need to change our habits of separation and not living in relation. We need to cultivate the habit of "interbeing," of being in relation. Such a change will also require us to reexamine the high value placed on autonomy that permeates so many of the theories of development, education, and behavior in our culture. There are a number of practices that will contribute to the formation of this habit of participating in interrelation.

One is a practice of thankfulness or gratitude. If we give thanks for our lives on a regular basis, then we may become more aware of how our lives are contingent and connected with the lives of others. In a way, we might realize our lives are not our own. In order to express gratitude, we need someone or something to address when we give thanks. Many of us direct our gratitude toward God in prayer. An everyday example is saying grace. Each time we say grace and give thanks, we are admitting that our lives are not all our doing, that what happens to us is not simply the direct result of our actions. If we begin to practice thankfulness regularly and think about where, along with God, to direct our gratitude, then we will begin to deepen a sense of interrelation. Imagine how our sense of relatedness might change if we thanked the chicken who gave its life for our dinner, or thanked the sun for providing warmth and energy, or thanked the person in China who made our clothes.

Giving thanks is a practice of mindfulness. It will help us become more aware of who we are and how our lives are intertwined with other lives, not only in the present but also in the past. African Americans refer to the shoulders on which they stand that brought them to this place in their lives. Other communities imagine the ancestors or the communion of saints who accompany them in their lives. It not only "takes a village to raise a child," but a child's life is also the village's and *vice versa*: village and child "inter-are."

Another practice of interrelation, one that flows from thankfulness, is reciprocity. To practice reciprocity does not mean to engage in "tit for tat" exchanges or to keep accounts. Reciprocity is not about balance, but about recognizing the depth of relation. If everything is interrelated, then there is always a going back and forth, a dynamic of mutuality.

My understanding of reciprocity is similar to the Christian idea of *perichoresis*. In Christian theology, *perichoresis* is a concept used to describe the relationship among the persons of the Trinity. It means mutual indwelling, such that the persons, while distinct, participate in one another. The persons of the Trinity are defined not by their separation but by their relations. In other words, the first person of the Trinity, who has traditionally been named Father, only is Father in relation to the second person, traditionally named Son. "Father" is a term of relation, not a name, which is to say, there is no "Father" and "Son" apart from one another. The Spirit also is Spirit in and through the relations of the Trinity. The three are defined by their relations.

When we practice reciprocity we, too, are participating in a type of *perichoresis* of the whole of creation. Given our finitude and the limits of our existence, we cannot achieve full indwelling, but we can approximate it as reciprocity. The character of reciprocity is dynamic; it results from the energy of relation. Interrelation is the energy flow between and among all that is. Because energy does not move in one direction but in all directions, reciprocity is a constant movement.

Another practice that both supports and is supported by the practices of thankfulness and reciprocity is generosity. To practice generosity is to eschew selfishness and fearfulness about scarcity. A generous spirit believes that there is abundance enough for all to live and that our living will be enhanced by giving freely of what we have. Generosity is a practice in the sense that, in any given circumstance, we are asked to consider how much we are willing to share and to give and to be open. Some people may seem to be generous by nature, but I think generosity is more a disposition that is formed through practice. As we practice generosity, we will become generous. The more aware we become of our interconnection, the more we will realize that sharing is not a giving away *per se*, but an act of nurturing dynamic relation.

Thus, generosity is not just a matter of sharing things or resources. It is an act of interrelation and an attitude. When we treat others with generosity, we accept them for who they are and think the best of them. We let go of any attempt to control them, and we approach them with open arms and hearts.

As we engage in these practices, we will become more attuned to interrelation. In turn, as that habit forms us, we will notice that who we are and what we want and need will no longer be the first and last consideration. We will begin to consider other perspectives; our own will not be the only reference point. We will not always automatically see ourselves as the center of the universe. Slowly, we will begin to de-center. Attention will shift to the dynamics of connection and interrelation.

At the same time, we will also develop more awareness of the value of our attachments. De-centering ourselves and valuing attachments may seem to be contradictory or opposed movements, but in actuality they are deeply connected. Psychologists who study the nature and dynamics of attachment are finding that we human beings are formed fundamentally by our attachments. The love, stability, and feedback provided through attachments are what allow us to develop whole selves. Attachment disorders, and related phenomena such as narcissistic personality disorders, can result from lack of appropriate attachment during a child's development. To be attached means to be connected, literally. Children and adults with attachment disorders are not able to connect in sustained and healthy ways. If we are to form a habit of interrelation, we need to be able to experience and practice authentic attachments.

Those who have been nurtured through healthy attachments are able to let go more easily. Children who have experienced appropriate and nurturing attachments have a much easier time differentiating themselves from their parents. Because they have known positive growth through relationship, they are able to trust the bonds of attachment and so not cling to them. Similarly for all of us, our attachments help us to take risks, rather than live out of fear and a need to be protective. The ability to trust, rooted in a sense of safety nurtured by attachment, enables us to let go.

Such letting go, however, does not mean being unattached. Rather, as we practice interrelation, our ability to connect will deepen, expand, and multiply. A self that is well-grounded in attachment is able to move along the webs of relation easily, as electric current flows through wires. The grounding provides safety enough for power to be released.

Implied in what I have been saying about attachment is the judgment that there are relationships that nurture healthy selves and those that are harmful. In actuality, most of the relationships we experience are a combination of both. And inevitably, our own relational practices are always a mixture. We cause harm, however much we try not to. Tragically, such harm seems unavoidable. The best we can do is to be aware of this inevitability and try to minimize the harm.

Therefore, the intent of our practice is not only interrelation but also right relation. Right relations seek to maximize the energy of connection through guaranteeing the conditions necessary for human flourishing. These include safety and care, justice and peace, and most especially freedom. There is no possibility of right relation without freedom. Freedom is the capacity to be fully present to others and the world. It is the ability to make connection, not out of fear or coercion, but from a desire for fullness of life. Freedom empowers connections and gives them life. Such freedom is different from autonomy and the freedom that has been opposed to finitude, which are so often defined by separation and an absence of connection, limitation, and contingency.

As discussed earlier, justice, peace, and freedom are not ends to be accomplished. As conditions necessary for human flourishing and life, they are values and ongoing tasks of the practice of right relation. By practicing right relation and cultivating a habit of interrelation, we will begin to inhabit the world differently. All the habits we have discussed so far contribute to such habitation.

Living in Wild Wonder

The last habit I would propose is living in wild wonder, as habit/at and "divine milieu" (to borrow a term from Teilhard de Chardin). That may seems a startling suggestion. What does wild wonder mean? Why should we nurture it as our habitat? How is it descriptive of the divine milieu? And in what sense is it a habit? I will respond to those questions in a somewhat roundabout way.

As we have seen, postmodernism has knocked the supports out from a modern worldview. In modernity, not only were human beings the center of the universe, but the universe was also understood to be subject to human decision and human control. Human beings saw themselves as being in charge of history and of the created order. That order was built on certain set foundations. History followed a given, overarching narrative. Postmodernism has dislodged human beings from center stage and dismantled the structures that supported universal foundations and given truths. Who or what then is postmodernism able to offer as the stand-in or as the replacement in the drama of life?

Various strains of postmodernism offer different answers. One strain would suggest that there is no fundamental order, that all is chance and/or the outcome of plays of power. Whoever may take center stage is only acting, pretending to know the play and the outcome. If they can make us believe them, then they have control of "reality." All of us are, in a sense, players in this drama: we are what we perform or speak. This strain of postmodernism reduces all of what we know either to the dynamics of power or to language or performance.

In addition, with no givens and no fixed universe, life is characterized by a kind of wildness. What we know as life is ultimately not rational or ordered. It is not a function of what, in the West, has been highly prized as civilization. There is a raw and potentially harsh character to this approach to life. Such a view of life may make many of us uncomfortable. We expect to live in an ordered universe—and a moral one—in which nature operates by set laws and, at the end of the day, fairness and goodness prevail. The suggestion that chaos or nonmoral forces are the heart of life is unsettling, if not threatening.

Another strain of postmodernism—or more accurately, reaction to postmodernism—emerges from a very different direction. It suggests that once the cold rationality of modern thought is cleared away, we will experience a re-enchantment of the world. Once we give up the illusion that human beings are the ones in charge and calling the shots, then we will encounter the world, the universe, and the divine anew. We will experience a sense of wonder, something like what has been termed a "second naiveté." Our whole stance toward life will shift toward a more receptive mode, one that is attuned and attentive to the fundamental mystery of life. Whether that mystery is termed God or life or the energy of the universe, it is something in which we participate. It is not something that we can manipulate or that is subject to our control. It is, however, good.

Some postmodern thinkers, who see the world moving into a time of re-enchantment, are often motivated by conservatism and a desire to retrieve tradition. They want to return to an earlier, pre-modern perspective, when God and the divine order were the ruling actors on stage. Other thinkers, however, see re-enchantment not as a return to an earlier worldview, but as a new and heretofore unexperienced perspective. Re-enchantment for them involves learning anew the nature of mystery and seeing that life is itself mystery. While not trying to reinstate foundations nor offer a meta-narrative, these thinkers find themselves experiencing amazement and wonder and deep appreciation.

My proposed habit/at of wild wonder combines elements of these seemingly divergent postmodern responses: one that underscores existence as raw and wild, the other that focuses on wonder. Each response contains apprehensions that deserve to be honored and that might be helpful in our efforts to learn a different way of inhabiting our lives. They can also keep each other honest, so to speak. A sense of enchantment and wonder in life would soften the edge off an approach to life that sees it as somewhat arbitrary, so much the outcome of plays of power. Meanwhile, keeping in mind the seeming arbitrariness of life, the untamed power of forces beyond any human control, and the terrors and tragedies that life holds would keep a sense of wonder from becoming too ungrounded and romantic or reactionary.

In this postmodern landscape, wild wonder describes our experience of the divine. The God of the Bible is neither tame nor predictable. That God is portrayed as both exquisitely tender and overwhelmingly forceful. God is imaged as a nursing mother and a thundering storm, as a still small voice and a violent wind. However God is experienced or imagined, the divine is most surely mystery that evokes from us a sense of wonder and awe. The long poem at the end of the book of Job, in which God questions Job, offers striking images of God's raw power, especially in and through the forces of nature: "Can you lift up your voice to the clouds, so that a flood of waters may cover you? Can you send forth lightnings, so that they may go and say to you, 'Here we are'? Who has put wisdom in the inward parts or given understanding to the mind?" (Job 38:34–36).

In the Bible, awe of God is often referred to as the fear of God. The idea of fear contains both the sense of wonder and of the wild. The early twentieth-century historian of religion Rudolf Otto spoke of the holy or the numinous as *mysterium tremendum et fascinans*—overwhelming, awe- or fear-inspiring, and fascinating mystery. Otto's description conveyed a sensibility similar to what I am proposing.

The divine is mystery that is known as wild and wondrous. As we cultivate the habits of honoring time, moving in place, imagining creatively, and participating in interrelation, we will move more into this divine milieu of wild wonder. We will find our hearts opening and our bodies grounding. We will feel surging energy of and for life. Knowing that we are encountering what is transcendent, we will also feel awe and even apprehension. The divine energy encountered in the wild does not offer comfort but life, in ways that may surprise us. It draws us into uncharted terrain, which we must learn to navigate differently.

The habits of honoring time, moving in place, imagining creatively, and participating in interrelation come together to help us live in this terrain of wild wonder. The practices of reverence, thankfulness, and receptivity, which thread through all the habits, contribute to grounding us in a habit/at of wild wonder. Instead of fighting what is unknown and that feels unsettling, these practices help us to receive and honor the challenges we encounter. In this milieu, we are not the center of the universe. As we human beings move out of center stage and are able to take in more of the wide, wild expanse of life, we begin to experience wild wonder as habit/at.

Another practice that helps that movement into wild wonder is ritual. Ritual is the experience of transcendence and communion: of being swept up, of drinking deeply, of entering into mystery as participants. Ritual is enactment. In ritual, all our habits can come together and find expression. Ritual is the performance of mystery. It is serious play that re-creates the world and transforms us.

It is through ritual that we experience, come to know, and give expression to mystery as our habitation. The practice of ritual teaches us that there is more to life than we can see or know, that we are fundamentally connected as life-forms across time and space, that our definitions of time and space are weak vessels to contain the wild wonder of the universe.

Ritual intensifies life. In ritual, the mundane and the extraordinary are wedded in performance that requires us to be fully present: in mind and body, with our senses and our sensibilities, with our intelligence and our intuition, feeling and acting and thinking all at once. At the same time, we are taken out of ourselves, de-centered and even destabilized, in a way that opens us up to the divine, wild power.

Ritual is a practice in two senses of that word. As performance, as something we do, ritual is practiced; it is enacted. But the performance of ritual also takes practice and requires intentionality. We are able to learn the ways of ritual and become better practiced at the creating and doing of ritual. It is a sensibility and a skill that we can develop. The more we develop our ritual capabilities, the more we will cultivate the habit of living in wild wonder.

We so often think of ritual as ordered, patterned behavior that includes a good deal of repetition. We view ritual as something static and unchanging. Ritualists tend to be traditionalists whose slogan is: "This is the way we have always done things." If ritual is so ordered and so unchanging, so tame, how does it help us live in wild wonder?

The answer is that ritual is not something rigid or tame, though its practitioners often make it so. Then ritual devolves into ritualism. Ritual itself, however, is alive. It orders performance to provide an overall structure, but the purpose of the structure is to make connections and to release energy. It is the context for improvisation, especially if we are attune to wild wonder.

Many of the practices already discussed in this chapter contribute to good rituals, especially ones that help us be mindful and attentive and to think holistically. One other practice that would be helpful is humility. It may seem very surprising to suggest humility as a practice to cultivate a habit of wild wonder. I do not, however, mean humility as self-abasement. Too often the practice of humility has been equated with behaviors and attitudes that diminish the self. Humility has been imposed on the less powerful as a sign of their station, and in a way that is harmful.

Rather, I mean humility as a stance of agency, of going with the flow of energy and steering a course that uses the available power. Such humility is about de-centering ourselves. Humility requires recognition of our contingency and our dependence on the energy of life. It is about knowing we do not keep ourselves alive. Although we are agents, we are not in control or in charge. We are part of the action but not its lone director. In fact, there is no singular director. The practice of humility recognizes that. It yields to wild wonder.

Wild wonder is power and beauty and truth, all in living, breathing, pulsing connection. Wild wonder as divine milieu is so present and available that it permeates the very air we breathe. At the same time, it is constantly in motion, seemingly just beyond the edge of what we can grasp. Immanent and transcendent, immanent as transcendent, transcendent as immanent, wild wonder is life itself.

Life as We Know It

The prescription for hope is living. Any and all of the practices and habits discussed here are meant for just that, to make life possible, abundant, and whole. It seems so simple really. And yet it turns out to be the most difficult thing of all. We get in our own way, setting up roadblocks and detours, sometimes even stopping dead in our tracks. And why? Because we do not trust life. We make enemies of time and place and imagination and interrelation. We make enemies of ourselves. We develop harmful habits that sap the energy of life from us. As a result, we do not inhabit our own lives, fully and powerfully.

The remedy is in coming home and setting up housekeeping, not in order to domesticate the wild but rather to embrace the embodiedness of human life. In coming home, we are committing to the habitation of life with all its complexities and contradictions and with its wildness. We are joining the improvisational dance. We make no claims to have reached a final destination nor are we giving up hope for change. Rather we are seeking to cultivate habits of hope for today, able to renew ourselves and our world. We are, to put it simply, having the time of our lives.

For Further Reading

Many of the ideas and practices outlined in this chapter can be found in texts already cited, as well in numerous works devoted to ritual and spirituality. Also available are a multitude of books dealing with the dynamics of change in our postmodern world. For example, *Presence: Human Purpose and the Field of the Future* by Peter Senge, C. Otto Scharmer, Joseph Jaworski, and Betty Sue Flowers (Cambridge, MA: Society for Organizational Learning, 2004) is structured as a conversation among the four authors, discussing change, creativity, and the future, especially in terms of organizations and organizational behavior. Margaret J. Wheatley's works, such as *Finding Our Way: Leadership for an Uncertain Time* (San Francisco: Berrett-Koehler Publishers, 2005) apply ideas about change to dynamics of leadership in organization and communities. For a further understanding of the dynamics of ritual practice, see Catherine Bell's *Ritual Theory/Ritual Practice* (New York: Oxford University Press, 1992), a theoretical work that provides ways to think about habits and practices, embodiment, and power. A helpful book for looking at spiritual disciplines rooted in Benedictine spirituality is *Wisdom Distilled from the Daily: Living the Rule of St. Benedict Today* by Joan Chittister (San Francisco: HarperSanFrancisco, 1991).

EPILOGUE

Time's Tale

As we engage in intentional practices, cultivate new habits, and relearn the contours of hope, what will the effect be on how we tell time? How will time's tale change? We will find responses to such questions as we begin to live differently and understand ourselves in the world differently. The effects will emerge and grow from our practices and habits. Our narratives of time may well change to be less linear and ends-driven, not so relentlessly comedic and more multi-dimensional. We may become better schooled in living with complexity and multiplicity, ambiguity and indeterminacy. Hope may seem more muted than we have imagined it in the past, but no less real and perhaps more compelling. In fact, the character of hope, as we come to know it, will be better able to sustain and nurture us for life in this place and time. By giving us tools to live differently in this world, it will be a countercultural practice.

We are constantly choosing the cultural and religious practices we embrace and those we ignore, resist, or reject. In part, the intent of this book has been to make us more aware of these choices, especially the ones that the dominant cultural and religious narratives might ignore or hide. In these pages, I have brought to center stage marginalized experiences, traditions, and narratives. I have offered tools so that we can begin to perceive an array of options and, hopefully, choose more wisely.

I do not, however, mean to imply that our choosing is the independent action of an autonomous will. We are not lone dancers on the stage of life, directing our movements solely by ourselves. Our choosing is never unconnected or without constraint. Who we are is shaped in and through the matrix of all the competing and complex narratives, practices, and habits that form the dynamics of living today. Our "choosing" happens in and through our moving within that array, attuned to what is seen to be authentic and life-giving.

As we have seen, such movement has the character of improvisation. It is a dance of discovery and commitment, enacting freedom and expression. For those of us used to the prescribed choreography of ballet or ballroom dancing, improvisation can be intimidating. Trusting in ourselves and in others and in the connections between and among us all can be a fearful thing. In order to give ourselves over to improvisation, we need to risk that trust. If we try to control the process too much or if we hold back, the improvisation that is life will be stiff and even thwarted. Learning to trust is itself a challenge. What will help is the process itself. This improvisational dance moves back and forth among risk and reception and reflection, as we find our way anew, again and again.

Narrative Elements for Improvisation

In the introduction, I offered my own experiences of growing up in mid-twentieth-century America and described the two worlds I lived in as a child. I close this book by returning briefly to those worlds I inhabited.

In my recollection, when my grandmother lit incense and carried it through our house on the eve of the Sabbath, the rest of us did not accompany her. It was not a family ritual. We kept on doing whatever we were doing and, in essence, paid little attention to her. It was her ritual act, not ours, though we could not help but experience the effects of it: the lingering smoke and scent. When I think about that scene now, I am aware that it contained an odd juxtaposition of attention and inattention—or of divided attention. It seems an apt metaphor for the way we live in time and in the world.

In the context of my family's home in mid-twentieth-century America, my grandmother's actions were counter-cultural. Perhaps it would be more accurate to say they offered an alternative cultural practice and potentially a different way of being. But that practice was itself a cultural product vying for my allegiance amid other contenders. It represented the "old world" of Armenian, pre-modern, religious sensibilities. The rest of the family, having bought into the "new world" meaning of Saturday evening, was usually engaged in a variety of leisure activities, most notably watching television. Each Saturday at sunset, the juxtaposition of worlds was enacted, week after week.

These two worlds are not the only choices. They were not even the only two in my familial household. The submerged and not so submerged world of genocidal trauma was there as well, as was the world of first generation immigrants, caught between assimilation and resistance to assimilation, valuing achievement in the dominant culture and fearing it.

Most of us live in a complex of worlds, even though we may not always be attuned to them. The "mix" of worlds may vary widely among us, but the presence of some multiplicity is common and persistent. In keeping with the multiplicity of worlds, in these last pages, I offer, from the mixed world of my childhood, juxtaposed images of times—left side by side, with conflicts and contradictions unresolved.

Welcoming the Sabbath

One image of time is that of Sabbath. Our hope will be more nurtured as we come to understand the need for time as Sabbath. Sabbath time has a particular quality and character. It is time set aside, which is not time, at the same time. Sabbath is a stepping out of time, which yet reflects multiple views of time.

Sabbath time implies linearity. In the Genesis story of creation, God acted and "worked" for six days and rested on the seventh. Sabbath rest came after work, at the end of the process of creation. In this sequential view of time, which contains purpose and direction, the day of rest can be read not only as the end of the sequence, but also as a culmination and completion. Sabbath is earned, so to speak, by work. The character of Sabbath is known in contrast to the days of creation and of work. For Augustine, who closes *City of God* with the image of Sabbath rest to describe eternal life, the "seventh day," as he calls it, is the final epoch. It is about restoration and perfection, the final and full realization of God's intended purposes. It is the end of the journey through time of the City of God.

The practice of Sabbath, however, is cyclical. The Sabbath comes around again every week. It recurs regularly. Imagery for the Sabbath tends to highlight themes of return and restoration and reconciliation. A major emphasis is on being in right relation, with ourselves, one another, the world, and the divine. We step out of our daily work routines to remind ourselves of life and its value. We rest to restore ourselves. We return to our focus and true purpose. We also come back to the beginning of the weekly cycle. Sabbath rest ends by returning us to work, which, in turn, returns us to Sabbath rest.

The weekly cycle is repeated on a daily basis, in the rhythms of work and rest. It is also repeated in the cycles of Sabbath years, normally every seven, and in the Jubilee tradition, every fiftieth year. However the time of Sabbath is counted—by days or weeks or decades—the intent is for rest, restoration, reconciliation, and return. The imagery is of harmony and peace and balance.

Sabbath time is also in the moment. It is the time of mindfulness. It requires us to be attentive to time, slow time down, set it aside, live it in a particular way. Sabbath befriends time as our lives' milieus. It also recognizes time as God's. In those ways it seeks to honor time.

Most of all, however, Sabbath intensifies time by seeming to suspend what we think of as ordinary time. The point of Sabbath is to approximate eternity and to experience it in some small way. To be in Sabbath time is to be in God's time. Especially in Christianity, Sabbath rest is often a metaphor for life in eternity. Eternity is not, as we have seen, endless time, but without time. Paradoxically, Sabbath, by focusing on time and the qualities of our living in time, takes us out of time.

The intensification of time in Sabbath spills over into the week or into ordinary time. It is, in part, from the perspective of a Sabbath vision of eternity that we take note of life in ordinary time and see how it is lacking in justice and harmony, how we are not in right relation with one another and with creation. In this way, hope means putting Sabbath into history, an extension of what Rosemary Ruether is proposing through the idea of Jubilee (as discussed in chapter 3).

Day by Day, Work without End

When I was a child, I not only had chores in the household, such as drying dishes, but I also had jobs in the grocery store my parents owned and operated. We all did. It was a family business. One of the tasks my brother and I were responsible for was restocking the shelves that held canned goods and other non-perishable items. Every week, we would make a list of what was needed and then retrieve those items from the storage area. This was a never-ending task since, happily, the shelves would become increasingly bare as items sold during the week.

Work is never done. Alongside the image of Sabbath rest, I place that of work without end. For too long, the Genesis story has been read as narrating an opposition of work and rest, with work being a punishment for sin. Despite efforts by theologians to dignify work and afford it a place in God's intended order, the sense that work is something we have to do and that has been imposed upon us remains. In paradise, if we had not sinned, there would have been no compulsion to work.

Work, however, is part of living. As long as we are living, we are working in order to establish and maintain the necessary conditions of life, as well as that which makes life enjoyable. We are not only providing for basic needs but also toiling without ceasing for right relation. We are engaged in the tasks of restoration, restocking the shelves with justice and peace, freedom and harmony. As we have seen, these are not accomplishments, but values, processes, and tasks that require our diligence and endless energy.

Work time is both linear and cyclical. It is linear in the sense that there are tasks that we set as goals to be accomplished. Whether we are building a house or ridding the world of AIDS, we measure our work by how close we have come to achieving our goals. It is good and important and necessary that we set goals and move forward to reach them. But we ought not think of these accomplishments as once and for all.

Work time is also cyclical. In order to maintain and sustain life, there are tasks that need to be repeated again and again. Much of our work lives are taken up with the ongoing jobs of life: educating children, paying bills, making justice, working for peace, doing the laundry.

The cycles continue as more children are born, more bills are incurred, different or renewed demands for justice and peace are expressed, and dirty clothes pile up.

Work also catches us up in the moment with an intensification of time. Mindfulness in relation to the most mundane of tasks may open a window into eternity. The experience that has been described as "flow" can take us out of ourselves even as we are most inhabiting ourselves. Moments of solidarity with others and satisfaction in what we are doing carry their own intensity. Feeling community and deep connection through shared work is a profoundly powerful experience. Such a sense of connection is also a way into eternity, as is the joy we may derive from work itself and from seeing the results of our labors.

Hope then does not take us away from toil but into work in a different way. A narrative of hope is about work as a given of life and a blessing.

Playtime

When we were children, my brother created an imaginary day. He named this day Twensday, because it fell between Tuesday and Wednesday. On Twensday, my brother was in charge of all that happened. He made the rules. He wrote the narrative of life on Twensday. This game gave my brother tremendous power of which he was well aware. For example, once he told me that I had broken my arm on Twensday. For him, the creation of this day was a sibling's wish come true.

Along with being a wonderful tribute to my brother's imaginative power, the fantasy of Twensday provided him a way to negotiate the uncertainties and sense of powerlessness any child may experience in daily life. Since he was in charge of the narrative, he could make things turn out the way he wanted. Everyone and everything was subject to him.

My brother realized he was engaging in fantasy. He knew that Twensday was not a real day. However, the fantasy provided a very real way for him to deal with feelings and desires, both positive and negative. He could cause my arm to break and suffer no consequences. He could indulge himself however he wished.

Fantasy is an important element in a narrative of hope. It is a way both to intensify and also to step out of time and do so simultaneously.

It is a form of spontaneous play, able to help us deal with a whole range of feelings and realities of our lives.

Fantasies have the power to aid us with our fears and our terrors. They also allow us to deal with evil in a way that gives it power but does not necessarily leave us powerless. However, fantasies can work in the opposite way, too. As trauma survivors know, fantasies can be frightening and controlling. They can take over and render us more vulnerable to evil and to terror.

Problems also arise when we forget that we are playing and come to believe our fantasies as true. Then we are living in them, rather than having them help us live. We are able to mitigate such problems when we recognize that our fantasies as just that—fantasies.

Therefore, the key to a positive role for fantasy is realizing that we are engaged in play. Then fantasy can be a powerful tool for indulging our feelings, projecting at will, and managing our uncertainties and even fears. The thing about Twensday was that the Wednesday always came. My brother did not live in Twensday. He just played there for a while.

Because time is not set or absolute, because ultimately time is not a fixed thing, because we realize we are the authors of time's tale, we know these elements of telling time are just that: our stories about time. But they are the tales we live by, so what stories we tell and how we tell them shapes the character and power of our hope. Out of the mix of Sabbath rest and endless work and indulgent play, maybe, just maybe, hope will be born anew, again and again.

God's Story and Ours

The living God is known in and through the process of living. This is a God of improvisation, an abundant energy, powerful and ever-moving. This God is ground of our hope.

The monarchical God, reigning in heaven, so often portrayed as the object and goal of our hope, is not adequate for the dynamic and complex vision of life we need today. Nor is a God made in our image as loving parent, granting our every desire, able to provide the hope needed in our day.

The God of life, ground of hope, speaks forcefully out of the whirlwind. God's power for life makes resurrection happen. This God is not person, but is relation: the energy of life that swirls and conjures all into being, all into "interbeing." This divine energy is the breath of life. It is present in all living beings and beyond all.

God in Godself is both out of time and in time. The God we know, the narrative of God we tell, puts God in time, but this is fundamentally our story more than God's own. Because we human beings need narratives to live by, we tell a story about God and our lives. Our insight into the nature and being of God is always limited, always an approximation in narrative form. We tell the narrative best as a love story, about God's desire and ours, about yearning for connection and feeling the pain of separation. This story constitutes our history. How we understand God is intertwined with the way in which we live in the world and understand who we are.

Our story of God and with God is ongoing and has no end. Not only is it everlasting, but also it has no resolution. This is to say that our narratives remain open-ended as well, and there is no conclusion to this book. Who God is and who we are continue to be revealed in and through our faithful embrace of life. As long as the God of life is with us, time's tale continues . . .

And hope abides.

INDEX